D0200788

San Diego Christian College
2100 Greenfield Drive
El Cajon, CA 92019

344.099
C296t

39.60

TITLE IX

Linda Jean Carpenter, PhD, JD
R. Vivian Acosta, PhD

Professors Emeritae, Brooklyn College,
City University of New York

Human Kinetics

Library of Congress Cataloging-in-Publication Data

Carpenter, Linda Jean, 1943-
Title IX / Linda Jean Carpenter, R. Vivian Acosta.
   p. cm.
Includes bibliographical references and index.
ISBN 0-7360-4239-3 (hbk.)
   1. Sex discrimination in sports--Law and legislation--United States. 2. College sports--Law and legislation--United States. 3. United States. Education Amendments of 1972. Title IX I. Title: Title nine. II. Acosta, R. Vivian. III. Title.
   KF4166.C37 2004
   344.73'099--dc22
                 2004009221

ISBN: 0-7360-4239-3

Copyright © 2005 by Linda Jean Carpenter and R. Vivian Acosta

All rights reserved. Except for use in a review, the reproduction or utilization of this work in any form or by any electronic, mechanical, or other means, now known or hereafter invented, including xerography, photocopying, and recording, and in any information storage and retrieval system, is forbidden without the written permission of the publisher.

The Web addresses cited in this text were current as of June 4, 2004, unless otherwise noted.

Acquisitions Editors: Amy N. Clocksin, Myles Schrag; **Developmental Editor:** Renee Thomas Pyrtel; **Assistant Editor:** Ann M. Augspurger; **Copyeditor:** Bob Replinger; **Proofreader:** Erin Cler; **Indexer:** Betty Frizzéll; **Permission Manager:** Dalene Reeder; **Graphic Designer:** Nancy Rasmus; **Graphic Artist:** Dawn Sills; **Photographer (interior):** all photos © Human Kinetics unless otherwise noted; **Photo Manager:** Kareema McLendon; **Cover Designer:** Jack W. Davis; **Art Managers:** Kelly Hendren, Kareema McLendon; **Illustrator:** Kelly Hendren; **Printer:** Edwards Brothers

Printed in the United States of America   10   9   8   7   6   5   4   3   2   1

Human Kinetics
Web site: www.HumanKinetics.com

United States: Human Kinetics
P.O. Box 5076
Champaign, IL 61825-5076
800-747-4457
e-mail: humank@hkusa.com

Canada: Human Kinetics
475 Devonshire Road Unit 100
Windsor, ON N8Y 2L5
800-465-7301 (in Canada only)
e-mail: orders@hkcanada.com

Europe: Human Kinetics
107 Bradford Road
Stanningley
Leeds LS28 6AT, United Kingdom
+44 (0) 113 255 5665
e-mail: hk@hkeurope.com

Australia: Human Kinetics
57A Price Avenue
Lower Mitcham, South Australia 5062
08 8277 1555
e-mail: liaw@hkaustralia.com

New Zealand: Human Kinetics
Division of Sports Distributors NZ Ltd.
P.O. Box 300 226 Albany
North Shore City
Auckland
0064 9 448 1207
e-mail: blairc@hknewz.com

For family and friends, students and colleagues, absent and still near, all of whom have made our lives richer.

CONTENTS

PREFACE

Unless you're just intrigued by the cryptic title of this book, you already have an idea what Title IX is. This book is intended to provide you with a complete, accurate, and up-to-date understanding of the depth and breadth of Title IX, its requirements, its history, its enforcement, its challenges, its place in society in general, and its place in the diverse realms of sport in particular, including physical education, intramural and recreational sports, and athletics.

Title IX and its provisions have been well settled in the law for a number of years despite the continuing and at times heated discourse concerning its effect. Whether you are a college president or a high school principal, a parent or a student, a coach or an athlete, a lawyer or a lay person, a professor of women's studies or a professor of sociology of sport, a master teacher or a student teacher, an athletic director or a physical educator, you'll find clear, complete, and comprehensive information about Title IX that will help you in your specific daily endeavors. Your only prerequisite is a need to know about Title IX and its role in your professional and personal life or an interest in the topic of gender equity.

Because the book is complete as well as conceptually based, no matter how much or how little you understand about Title IX and gender equity, you'll know and understand more or have greater confidence in the accuracy of your understanding by the time you arrive at the final pages of the book. For instance, lawyers will see the applicability of Title IX in context; athletic directors will see Title IX requirements presented in ways easily transferable to their particular situations, physical educators will understand the application of Title IX to course selection and coed classes while also finding sources for assistance in meeting its requirements, and athletes will gain an understanding of their rights and responsibilities.

Title IX is unique in organization and contents. It can be read cover to cover for a complete, precept-upon-precept understanding of everything Title IX is and does. It can be picked up and used as a desk reference to provide information about a specific equity issue that appears to be developing in your program. It can serve as the key to a world of information about equity in sport through its inclusion of a wealth of useful Internet resources. It can be opened to a discussion of a particular lawsuit for an explanation of the legal reasoning used to decide a particular issue.

It can serve as a helper and strategist in deciding enforcement avenues to pursue. It includes additional information in chapter notes for readers who want more, and it includes situational questions and answers to assist you in applying and testing for accuracy your understanding of Title IX requirements in action.

Title IX is divided into three parts. The first part provides a clear understanding of the source and contents of the law, its regulations, policy interpretations, and other corollary materials. Then it walks you through the application of the requirements of the law within physical education, intramural and recreational sport, and athletics programs and does so acknowledging that these areas are not synonymous or interchangeable. The second part reviews the place of Title IX in society by reviewing the sociological milieu into which it was born and through which it has lived for over three decades. Lawsuits and settlements of note are discussed and dissected.

The third part looks at the changes wrought in the sport-related areas within reach of Title IX and the current controversies that Title IX faces. So that you don't have to go elsewhere for background documents, the appendixes include the regulations, policy interpretations, 1996 clarification letter, 1998 clarification letter, 2003 clarification letter, and an extensive listing of resources for help and further information, most of which are available online.

The tone of the book is light and straightforward. We even tuck in a bit of humor now and then. We intend the book to be your Title IX desk reference, primer, source book, and companion textbook for legal issues in sport—the first and last book you'll reach for whenever you have a Title IX question.

Disclaimer

Dear Kind and Gentle Reader,

No book about legal issues would be complete without a small disclaimer suggesting that you should consult your own attorney for specific legal advice and that our words in this book are not intended to replace that individualized legal advice. So, please consider the above as the obligatory disclaimer.

ACKNOWLEDGMENTS

Our professional lives have been made more challenging and rewarding by mentors who opened doors we thought locked, who wanted us to succeed rather than dared us to endure, and who raised the bar by their own examples. To these professional mothers and fathers, sisters and brothers, we owe the joy that has filled our working lives. Among the names written on the scrolls of our hearts are Leona Holbrook, Irma Schalk, Lucille Bacon, and Tillman Hall.

PART I

Title IX and
Its Applications

Title IX and its provisions have been well settled in the law for a number of years despite the continuing and at times heated discourse concerning its authority. Familiarity with the topic may not always translate to accurate understanding. Part I will give you material that will lead you from familiarity to accurate understanding.

Part I will review the law, its source and resources, and enforcement mechanisms. Then we'll review how the law applies specifically and independently to the areas of physical education, intramural club and recreational sport programs, and athletics.

1

The Law

No person in the United States shall, on the basis of sex, be excluded from participation in, be denied the benefits of, or be subjected to discrimination under any education program or activity receiving Federal financial assistance.[1]

These 37 words are the sum of the law known as Title IX. Although the words "athletics," "physical education," and "recreation" are not among the 37, the solitary sentence of Title IX has changed the face of American sport forever.

Title IX was enacted on June 23, 1972, against a backdrop of changing social awareness about discrimination. Only nine years earlier, President Kennedy had ordered the Alabama National Guard to escort two African American students through the University of Alabama doors blocked by Governor George Wallace.[2] By the time Title IX became law, America had become fully engaged in a sometimes rancorous dialogue about the fuller participation of a broader spectrum of society's members. The dialogue, perhaps more muted, continues even today. Although the dialogue continues, the jurisdiction, requirements, and enforcement protocol of Title IX are well settled.

When enacted, Title IX provided a six-year period in which schools could move toward compliance and in which the regulations could be written to determine whether schools indeed met compliance. For postsecondary schools, that date, known at the mandatory compliance date, was 1978. The mandatory compliance date came and went without compliance existing, but it at least provided a date from which institutions were at risk for the penalties of failing to comply.

On the following pages we'll take a close look at Title IX, including its structure, evolution of requirements, and the mechanisms for enforcing its requirements. You'll find an illumination of the interplay between the solitary, 37-word sentence that is the actual law known as Title IX, the regulations that define the meaning of the sentence in

3

practical terms, and the policy interpretations that bring into focus the application of the law to sport programs. An understanding of these concepts is necessary for achieving compliance with the mandates of Title IX and creating a foundation on which rational consideration and critical thought processes can build intelligent, well-grounded perspectives concerning Title IX.

To get a sense of the context in which Title IX developed and was enacted, see figure 1.1, the Title IX timeline, which runs across several pages of this chapter.

Before we begin, clarifying a few terms will be helpful. Enactment, the creation of a statute by a legislative body such as Congress, is an empty exercise if no method of enforcement (causing people to live up to the law) exists. In the United States we enjoy a system of checks and balances, or, in other words, compartmentalized responsibilities. Are memories of your civics classes coming back?

The legislative branch of government proposes and votes on (enacts) laws and statutes. On the federal level, the legislative branch is Congress.

Making sure that people live up to the laws is the job of the executive branch. On the federal level the executive branch is the president and various departments under the president's control, such as the Department of Education and the Department of Justice.

The judiciary steps in when it is necessary either to evaluate the constitutionality of a law or to interpret the language of a law or its

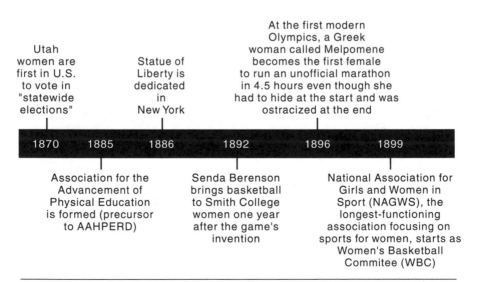

Figure 1.1 World events, women's sport, and Title IX timeline.

regulations. On the federal level the judiciary is made up of district courts, circuit courts of appeal, and finally, as a last word, the United States Supreme Court.

All three branches of government have played a role in the development of Title IX. Now, let's get started.

THE REGULATIONS

First came the law and its 37 words; enacting the law was the task of Congress in its role as the legislative branch. Although the task of enacting laws resides with the legislative branch, the task of enforcement lies with the executive branch. The 37 words of the law say, in effect, "be fair," but without details, definitions, and exceptions, enforcing the law is difficult. Thus, the Office for Civil Rights (OCR), part of the Department of Education,[3] was charged with both developing the details in the form of regulations and then enforcing the regulations.

Regulations are not created by one person sitting alone in an office with a pen and paper. Much debate, comment, interchange of ideas, and numerous hearings go into the formulation of regulations. Title IX regulations, which detail and define the law and identify exceptions to it, were created just this way. Over 10,000 comments were received during the review process. The comments came from lobbyists, athletics directors, parents, teachers, lawyers, coaches, and educational administrators; the comments came from a broad spectrum of interested individuals and

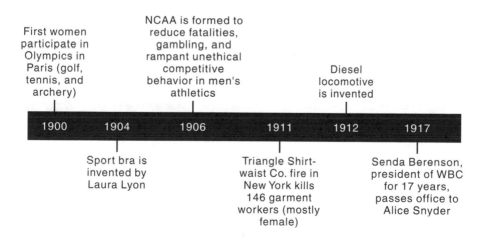

Figure 1.1 *(continued)*

groups. Over 90 percent of those comments related to the application of Title IX to athletics, yet less than 10 percent of the regulations deal directly with athletics, physical education, recreation, or sports.

Once OCR completed the process of assimilating, balancing, writing, and rewriting the regulations that would breathe an enforceable life into Title IX, OCR presented the draft regulations for Title IX to Congress on June 18, 1974. Congress, which had enacted the law two years earlier, had 45 days to review the draft regulations. During that period Congress had the opportunity to evaluate the details, definitions, and exceptions of the regulations to determine whether they would allow enforcement of the law to produce an outcome that Congress envisioned when it enacted the law. Unless Congress rejected the draft regulations during the 45-day review period with a concurrent resolution and told OCR to go back and try again, the draft regulations would become the final regulations and carry the force of law, just as the 37 words of the law do. That's what happened on July 21, 1975. On that day, Title IX consisted of the one-sentence law and the multipage regulations. (See appendix A, page 203, for an abridged copy of the final regulations.)

Regulations such as those of Title IX are not law; Congress did not enact them. Instead, the executive branch developed and promulgated the regulations in its role as enforcer of the law. But once Congress accepted the regulations as being an accurate and appropriate method of measuring and enforcing compliance with the law, the regulations were given the "force of law," and the courts were required to give the

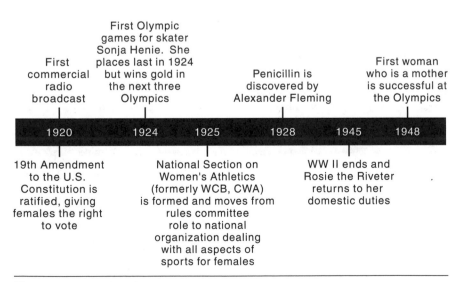

Figure 1.1 *(continued)*

regulations the same weight as they would the actual language of the law from which they came.

Yet the regulations, which tell us only a little about what is required within athletics programs and even less about physical education and recreation, do so without any detail or instruction about how to measure compliance. Section 106.8 of the regulations requires the institution to designate a responsible employee to coordinate compliance and investigate any in-house complaints received. Sections 106.33 and 106.37 contribute to the knowledge base about such points as when single-sex teams may be offered, what is a contact sport, on what basis providing financial aid is considered equitable, and whether separate locker-room facilities are acceptable. Another section, 106.41, gives us a list of areas within athletics programs that should be evaluated for fairness. In taking a close look at each of these sections, we will be able to see more clearly the direction of the regulations and their lack of specificity about measuring compliance.

Let's start with section 106.8. Here is that text:

Section 106.8 Designation of responsible employee and adoption of grievance procedures.

(a) *Designation of responsible employee.* Each recipient shall designate at least one employee to coordinate its efforts to comply with and carry out its responsibilities under this part, including any investigation of any complaint communicated to such recipient alleging its noncompliance with this part or alleging any actions which would be prohibited by this part.

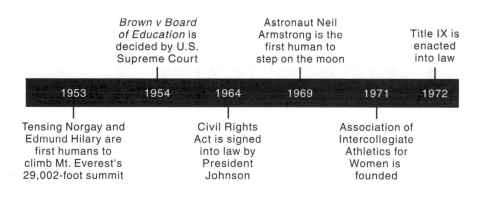

Figure 1.1 *(continued)*

> The recipient shall notify all its students and employees of the name, office address and telephone number of the employee or employees appointed pursuant to this paragraph.
>
> (b) *Complaint procedure of recipient.* A recipient shall adopt and publish grievance procedures providing for prompt and equitable resolution of student and employee complaints alleging any action which would be prohibited by this part.

In the mid-1970s, in response to section 106.8, schools designated a responsible employee and developed grievance procedures. Other than posting a name and title on a back-corridor bulletin board, many schools did little to disseminate to the campus community information about the requirements of Title IX. Over the years, few schools appointed successors to those designated employees who retired or changed jobs. Although this failure placed many institutions in technical violation of a provision of Title IX, the greater result was that the campus community had no one to educate it about Title IX.

In the late 1970s, a few years after enactment of Title IX, each institution developed and filed in-house grievance procedures. Each institution developed specific procedures; similarity to the procedures of the Office for Civil Rights was not needed. Duke University's grievance procedures might be very different from those of Queens College, and both might be very different from the OCR procedures. Rarely were an

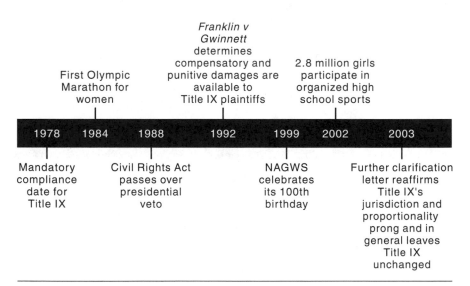

Figure 1.1 *(continued)*

institution's in-house grievance procedures reviewed or used because Title IX enforcement during those years was minimal.

Here is the text of section 106.33:

Section 106.33 Comparable facilities.

A recipient may provide separate toilet, locker room, and shower facilities on the basis of sex, but such facilities provided for students of one sex shall be comparable to such facilities provided for students of the other sex.

As with many of the regulations, no mention was made as to how to measure "comparable facilities." Section 106.33 served more to set minds at ease that Title IX did not require nor propose coed bathrooms or locker rooms. Section 106.33 would have to wait until 1979, when the policy interpretations of Title IX were created, to find fuller definition. (We will discuss the policy interpretations in more detail later in this chapter.)

Here is the text of section 106.37:

Section 106.37 Financial assistance.

(1) To the extent that a recipient awards athletic scholarships or grants-in-aid, it must provide reasonable opportunities for such awards for members of each sex in proportion to the number of students of each sex participating in interscholastic or intercollegiate athletics.

(2) Separate athletic scholarships or grants-in-aid for members of each sex may be provided as part of separate athletic teams for members of each sex to the extent consistent with this paragraph and section 106.41.

Before Title IX, no financial aid or athletic scholarships of any import had been awarded to female athletes. Section 106.37 provides for "reasonable opportunity" for gaining those scholarships but omits mention of how to judge what "reasonable" means. Although the regulation clearly states that opportunities must be in proportion to the ratio of male and female athletes, without details about what "reasonable" means, confusion remained.

Here is the text of section 106.41:

Section 106.41 Athletics.

(a) *General.* No person shall on the basis of sex, be excluded from participation in, be denied the benefits of, be treated differently from another person or otherwise be discriminated

© Smith College archives

Female college hurdlers would not have been awarded athletic scholarships or financial aid of any kind in the late 1920s, despite their competitive spirit and athleticism.

against in any interscholastic, intercollegiate, club or intramural athletics offered by a recipient, and no recipient shall provide any such athletics separately on such basis.

(b) *Separate teams.* Notwithstanding the requirements of paragraph (a) of this section, a recipient may operate or sponsor separate teams for members of each sex where selection for such teams is based upon competitive skill or the activity involved is a contact sport. However, where a recipient operates or sponsors a team in a particular sport for members of one sex but operates or sponsors no such team for members of the other sex, and athletic opportunities for members of that sex have previously been limited, members of the excluded sex must be allowed to try-out for the team offered unless the sport involved is a contact sport. For the purposes of this part, contact sports include boxing, wrestling, rugby, ice hockey, football, basketball and other sports the purpose or major activity of which involves bodily contact.

(c) *Equal opportunity.* A recipient which operates or sponsors interscholastic, intercollegiate, club or intramural athletics shall provide equal athletic opportunity for members of both sexes. In determining whether equal opportunities are available the Director will consider, among other factors:

(1) Whether the selection of sports and levels of competition effectively accommodate the interests and abilities of members of both sexes;

(2) The provision of equipment and supplies;

(3) Scheduling of games and practice time;

(4) Travel and per diem allowance;

(5) Opportunity to receive coaching and academic tutoring;

(6) Assignment and compensation of coaches and tutors;

(7) Provision of locker rooms, practice and competitive facilities;

(8) Provision of medical and training facilities and services;

(9) Provision of housing and dining facilities and services;

(10) Publicity.

Unequal aggregate expenditures for members of each sex or unequal expenditures for male and female teams if a recipient operates or sponsors separate teams will not constitute noncompliance with this section, but the Assistant Secretary may consider the failure to provide necessary funds for teams for one sex in assessing equality of opportunity for members of each sex.[4]

The 10 areas listed in section 106.41, and financial aid, which is found in section 106.37 of the regulations, are those that institutions should consider when assessing equity under Title IX. Later, the policy interpretations (discussed later) added 2 more areas to the list—recruitment and support services—for a total of 13 areas. The list is not exhaustive and other areas may be considered, but the phrase, "13 program areas/components" has found its way into the enforcement jargon of Title IX.

The final paragraph of Section 106.41 relates to the Javits amendment to Title IX.[5] The paragraph acknowledges that using a yardstick strictly based on expenditures is an unfair method for evaluating equity. The assistant secretary for civil rights, however, retains the ability to review significant differences in financial support of one sport over another, not supported by gender-neutral considerations, as a possible pretext for gender discrimination.

Considering that Title IX applies not just to athletics but to all segments of the educational endeavor, the presence of sections relating specifically to athletics places an inordinate amount of attention on a solitary segment. The sex-segregated nature of athletics, unlike art or biology or sociology, brings with it a greater opportunity for overt discrimination and may explain why the regulations say so much about it. Indeed, Caspar Weinberger, the secretary of HEW at the time of the comment period, said, "I had not realized until the comment period that the most important issue in the U.S. today is intercollegiate athletics."[6]

POLICY INTERPRETATIONS

At first glance the fine print of the regulations seems clear, but as we've seen, the regulations leave many questions unanswered. For example, how is compliance with the requirement to provide equitable locker rooms or assignment of coaching or travel and per diem allowance determined? If the male basketball team has a head coach and the female basketball team has a head coach, has that arrangement met the requirements of Title IX concerning assignment of coaches? If both teams occupy private locker rooms, has that arrangement met the Title IX requirements

© Smith College archives

Is it likely that the coach of this pre–Title IX 1966 college varsity basketball team received fair pay for her dedication and skill?

for the provision of locker rooms? If a male coach of a males' team is paid less than the male coach of the corresponding females' team, is it different, from a Title IX standpoint, than if a female coach of a females' team is paid less than her male counterpart? Details, details, details. The policy interpretations eventually provided them.

On December 11, 1978, a few months after the mandatory compliance date for Title IX, the Department of Health, Education, and Welfare published draft policy interpretations. A year later, after over 700 comments were received and reviewed, and following on-site visits to eight colleges to assess the potential effect of their application, a final set of policy interpretations became effective on December 11, 1979. (See appendix B for abridged policy interpretations.) Thus, as of December 11, 1979, Title IX consisted of three components:

The law (mission statement), 1972

The regulations (goals), 1975

Policy interpretations (yardstick for measuring goal attainment), 1979

The policy interpretations arrived none too soon. "By the end of July 1978, the Department [OCR] had received nearly 100 complaints alleging discrimination in athletics against more than 50 institutions of higher education."[7] The policy interpretations were needed. Because of the level of detail found in the policy interpretations, we'll be discussing them more fully in chapters 2, 3, and 4. But let's look at an example to see how the regulations and policy interpretations work together. Section 106.33 of the regulations states the following:

A recipient may provide separate toilet, locker room, and shower facilities on the basis of sex, but such facilities provided for students of one sex shall be comparable to such facilities provided for students of the other sex.

The related section of the policy interpretations (section 86.41) by contrast, says this:

f. Provision of Locker Rooms, Practice and Competitive Facilities.

Compliance will be assessed by examining, among other factors, the equivalence for men and women of:

(1) Quality and availability of the facilities provided for practice and competitive events;

(2) Exclusivity of use of facilities provided for practice and competitive events;

(3) Availability of locker rooms;

(4) Quality of locker rooms;

(5) Maintenance of practice and competitive facilities; and

(6) Preparation of facilities for practice and competitive events.

The regulations suggest that comparable facilities are needed; the policy interpretations provide more details about what one might consider in determining comparability.

The law and regulations both have the force of law.[8] The policy interpretations do not have the force of law but are given considerable deference.[9] What is the difference between "force of law" and "deference"? When something has the force of law, such as the regulations, the courts are required to give its language weight as though its words were actually part of the law that the legislative branch enacted. A second level of importance is known as deference. Although the policy interpretations do not have the force of law, their content must be given great weight, although not as much as the law, when they are offered to support what the law (and the regulations) require. In other words, the policy interpretations must be deferred to over an individual's testimony or a document of lesser weight, such as an investigator's manual, but not deferred to when compared with the regulations.

Sometimes, the presence in the policy interpretations of a method for measuring compliance with a requirement found in the regulations can become the focus of heated discussion based, in part, on the differing weight of the two documents.

The most well-known example of this is found in the compliance measurement of the policy interpretations regarding the requirement of the regulations for equal access to participation opportunities and its three-prong test. Although chapters 4, 7, and 9 discuss the three-prong test more fully, let's briefly use it here as an illustration of the difference between the regulations and the policy interpretations.

In effect, the participation requirement of the regulations says that equitable athletic opportunities must be provided for members of both sexes. But the regulations don't say how to measure compliance. The policy interpretations do. They provide a list of three options ("three-prong test"), of which only one needs to be met to comply with the participation requirement. Briefly stated, the three options are the following:

- Provide participation opportunities substantially proportionate to the ratio of males to females in the student body (an option known as the "proportionality prong")

- Show a history and continuing practice of upgrading girls' and women's programs
- Meet the interests and abilities of the females

Some people don't like the presence of the proportionality prong and see it as their only option because they've found it difficult to comply with either of the other two. These same people want to have it altered, removed, or ignored. To bolster their argument, they point out that the three-prong test lacks the force of law because it appears only in the policy interpretations, not the regulations. Chapters 4, 7, and 9 discuss the failure of their argument, but at least you now know what proportionality refers to and the nature of the arguments made against it based on regulation versus policy interpretation.

Most of the continuing debate regarding Title IX arises from the policy interpretations rather than from the law or the regulations. This is the case probably because only the policy interpretations outline *how good* an institution has to be in order to comply.

The law mandated institutions to "be fair." The regulations expanded the law to "be fair *in these specific areas.*" When even the details located in the regulations were found to be insufficient for determining correct behavior, at least in the rule-bound domain of athletics, it was necessary to find a way to provide additional specificity sufficient to produce compliance. The policy interpretations were created to provide the additional specificity needed in the realm of athletics. In effect, the policy interpretation says, "Be fair, in these specific areas, *as measured by this yardstick.*"

INVESTIGATOR'S MANUAL

The policy interpretations told us a lot, but there was still a need for even more information. The Office for Civil Rights, charged with administrative enforcement of Title IX in its role as part of the executive branch, found it needed to assist its own investigators in applying the yardstick to specific, actual athletics programs. On July 28, 1980, only seven months after the issuance of the policy interpretations, OCR produced the *Interim Title IX Intercollegiate Athletics Manual.* Thus, investigators received instruction in how to investigate.

Although the manual was titled "interim," it and the narrow *Guidance on Writing Title IX Intercollegiate Athletic Letters of Findings,* issued on March 26, 1982, both held their place until 1990, when the *Title IX Athletics Investigator's Manual* replaced them.

Why did it take eight years to replace the interim manual? In the intervening years, from the early 1980s to 1990, the terrain for application of

Title IX to athletics shifted greatly. From the 1984 *Grove City* case[10] (which effectively removed intercollegiate athletics from the jurisdiction of Title IX) through the 1988 passage of the 1987 Civil Rights Restoration Act[11] (which restored the jurisdiction of Title IX), Title IX did not apply to intercollegiate athletics, physical education, intramural programs, or recreation programs. Because Title IX didn't apply to these sport-related areas from 1984 to 1988, there was no need to update or expand any of the investigators' materials.[12] No investigations were moving forward. Indeed, OCR had dropped most athletic cases within weeks of the *Grove City* decision.[13] But with the passage over presidential veto of the Civil Rights Restoration Act in 1988, the terrain for inclusion of athletics, physical education, intramurals, and recreation within the jurisdictional rubric of Title IX became bedrock, and people looked to Title IX with expectant eyes to move forward after its four-year hiatus from enforcement. Thus, less than two years following the Civil Rights Restoration Act, OCR issued a permanent, not interim, *Investigator's Manual.*

In the years following the issuance of the *Investigator's Manual*, OCR indicated that it would issue a revised manual, but it has not. The absence of a revised manual doesn't mean that all parties agree that the *Investigator's Manual* accurately reflects the law, regulations, and policy interpretations. Among criticisms of the *Investigator's Manual* were those taking issue with the efficacy and validity of the specific statistical format used to determine participation compliance. The lack of the publication of a revised manual does reflect perhaps a weakening of the enforcement will of OCR, a reduction in its budget, or perhaps even a developing satisfaction with the main portion of the 1990 *Investigator's Manual*. In any case, the *Investigator's Manual* does not have the force of law, nor is it even entitled to the judicial deference afforded the policy interpretations; it is another voice, not a different voice. Thus, the lack of an updated version doesn't affect one way or another the tenets of Title IX.

The presence of the *Investigator's Manual* in the library of Title IX materials is significant more for its participation in the development of the "official" enforcement literature than for the uniqueness of its content. The *Investigator's Manual* was drafted not to interpret the law and regulations but to give OCR investigators a systematic guide to follow as they evaluated the degree of compliance on a particular campus or in a particular program. In spite of its intended use as an internal guide for OCR investigators, however, the *Investigator's Manual* has been frequently cited in Title IX lawsuits as an unofficial glimpse into how OCR sees various portions of the regulations or policy interpretations. Thus, an understanding of its placement in the library of Title IX materials is important.

Bound with the 1990 *Investigator's Manual*, however, is a two-page policy clarification concerning coaching compensation, issued on June 27, 1983, by the assistant secretary for civil rights within the Department of Education. The letter addressed a question from a regional civil rights director concerning the applicability of section 106.54 of Title IX to disparate coaching salaries based on the sex of the students receiving the coaching rather than on the sex of the coach providing the coaching services.

Section 106.54 says this:

> A recipient shall not make or enforce any policy or practice which, on the basis of sex:
>
> (a) Makes distinctions in rates of pay or other compensation;
>
> (b) Results in the payment of wages to employees of one sex at a rate less than that paid to employees of the opposite sex for equal work on jobs the performance of which requires equal skill, effort, and responsibility, and which are performed under similar working conditions.

The answer to the regional director's question was that absent a showing that female coaches are assigned discriminatorily to female teams, any actionable disparity under Title IX flows from the sex of the employee rather than the sex of the student. But if an employer assigns males only to higher paying positions and females only to lower paying positions, "there is a very strong presumption that the sex of the employee controls the resulting compensation."

The 1983 clarification letter bound in the 1990 *Investigator's Manual* may have received more attention if *Grove City* had not intervened and delayed the publication of the manual.

LETTERS OF CLARIFICATION

The agency enforcing a law, OCR in the case of Title IX, has the right and perhaps the responsibility to clarify apparent ambiguity.[14] Based on the decibel rating and length of the debate about the proportionality prong and several other topics, clarification of apparent ambiguity was needed. Therefore, OCR has issued three letters of clarification over the years.

1996 Letter of Clarification (Proportionality)

In 1996, after debate, hearings, and comment review, OCR issued a letter known as the 1996 clarification letter, over the signature of Norma

Cantu, then the assistant secretary for civil rights, which attempted not to change the proportionality test of the policy interpretations, but to clarify it. (See appendix C for a copy of the 1996 clarification letter.) The clarification letter of 1996 neither adds to nor changes material already found in the policy interpretations. By its attempt to clarify rather than change, it has gained a central place in the continuing postmillennial debate about proportionality.

1998 Letter of Clarification (Financial Aid)

The 1998 letter of clarification dealt with the meaning of "substantially equal" as used in the requirement to provide equitable financial aid to both males and females (see appendix D for the 1998 clarification

An athletic department's overall budget for financial aid (such as this woman's tennis scholarship) must be divided proportionally to the number of males and females in the athletics program, not in the student body as a whole.

letter). The genesis of using the proportion of male and female students as a yardstick against which to measure compliance is found in section 106.37 of the regulations and deals with the granting of financial aid. The proportionality test for *financial aid* found in section 106.37 of the regulations compares the distribution of aid to the ratio of males and females within the athletics program, unlike the proportionality test for *participation* opportunities found in the policy interpretations, which uses the student-body ratio of males to females. Although the comparator (athletics program or student body) differed, defining the meaning of "substantially equal" for financial aid with the 1998 letter of clarification affected the interpretation of the same term as applied to participation.

2003 Letter of Clarification (Proportionality and Reaffirmation)

The latest letter of clarification, issued in July 2003, related to the proportionality prong of the test for participation opportunities. The 2003 letter of clarification does not alter the material found in the 1996 letter of clarification; it simply reaffirms it but does so after a series of hearings and commission discussions. See chapter 9 for a further discussion and appendix E for the complete letter.

LAWSUITS, CASE LAW, LETTERS OF FINDINGS

The law, the regulations, the policy interpretations, the *Investigator's Manual*, and the 1996, 1998, and 2003 letters of clarification have contributed in one degree or another to the body of literature that defines the meaning of Title IX. These documents all flow out of the statutory process. They are either the statute or the official interpretations of the statute, or they receive deference of some degree in the judicial review of the statute because their creation was grounded in the statutory process. Table 1.1 lists these documents and summarizes their respective legal strengths.

Table 1.1 The Documents That Define Title IX	
Document	**Legal strength**
Title IX (37 words)	The law
Regulations	Force of law
Policy interpretations	Worthy of judicial deference
Letters of clarification	Worthy of judicial deference

Besides the documents that flow from the statutory process, a growing mountain of OCR complaints, OCR letters of findings or letters of resolution, and lawsuits have resulted from the enforcement process. These materials also lend weight to the policy interpretation as the "controlling authority" [15] in its role as a reasonable and "considered interpretation of the regulations."[16]

The case law that has developed by virtue of decisions in a long line of Title IX lawsuits provides another source of information about Title IX and its requirements. Decisions in lawsuits reflect the court's opinions on various topics and, as courts make more decisions as the result of more lawsuits, a body of opinion known as case law develops. Some case law carries the unique weight of being precedent setting. A precedent is created when the highest court in a particular jurisdiction makes a decision on a particular issue. For example, when a U.S. circuit court of appeals hands down a decision on a particular Title IX issue, the point of view of the decision serves as a precedent (very strong guidance) for future cases relating to the same issue in the geographic region over which the particular circuit court of appeals has jurisdiction. Even when not carrying the weight of being a precedent-setting case, the decisions in lawsuits (case law) help illuminate the general state of the law concerning a particular issue. In general, the case law has strongly supported the statutory sources of Title IX information, including the power of the policy interpretations.

Decisions of OCR complaints are called letters of findings (LOF) or letters of resolution (LOR). Unlike the Title IX case law that has typically provided strong support for the policy interpretations and other statutory sources of Title IX information, LOFs, and LORs have been more difficult to predict and have sometimes provided less support. Case law, however, carries more weight than do OCR LOFs or LORs.

Issues such as the validity of the proportionality test,[17] amount of notice required to place liability, availability of punitive or compensatory damages, application to employees, and so forth have all been litigated and add to the sources of Title IX understandings. Chapters 6 and 7 include a fuller discussion of the sequence of Title IX case law.

In summary, the sources of statutory-based Title IX information are found in

Title IX (law),

regulations (force of law) (see appendix A),

policy interpretations (deference) (see appendix B),

Investigator's Manual,

1996 letter of clarification (see appendix C),

1998 letter of clarification (see appendix D), and

2003 further clarification letter (appendix E).

In addition, sources of complaint and lawsuit-based Title IX information are found in

letters of findings (LOFs) and letters of resolution (LORs) and

case law produced through lawsuit decisions.

Now that we've talked about sources of the requirements of Title IX, let's turn our attention to enforcement options.

> ". . . an athletics program is gender equitable when the men's sports program would be pleased to accept as its own, the overall participation, opportunities, and resources currently allocated to the women's sports program and vice versa."
>
> *NACWAA, Summer 1993*

AVENUES OF ENFORCEMENT

Theoretically, once the regulations, policy interpretations, and other sources of statute-based Title IX information were in place, Title IX would be easy to enforce. The three avenues of enforcement are in-house complaints, OCR complaints, and lawsuits. None is a prerequisite or precursor to pursuing any other.

In-House Complaints

The method that has proven least effective is the in-house complaint. According to section 106.8 of the regulations, each institution must have a responsible employee and a complaint procedure. All students and employees are, according to section 106.8, supposed to be made aware of the identity of the "responsible employee" as well as the complaint process. The reality is that the most students and employees are aware of neither. In addition, because most "Title IX responsible employees" work at the pleasure of the institution's chief executive officer, the on-campus person charged with enforcing Title IX is often hoping *not* to find discrimination for fear of alienating the employer.

Loyalties, enmities, campus politics, and concerns about job retention are external variables that can have great bearing on the outcome of in-house complaints. Even when such variables are held at bay, the resolve to comply more closely with Title IX is sometimes not fueled by judicial threats of damages or withdrawal of federal financial aid but rather relies on an intrinsic desire to do what is right. On campuses where that intrinsic desire is in short supply, pursuing an in-house complaint is fruitless. In any case, the law, regulations, and policy interpretations are silent about *how* the responsible employee is to educate and investigate; all is left up to the institution to decide.

One key fact about in-house complaints, however, is that to file one there is no need for legal standing. (Legal standing means that the plaintiff is someone who has something to gain or lose by the outcome of the case.) Thus, a third party may submit an in-house complaint on behalf of another party.

OCR Complaints

OCR personnel are charged with enforcement. They are not advocates for equity. The zealousness of an OCR investigation depends largely on the administrative climate of a particular regional OCR office or the commitment of the specific OCR employees assigned. On the other hand, plaintiffs in a lawsuit assume that their attorneys will be committed advocates. It would be naive to assume the same of OCR. OCR's role relating to a Title IX complaint is quite different from the role an attorney for a plaintiff should perform. A clear understanding of the different roles played by OCR compared with an attorney for a Title IX plaintiff is one factor to consider when deciding whether to file an administrative complaint with OCR or a lawsuit.

OCR has the power but often neither the will nor the budget to initiate investigative enforcement procedures on its own accord. OCR is required by law, however, to investigate all Title IX complaints it receives unless for some reason it finds that there is no jurisdiction because of a lack of one of the three required elements: education program, allegation of sex discrimination, and federal financial assistance. OCR's only discretion in deciding whether to act on a complaint arises if (1) the complaint is baseless on its face, (2) the complaint is not filed in a timely fashion[18] (within 180 days of the last occurrence), (3) the complainant and institution have reached an agreement by themselves that, in effect, withdraws the OCR complaint from the table, or (4) the complainant is unwilling to cooperate with the investigation.

The average time from the initiation of an OCR complaint to the dissemination of a letter of findings or letter of resolution[19] is 206 days[20] according to one study, but often Title IX cases involving athletics take even longer because of their multifaceted nature. OCR has an internal time frame for completion of their investigation, but no permission from the complainant is needed for the time to be extended, nor are there any penalties placed on OCR for failing to meet its internal deadline.

In-house and OCR complaints do not require legal standing. If a person with legal standing files an OCR complaint, that person may also contemporaneously or afterward file a Title IX lawsuit. The complainant has no requirement to exhaust remedies potentially available through either an in-house or an OCR administrative complaint before filing a lawsuit. Neither does the complainant have any requirement to select only one avenue of enforcement at a time. OCR will toll a Title IX complaint, however, if the complainant also files a lawsuit. Tolling means that the clock used to time the passage of OCR's internal time limitations is turned off until the occurrence of a specific situation, such as the completion of a related lawsuit. Once the lawsuit is completed, OCR will resume its investigation if the outcome of the lawsuit is not to the liking of the plaintiff or complainant.

Another factor to be considered is whether the complainant or plaintiff has legal standing. A plaintiff in a lawsuit *must* have legal standing. An OCR complainant does not. Although a lawsuit may have remedial advantages such as the potential for damages, its requirement that the plaintiff have legal standing may be sufficiently off-putting to make an OCR complaint a better choice.

For example, many coaches of women's teams are employed on one-year contracts and are astute enough about the political climate on their particular campus to know that being the filer of either a Title IX complaint or a lawsuit is likely to result in their not being reappointed, as well as their carrying the burden of a future identity as a Title IX pariah. Once a lawsuit is filed, the institution becomes aware of the coach's central role in the controversy. But because an OCR complaint does not require the complainant to have legal standing, a person more insulated from retaliation can sign the complaint. A parent, community member, or even a professional organization can file the complaint.[21] The institution may suspect the identity of the motivating force behind the complaint but will not be certain.

Retaliation is a separate cause of action under Title IX. The employee who files a Title IX complaint or lawsuit who is then the victim of retaliation may file a separate complaint or lawsuit based on that retaliation. In reality, however, employers have learned to be subtle in their retaliation, making retaliation complaints or lawsuits often difficult to prove. Avoiding retaliation from the outset is the better strategy. The avoidance may be accomplished either by having a third party file the OCR complaint or, more happily, by finding people of goodwill in positions of authority on campus who will do the right thing about equity before a complaint or lawsuit is even filed.

What is the best expectation of someone who files an OCR complaint? The greatest enforcement power available to OCR is to withhold federal dollars from an institution that is found to be violating the requirements of Title IX. No damages are allowed to the complainant. The presence of federal dollars at most institutions is considerable; research grants, student financial aid programs, and grants to improve facilities and instructional endeavors are among the sources of federal dollars on campus. If federal dollars were to be withheld from an institution, most institutions would certainly feel the pain. But the threat of withholding federal dollars is a hollow one. OCR has never withheld one dollar of federal financial aid because of a finding of an institution's noncompliance with Title IX. Considering that Title IX is more than three decades old and that mandatory compliance has been required for a quarter of a century, the threat, unused, has grown frail with rust.

> "Congress surely did not intend for federal monies to be expended to support the intentional actions it sought to proscribe."
>
> Franklin v Gwinnett, *112 S. Ct. 1028 (1992)*

Lawsuit

Until the U.S. Supreme Court's 1992 *Franklin v Gwinnett* decision, the difference in the potential outcome of an OCR complaint and a lawsuit was negligible; neither could result in monetary damages but only in a promise from the institution to "go forth and sin no more." Only educational and moral imperatives existed; any financial imperative was solely illusory. Following *Franklin* (see chapter 6 for a full discussion of this important case), however, a successful plaintiff of a lawsuit alleging intentional discrimination under Title IX has available remedies that include monetary damages, both compensatory and punitive. Compensatory damages represent money paid by the defendant to compensate for financial loss such as salary or scholarships. Punitive damages represent money paid by the defendant to produce a sense of punishment within the defendant and to send an enforcement message to other potential defendants. Both kinds of monetary damages focus the attention of defendants in a way that the potential loss of federal financial aid does not. Thus, institutions, noting the potential financial consequence, began to take a more proactive view to implementing Title IX on their campuses. Attorneys who had previously found no incentive for pursuing a Title IX case now found the potential for contingency awards based on monetary damages a strong motivation to represent Title IX plaintiffs.

Complaints and lawsuits differ considerably as avenues for enforcing Title IX. Depending on the complainant or plaintiff's individual situation, the differences can be perceived as either negative or positive:

- Lawsuits require the plaintiff to be someone with legal standing, thus often targeting an employee for retaliation; an OCR complaint does not.

- Lawsuits require the plaintiff to pay for the costs of a lawsuit (transcripts, filing fees, and so forth) even if the attorney is serving on a contingent basis; an OCR complaint does not.

- Lawsuits have characteristically produced outcomes favoring the Title IX plaintiff; the outcomes of OCR complaints have been difficult to predict.

- Lawsuits carry the opportunity to sue for monetary damages; an OCR complaint does not.

- Lawsuits generally take longer than an OCR complaint does to reach resolution, but during the process the plaintiff often feels supported by the advocate role played by the attorney, which differs from the nonadvocate role played by OCR personnel.

- Lawsuits generally involve the plaintiff more actively in the process; an OCR complaint often proceeds with little concern for the desire of the complainant to be involved, thus increasing the complainant's isolation and frustration or, in the alternative, permitting the complainant to step back out of the fray and allow the investigation to proceed.

- A lawsuit's successful plaintiff can look to the court to oversee the enforcement of the remedy obtained; a successful complainant in an OCR case must rely on OCR, in an environment of fluctuating vigor depending on who occupies the White House, to monitor and enforce the letter of findings or resolution.

> "Victims are not going to have a problem finding a lawyer to bring suit any more."
>
> *Ellen Vargyas, attorney, commenting on* Franklin v Gwinnett *decision in* USA Today, *February 27, 1992*

How long does a complainant have before a complaint or lawsuit must be filed? The statute of limitations in Title IX complaints (in house or OCR) is 180 days from the occurrence of the discriminatory act. If the discrimination is continuing, as it often is in athletics, then each new day starts the 180-day clock running anew. The defendant in a lawsuit similarly benefits from the daily renewal of the statute of limitations in cases where the discrimination is ongoing.

The statute of limitations in Title IX lawsuits is less precise. The answer to the question of the length of the statute of limitation when applied to a lawsuit (not an in-house or OCR complaint) must come from the state in which the Title IX case arises. The courts review any state legislation similar to Title IX, select the most appropriate law, and apply its statute of limitation to the Title IX case. If the facts of the case lend themselves to the argument either that the act of discrimination was a single discreet act or that the discrimination ceased at a specific time in the past, the subjective determination of the applicable statute of limitation for lawsuits becomes a critical argument. In athletics Title IX cases, however, the discrimination is typically ongoing, and thus the statute of limitations is not an issue in either OCR complaints or lawsuits.

IN BRIEF

The requirements of Title IX as they apply to all corners of the educational endeavor receiving federal financial assistance, including athletics, physical education, clubs, recreation, and intramurals, are found in the one-sentence law and the regulations. Additional details about the requirements as they apply to athletics programs are found in the policy interpretations, *Investigator's Manual*, clarification letters of 1996, 1998, and 2003, and, as with all areas, case law.

The three avenues of enforcement are in-house complaints, Office for Civil Rights complaints, and lawsuits. The first is usually ineffective but requires no financial outlay on the part of the person filing the complaint. The second, an OCR complaint, similarly involves no financial outlay on the part of the person filing the complaint nor does it promise any potential for the imposition of damages but may be more effective. The third, lawsuits, unlike the first two requires that the plaintiff be a person with legal standing. Money is at stake: Lawsuits carry with them the potential for imposition of both compensatory and punitive damages.

The source of the information concerning the requirements of Title IX is important because various sources carry differing legal weights. The selection of the form of enforcement concerning the requirements of Title IX is important because the potential outcome varies from the institution's promise to do better in the future to the imposition of compensatory and punitive damages.

Nineteen Questions and Nineteen Answers

1. **If you're a complainant or plaintiff, do you first have to pursue resolution of Title IX issues within the institution before seeking the outside help of OCR or the courts?**

    No. Title IX does not require the exhaustion of in-house complaint procedures before pursuing external remedies. The plaintiff or complainant should consider strategy, endurance, support system, job security, and financial resources when deciding which enforcement avenue to follow first.

2. **What are the statutory-based sources of Title IX information, and which have more strength than others?**

    *   The law, 1972
    *   The regulations, 1975 (force of law)
    *   The policy interpretations, 1979 (deference and weight as controlling authority because of its role in explaining, not changing, regulations)
    *   *Investigator's Manual*, 1990 (no legal weight except as evidence of what the OCR's in-house interpretation might be)
    *   Letter of clarification, 1996 (three-prong test) (deference and weight as controlling authority)
    *   Letter of clarification, 1998 (financial aid) (deference and weight as controlling authority)
    *   Further letter of clarification, 2003 (three-prong test) (deference and weight as controlling authority)

3. **Who can file a complaint? A lawsuit?**

    Anyone can file a complaint; the complainant need not have any official connection with the institution nor need he or she have legal standing (have something to lose or gain). Only people with legal standing can file a lawsuit. A person with legal standing for a Title IX case might be a coach, an athletic director, or a student-athlete.

4. **If you're a successful complainant in an OCR case, can you expect any monetary reward or benefit?**

    No. Compensatory damages are not part of the remedies available through an OCR complaint. Compensatory damages, however, are available through a lawsuit based on allegations for intentional discrimination.

5. **Can you file both an OCR complaint and a lawsuit?**

   Yes. OCR will toll the complaint, however, until completion of the lawsuit.

6. **How long can you wait from the discriminatory acts until you file an OCR complaint?**

   An OCR complaint must be filed within 180 days from the act of discrimination. In most Title IX instances, however, the discrimination is ongoing, so every new day starts the 180-day clock running anew.

7. **If you represent an institution accused of violating Title IX, what is the most that you (the institution) stand to lose?**

   If a Title IX complaint is filed with OCR, your institution theoretically stands to lose all its federal financial assistance, wherever it is located on campus. In other words, more than just the money related to athletics is at risk (theoretically). If a Title IX lawsuit is filed, the financial implications are without limit. Besides compensatory damages, the institution stands to lose punitive damages, which have no cap. Additionally, in both instances, the institution loses the value of the attorneys' time used in defending a complaint or lawsuit. The goodwill of potential donors, both male and female, may be lost because of the negative publicity resulting from a legal battle if the institution is perceived to be resistant to doing what Congress has deemed fair.

8. **Where should you look for the "yardstick" to measure compliance with Title IX?**

   The "yardstick" for measuring compliance with Title IX requirements related to athletics is located in the policy interpretations. Documents that followed the policy interpretations such as the *Investigator's Manual* carry less legal weight but may still provide additional insight.

9. **What are the duties of a "responsible employee," and does every institution need one?**

   The "responsible employee" receives and investigates, according to the institution's policies and procedures, in-house Title IX complaints. The "responsible employee" also educates the faculty, staff, and students about the rights and responsibilities flowing from Title IX. Every institution needs one.

10. Did Congress draft the regulations? Policy interpretations?

No. Congress enacted the one-sentence law known as Title IX. The executive branch in the form of the Office for Civil Rights drafted the regulations and policy interpretations. When each was proposed, Congress had the opportunity to reject each but did not.

11. On what basis do the courts give deference to the policy interpretations?

When an agency's duly adopted regulations are ambiguous, the agency that created the regulations is considered the appropriate agency to explain them by way of policy interpretations. When policy interpretations are adopted, they are given deference as the controlling authority in their role as a reasonable and considered interpretation of the regulations.

12. A form of proportionality is used to determine whether financial aid is provided in an equitable fashion. Is the basis of the financial aid proportionality the ratio of males and females in the student body or the ratio of males and females in the athletic department?

The ratio used for financial aid, unlike the ratio used for participation opportunities, is the ratio of males and females within the athletics program rather than within the student body.

13. The regulations identify 10 program areas plus financial aid as places to check for discrimination. Where do the remaining 2 areas, for a total of 13 program areas, come from, and what are the remaining 2 areas?

The remaining 2 areas, recruitment and support services, are found in the policy interpretations.

14. Why do you think that the press has focused mostly on the application of Title IX to athletics? What is the central difference between sport-related programs and the rest of the institution's educational programs, which perhaps play a major role in the focus of Title IX?

Athletics is fundamental to the American psyche. In addition, because athletics programs are generally sex segregated, any disparity in opportunity or support is relatively easy to see.

15. **Consider your own institution. Which enforcement avenue might be the best choice for a coach who believes that your school is in violation of Title IX within its athletics or physical education department? Why?**

    Your answer should consider the likelihood of retaliation, the security of the coach's continued employment, the political support on campus for the coach and for equity, the ability and willingness of the coach to underwrite the costs of a lawsuit, and the potential availability of compensatory or punitive damages in the specific case.

16. **What is the difference between the roles of OCR personnel and an attorney for a Title IX plaintiff?**

    OCR personnel are charged with investigating the matter and, in cases where violations are present, arriving at a resolution to which the institution voluntarily agrees. If no such resolution is possible, OCR turns the case over to the Department of Justice for enforcement by way of withdrawing federal financial assistance. OCR investigators are not advocates for equity.

    An attorney for a plaintiff in a Title IX lawsuit plays the role of advocate and engages the plaintiff in the process of investigation, litigation, and requesting a remedy. OCR's efforts are without cost. The plaintiff's attorney in a lawsuit is not without cost but will, if the case is won, take a portion of the damages as compensation. Additionally, the plaintiff bears the costs of litigation.

17. **Is the threat of losing federal money an effective enforcement motivator? Explain.**

    No, at least not to an institution that has followed OCR's history. No federal money has ever been lost because of an OCR finding of a violation of Title IX.

18. **Fear of retaliation is often present when someone files a Title IX complaint or lawsuit. Is retaliation a violation of Title IX? If retaliation becomes a reality, what recourse does the victim have?**

    Yes, retaliation is a separate cause of action in Title IX. The victim of retaliation may file either an additional OCR complaint alleging retaliation or an additional Title IX lawsuit alleging retaliation. Note that a lawsuit carries with it the potential for punitive damages and that a jury finding retaliation may be more inclined to award punitive damages.

19. **What is the significance of the U.S. Supreme Court's unanimous 1992 decision in *Franklin v Gwinnett* to the enforcement of Title IX?**

Money damages. Before the unanimous decision in *Franklin*, the only remedies available to the successful plaintiff were the same as those available under an OCR complaint. After *Franklin*, compensatory and, potentially, punitive damages became available. As soon as the U.S. Supreme Court handed down the *Franklin* decision, many institutions where the rumblings of Title IX complaints and lawsuits were heard decided to put their money into improving athletics programs for female athletes rather than into litigation that would attempt to maintain the status quo of discrimination.

NOTES

[1]Title IX of the Education Amendments of 1972, P.L. 92-318, 20 U.S.C.S. section 1681 et seq. was enacted on June 23, 1972. Its language is patterned after the pre-existing Title VI.

[2] On June 12, 1963, only two months after riots in Birmingham, Alabama, President Kennedy federalized the Alabama National Guard to force racial desegregation in response to Governor Wallace's overt unwillingness to accede to the requirements of federal law.

[3]The current Department of Education was the Department of Health, Education, and Welfare when the regulations were being drafted. The change from HEW to the Department of Education had no significant effect on Title IX.

[4]Sections 106.33, 37, and 41 of Title IX of the Education Amendments of 1972, P.L. 92-318, 20 U.S.C.S. section 1681 et seq. provide the meat of the regulations as they apply to athletics.

[5]The Javits amendment arose after the defeat of the Tower amendment, which proposed the removal of so-called revenue sports from the jurisdiction of Title IX. The Javits amendment acknowledges that some sports cost more to equip and otherwise support than do others. For instance, equipping a football player may cost $1,000, whereas equipping a member of the track team may cost only $200. The dollar discrepancy is a function of the sport, not of discrimination.

[6]Caspar Weinberger shared his new view of the apparent importance of athletics in the minds of the American public while testifying in support of the notion that HEW had early on felt that athletics was squarely within the purview of Title IX. See *Sex Discrimination Regulations, Hearings Before the House Subcommittee on Post Secondary Education of the Committee on Education and Labor*, 94th Congress, 1st Session at 438-9 (1975).

[7]*Policy Interpretations: Title IX and Intercollegiate Athletics. Federal Register*, vol. 44, no. 239, at 71413, December 11, 1979. The initial batch of Title IX complaints focused almost universally on applications of Title IX to athletics.

[8] The force of law of the regulations has been challenged in the courts. The regulations of Title IX have withstood challenge. See *Kelley v Board of Trustees of University of Illinois*, 35 F. 3d 265 (7th Cir. 1994) and *Yellow Springs Exempted Village Sch. Dist. Bd. of Ed. v Ohio High School Athletic Association*, 647 F. 2d 651, 658 (6th Cir. 1981).

[9] See *Roberts* 998 F. 2d at 828 citing *Martin v Occupational Safety and Health Commission* 499 U.S. 144 (1991). Also see *Thomas Jefferson University v Shalala* 512 U.S. 504 (1994): "We must give substantial deference to an agency's interpretation of its own regulations." Also see *Chalenor et al. v University of North Dakota*, U.S. Court of Appeals, 8th Cir. #00-3379ND, May 30, 2002 at p. 8. See also *Auer v Robbins* 519 U.S. 452 (1997)—required to give deference to agency, *Glover v Standard Fed. Bank* 283 F. 3d 953, 962 (8th Cir. 2002)—agency's policy interpretation of its own regulations is controlling authority.

[10] *Grove City College v Bell*, 104 S.Ct. 1211 (1984). Within days of the *Grove City* decision, scholarship programs for women were canceled at a number of colleges and universities even though *Grove City* only removed the teeth from Title IX rather than affecting the definition of equitable treatment of male and female students, which had caused its enactment 12 years before. See chapter 6 for the details of the effect of *Grove City* on the enforcement ability of Title IX in intercollegiate athletics programs.

[11] Civil Rights Restoration Act of 1987, 20 U.S.C. section 1687 (1988). Although the CRRA became law in 1988, it is more accurately known as the CRRA of 1987. Congress did not pass the 1987 act over President Reagan's veto until 1988.

[12] Included in the 1990 *Investigator's Manual* was a policy clarification regarding coaching compensation from June 1983. Had Title IX been in force more than a few months after the coaching clarification was issued, the clarification might have had greater discussion, but the 1984 *Grove City* Supreme Court decision intervened.

[13] See *Bennett v West Texas State University* 799 F. 2d 155, 159 (5th Cir. 1986), which dismissed all Title IX claims including athletic financial aid. See also *Haffer v Temple University* No. 80-1362 (E.D. Pa. Feb. 14, 1985), which dismissed all Title IX claims except scholarships through the financial aid office.

[14] See *Cohen* 991 F. 2d at 896. Chapter 7 more completely discusses the *Cohen* case. The case brought much attention to the varying weight of the regulations versus the policy interpretations.

[15] See *Glover v Standard Fed. Bank* 283 F. 3d 953 (8th Cir. 2002) for a discussion of the weight conferred on policy interpretations.

[16] *Cohen* 991 F. 2d at 896. The proportionality prong of the test for compliance in the area of access to participation opportunities was the primary focus of the *Cohen* case. See chapter 9 for current and continuing controversy concerning proportionality.

[17] Indeed, in the area most debated regarding Title IX, proportionality, no lawsuit that has addressed the issue has ever found it to be an impermissible choice as a method when selected by the institution for determining compliance with the regulation to provide equal opportunities to participate. A review of courts that have rendered decisions concerning the relationship of Title IX and its policy interpretations demonstrates almost unanimity of thought; it is permissible to move toward compliance with the requirement to provide access for the historically underrepre-

sented sex (generally women in athletics) by either increasing their opportunities or by decreasing the opportunities of the historically overrepresented sex (generally males). A review of the stated purposes for including athletics in the broader educational endeavor, however, might support the notion that the first method is vastly preferable to the second.

[18]An OCR complaint must be filed within 180 days of the act of discrimination (see 34 CFR, sec. 100.7(b) 1992). Continuing discrimination results in a rolling statute of limitations starting over each new day. The 180-day statute of limitations does not apply to a lawsuit; it applies only to OCR complaints. Where lawsuits are concerned, the statute of limitations is borrowed from the state statute that most nearly mirrors the federal law, Title IX. See *Bougher v University of Pittsburgh*, 882 F. 2d 74 at 77 (3d Cir. 1989), which reaffirmed the inapplicability of the administrative 180-day statute of limitations within lawsuits, as also noted in *Burnett v Gratan*, 468 U.S. 42 (1984) at 51, and *Minor v Northville Pub. Sch.*, 605 F. Supp. 1185 (E.D. Mich. 1985) at 1199.

[19] The term "letter of resolution" replaced the term "letter of findings" in the mid-1990s. This change was made, in part, as a verbal token of OCR's greater emphasis on developing an agreement with the institution earlier in the process through a let's-get-this-resolved attitude. Some would argue that the kinder, gentler, more conciliatory approach did little to shorten the time but did lessen the institution's discomfiture with the process.

[20]*A License for Bias*, American Association of University Women, Legal Advocacy Fund, 2000 at 55. The study that served as a basis for much of the material in *A License for Bias* focuses mainly on nonathletics programs. But the discussion of enforcement mechanisms and OCR's response to allegations of Title IX noncompliance are broadly applicable. *A License for Bias* provides good insight into application of Title IX beyond the fields of play.

[21]For example, on the 25th birthday of Title IX, the National Women's Law Center filed complaints at 25 schools even though the NWLC had no legal connection or specific interest in any of the 25 schools.

2

The Law As Applied to Physical Education

Title IX and athletics go together. The effect of one on the other has been massive; the media have found nourishing fodder in the Title IX–athletics relationship. But Title IX has had a similar effect but with considerably less media attention in the related area of physical education.

THE REGULATIONS

Some of the sections in the regulations apply to physical education as well as to athletics and other areas of the educational endeavor. For example, section 106.33, which requires comparable facilities, is universally applicable. But sections 106.31 and 106.34 single out physical education for attention:

> **Section 106.31 Education programs or activities.**
>
> (a) [omitted, not applicable to current discussion.]
>
> (b) *Specific prohibitions.* Except as provided in this subpart, in providing any aid, benefit, or service to a student, a recipient [of federal money] shall not, on the basis of sex:
>
> (1) Treat one person differently from another in determining whether such person satisfies any requirement or condition for the provision of such aid, benefit, or service;
>
> (2) Provide different aid, benefits, or services or provide aid, benefits, or services in a different manner;
>
> (3) Deny any person any such aid, benefit, or service;
>
> (4) Subject any person to separate or different rules of behavior, sanctions, or other treatment;

(5) Apply any rule concerning the domicile or residence of a student or applicant, including eligibility for in-state fees and tuition;

(6) Aid or perpetuate discrimination against any person by providing significant assistance to any agency, organization, or person which discriminates on the basis of sex in providing any aid, benefit or service to students or employees;

(7) Otherwise limit any person in the enjoyment of any right, privilege, advantage, or opportunity.

Did you notice that item number 5 is missing in the previous list? On July 28, 1982, item number 5 was revoked. Item number 5 prohibited "(5) Discriminat[ion] against any person in the application of any rules of appearance." Dress codes are common in sport as well as in other areas of the educational endeavor. Many believe that school uniforms reduce the amount of theft and gang violence at school. Others feel that wearing jewelry during physical education classes or other sport participation carries with it risk of injury for the wearer and for those around the wearer. These and other dress codes may seem both reasonable and gender neutral, but sometimes they are not. For instance, when a code of appearance for schools in New York City was recently being considered, the proposed rules requiring slacks for males and skirts for girls appeared at first blush to be gender neutral. The proposed rule, however, would have meant that girls would face the winter weather with bare legs as they ran, jumped, and engaged in other freedom-of-movement activities. Such activities would be more limited for individuals wearing skirts than for those wearing slacks.

The revocation of item 5 does not mean that local authorities cannot set and enforce appearance codes, but it does mean that the enforcement effort of Title IX will not be expended on appearance codes. OCR received 53 comments from interested parties concerning item 5. Thirty-one of those comments supported the revocation of item 5, with most noting that federal intervention into appearance codes would both sap the enforcement energy of OCR and constitute overregulation by the federal government. Although the intervention of Title IX into appearance codes has been revoked, discrimination in the application of appearance codes may still be actionable through such means as 14th Amendment constitutional claims.

Let's look at examples of how the other items in section 106.31 apply to physical education classes.

It is prohibited to

(1) Treat one person differently from another in determining whether such person satisfies any requirement or condition for the provision of such aid, benefit, or service.

Here are three examples of how this prohibition affects physical education:

- Teachers cannot require attendance, skills, or written tests for female students in order to pass a physical education class while giving class credit to males just because they are varsity athletes.
- When a teacher uses a single standard to measure skill but that method adversely affects one sex because of such things as anatomical or physiological differences between the sexes, a Title IX issue arises. For instance, if a swimming teacher deducts 10 percent from the grade each time a student observes rather than swims, the single standard that is gender neutral on its face would have a disparate adverse effect on menstruating females who elect to use pads rather than tampons and thus observe rather than swim during their menstrual periods.
- Using two different skill tests, one for boys and another for girls, is problematic if the tests are based on sex rather than on neutral standards such as body size, weight, or maturation. If such skill tests result in an adverse, gender-based effect on one sex, the institution administering the test may face Title IX sanctions.

Does it seem as though a physical education teacher has to put some energy into developing nondiscriminatory testing protocol? Yes, and doing so is difficult unless the teacher puts aside previously established habits and starts with a clear understanding of exactly what is being tested. Consider, for example, a volleyball skills test for girls that requires a 12-inch vertical jump and a similar test for boys that requires a 14-inch vertical jump. What is being tested? Is an assumption being made that girls cannot perform as well on a vertical jump as their male counterparts? Rather than having two standards, one for boys and another for girls, a more appropriate dual standard, if one is needed, might be based more on student height or student weight (factors not based on gender that would have more direct correlation with vertical-jumping skill.)

It is prohibited to

(2) Provide different aid, benefits, or services or provide aid, benefits, or services in a different manner.

Here are two examples of how this prohibition affects physical education:

- Teachers can group students in many ways—by sex, age, skill, weight, or grade in school. When students are grouped by sex, Title IX is probably being violated.
- Hiring experienced teachers for male students and employing inexperienced teachers for female students equates to providing the services of a teacher differently for the female students, thus contravening section 106.31 (b)(2) of the regulations.

It is prohibited to

(3) Deny any person any such aid, benefit, or service.

One example of this prohibition in action is the availability of weight rooms. Weight rooms have long been the domain of male physical education students. But if female physical education students are denied access to weight rooms, Title IX is being violated.

It is prohibited to

(4) Subject any person to separate or different rules of behavior, sanctions, or other treatment.

One example of this prohibition in action is how teachers respond to misbehavior. Both boys and girls misbehave. But teachers often respond differently to that misbehavior. A teacher who punishes a female student's misbehavior in class but acquiesces to a male student's similar misbehavior by saying, "Boys will be boys," has violated the principle found in section 106.31(b)(4).

It is prohibited to

(5) Apply any rule concerning the domicile or residence of a student or applicant, including eligibility for in-state fees and tuition.

One example of this prohibition in action is out-of-district enrollment. Allowing an out-of-district male student to enroll simply because he would be an asset to the varsity program while denying a female student the same waiving of the residence requirement is a violation of Title IX.

It is prohibited to

(6) Aid or perpetuate discrimination against any person by providing significant assistance to any agency, organization,

or person which discriminates on the basis of sex in providing any aid, benefit or service to students or employees.

One example of this prohibition in action is use of facilities and equipment. When a school significantly aids an off-campus group that prohibits participation by females by allowing it to use school facilities or equipment, Title IX issues arise. For instance, if Itty Bitty League Baseball, which permits only boys to participate, rents a school's fields for the season, the organization, Itty Bitty League Baseball, which "discriminates on the basis of sex" by not "providing aid, benefit or services" to girls, may trigger an accusation of Title IX noncompliance against the school supplying the facilities or equipment.

It is prohibited to

(7) Otherwise limit any person in the enjoyment of any right, privilege, advantage, or opportunity.

Here are four examples of how this prohibition can affect physical education:

- Banning females from an advanced basketball class would raise Title IX issues.
- Allowing free play in the gym for boys after school but not allowing girls to play would also raise Title IX issues.
- If an award is given to the boy in class who makes the highest score or shows the greatest improvement, but no comparable award is available to female students, Title IX issues arise.
- Permitting a highly skilled male basketball player to bypass a prerequisite required to enter an advanced basketball class by virtue of his membership on the school team but banning a female from the same advanced basketball class or requiring the female to audition for the class by proving her skills even though she is a member of the school's basketball team would violate this subsection.

Coeducational Requirements

Teachers and administrators of goodwill find it reasonably easy to live up to the regulations found in section 106.31. Observing those regulations requires little, if any, staffing expenditure or alteration of facilities. Living up to them requires only commitment, unbarring doors, and minor curricular and grading-protocol reassessment. The regulations found in section 106.34 (access to course offerings), however, have presented greater hurdles for physical educators.

Section 106.34 Access to course offerings.

A recipient shall not provide any course or otherwise carry out any of its education program or activity separately on the basis of sex, or require or refuse participation therein by any of its students on such basis, including health, physical education, industrial, business, vocational, technical, home economics, music, and adult education courses.

(a) [omitted, not applicable to this discussion.]

(b) This section does not prohibit grouping of students in physical education classes and activities by ability as assessed by objective standards of individual performance developed and applied without regard to sex.

(c) This section does not prohibit separation of students by sex within physical education classes or activities during participation in wrestling, boxing, rugby, ice hockey, football, basketball and other sports the purpose or major activity of which involves bodily contact.

(d) Where use of a single standard of measuring skill or progress in a physical education class has an adverse effect on members of one sex, the recipient shall use appropriate standards which do not have such an effect.

(e) Portions of classes in elementary and secondary schools which deal exclusively with human sexuality may be conducted in separate sessions for boys and girls.

In sum, section 106.34 mandates coeducational classes, with a few exceptions. Coeducational social studies classes, language arts classes, and chemistry classes seem to need no explanation (although one of the authors was the first female allowed to participate in her previously all-male, no-girls-allowed high school physics class). But when physical education classes are involved, coeducation seems to cause much consternation. As a reflection of this consternation, the Department of Education's Office for Civil Rights promulgated guidelines on single-sex classes and schools in May 2002[1] and, at the same time, also requested comments on the state of the coeducational requirement of the regulations on the educational process in anticipation of proposing changes.[2] The stated impetus for this regulatory activity is the enactment of the No Child Left Behind Act of 2001. The current discussion perhaps also reflects the reality that coeducational physical education classes carry inherent pedagogical and logistical challenges that only now, more than 30 years after the passage of Title IX, are being effectively dealt with so that the inherent and logistical benefits of a coeducational physical education experience can be realized in classes taught by dedicated, insightful, and creative teachers supported by similar administrators.[3]

Why don't we see as many physical education Title IX complaints and lawsuits as we do athletics Title IX complaints and lawsuits? OCR complaints and lawsuits concerning the coed requirements of Title IX remain almost nonexistent. Although there are some OCR complaints and lawsuits about Title IX violations in physical education, they are small in number compared with those focused on athletics, and they concern disparate, discriminatory treatment rather than compliance or noncompliance with the coeducation requirement. This is the case probably because often the students are content in a single-sex environment, having had little experience in a high-quality coeducational environment. Similarly, teachers who prefer single-sex classes because of habit or belief simply find subtle ways to pay lip service to the coeducational process while teaching in single-sex circumstances. Such teachers are among those least likely to file an OCR complaint or lawsuit to enforce the coeducation requirement.

Let's review a few frequently occurring scenarios that, although often uncontested by complaint or lawsuit, are likely to be violations of the coeducation requirements of Title IX.

- Taking roll as a coed class using dummy rolls and then separating into a boys' class and a girls' class.
- Scheduling classes such as football opposite aerobic dance with the intent of producing sex-segregated classes.
- Requiring girls to pass a skill test to enroll in an advanced class or a typically males-only class such as football, when boys do not have to pass such a test.
- Labeling a class as "girls' basketball" or "boys' wrestling."

It is not difficult to understand the motivation for using single-sex classes in some situations, even though doing so produces compliance issues. Older facilities often include locker rooms at opposite ends of the school so that when coed classes are offered, boys must run through the hallways to get to the girls' gym at the other end of the school from the boys' locker room and vice versa. Hormones increase discipline issues when classes are coed. Ingrained gender-based behaviors imprinted by parents who grew up before Title IX find expression in abusive or derisive behaviors or expectations in class. Teachers have experience teaching only single-sex classes, and retraining opportunities are not available.

Making coeducational physical education a reality can be difficult in some situations, but grouping children by skill rather than by gender fosters teamwork and respect.

But much can be gained by overcoming such roadblocks to coeducational physical education. Pedagogically, it is wiser to group by skill (related to the activity) than by gender (unrelated to the activity). Socially, students learn to respect members of the opposite sex when they are grouped by skill and strive together to increase proficiency. The teamwork and respect that follow may lessen male-female out-of-class disrespect and abuse.

In any case, coeducational physical education in activities other than those deemed contact activities is the current state of the law.

Contact Sports Exception

Physical education classes must be coeducational unless the activity being participated in is a contact sport. According to the Title IX definition formed in the 1970s, contact sports are wrestling, boxing, rugby, ice hockey, football, basketball, and any other sport in which bodily contact is its purpose or major activity. If a Title IX–designated contact sport is involved, single-sex classes may be used, but they don't have to be.

Let's take a look at examples of how the contact sport exception applies to physical education classes.

- A school in a town where basketball is extremely popular decides to offer three basketball classes. One will be coed, and the other two will be single sex. This arrangement would be acceptable within the constraints of Title IX because as a contact sport, basketball may be offered as a single-sex class but does not have to be.

- A school has a class that contains three units—basketball, karate, and volleyball. During the semester, the class may be, but doesn't have to be, separated by sex during the basketball and karate units, but it must be coed during the volleyball unit. Basketball is a named contact sport, and karate fits the definition of a sport in which bodily contact is its purpose or major activity.

- After several muggings of students near campus, a school decides to offer a self-defense class for girls. Designating a particular class or unit within a class as "boys only" or "girls only" is not permissible unless the class or unit falls into the contact sport exception. So in this scenario the legality of offering a single-sex course in self-defense depends on whether self-defense can be legitimately classified as an activity whose major purpose is bodily contact. If so, the school may offer it on a single-sex basis. If not, it must be coed.

- In some areas of the country, because of religious tenets, females cannot swim with males because females are not allowed to be in a state of undress comparable to wearing a swimsuit with males. Where these are strict and observed tenets, single-sex swimming classes may be scheduled even though swimming is not within the contact sport exception. When the closing of the swimming class to males in such instances is based on religion and is not a sham reason, the single-sex class is permissible within Title IX. However, the religious exception must be narrowly construed.

Why are contact sports excluded from the mandatory coeducational requirement? Historically, the participation of females in sport was limited not only by virtue of an intent to exclude their participation in a male domain but also by virtue of a paternalistic and maternalistic

Female Wrestlers Sue University of California-Davis for Title IX Violations, Fired Wrestling Coach Sues for Retaliation

Womens Sports Foundation, Media Relations, December 15, 2003

desire to protect them physiologically and anatomically from injury and overexertion. From the time when Title IX was enacted, 12 years would pass before women were allowed to run a marathon in the Olympics. Rosie the Riveter's shoulders carried a significant portion of the homeland defense effort in World War II, but at the end of the war, those shoulders were deemed too feminine and fragile to play on a basketball court divided into less than three sections, too delicate to dribble the ball more than three bounces, and too feeble to contact the opponent lightly without incurring a foul.

In the 1960s women's basketball *was* a noncontact sport. Society's view of women as too fragile to participate safely in sweaty, rough sports provided part of the impetus for the contact sports exclusion. But it has been argued that the then prevailing view of women also provided the NCAA with a good excuse for carving out a bit of protected male domain from the incursion of women. See chapter 5 for a fuller discussion of the attempts by the NCAA to remove all athletics from the jurisdiction of Title IX and, when that effort was unsuccessful, to construct firewalls to limit the effect of Title IX on those sports deemed most "male." In the meanwhile, consider from a sport and political point of view why basketball (considered by some to be a potentially revenue-producing sport in athletics programs) might have been included as a designated contact sport when the regulations were drafted in the 1970s (and thus a sport for which coed learning experiences were not required) and why others such as soccer or lacrosse, which may be equally contact oriented, were not. Also, ponder what the effect might be on both physical education experiences and athletics if the contact sport exception were to be removed.

The few lawsuits relating to the contact exception have dealt primarily with the sport of field hockey[4] and typically involve boys wanting to become members of girls' teams. Because field hockey is not one of the enumerated contact sports, the issue of whether it should be classified as one because bodily contact is its purpose or major activity becomes paramount. The courts have listened to experts explain the no-contact nature of the rules of field hockey and have heard other experts explain the heavy contact that actually occurs on the hockey field. Do the rules define a sport as contact in nature, or does reality define it? Because of the paucity of cases, all that can be said with surety is that when the contact versus noncontact nature of a sport is in question, the sports rules are not controlling. The reality of the play of the game is the focus.

Whatever the reason for the contact sport exception, the effect is that many physical education programs interpret the idea that they "may" offer single-sex classes when contact sports are involved to mean that they "must" offer single-sex classes. When physical education programs choose to exclude rather than include females in contact sport settings, they are creating a de facto exclusion of their female students from the opportunity to test themselves in coeducational settings and develop the character skills often stated as a strong reason to include contact sports

Since tennis is not a contact sport, physical education classes in tennis must be coeducational.

in the curriculum. Besides limiting opportunities for females, a reflexive exclusion of females from coeducational contact sport experiences perpetuates a message of feminine fragility to both males and females. The understanding and respect that can develop in coeducational programs (including contact sports) are also limited.[5]

Similarly, when girls are excluded from coed contact sports classes in their physical education experiences, they are deprived of the opportunity to learn and improve their skills in contact sports altogether unless a school offers a full range of single-sex classes for girls in contact sports such as wrestling and football. The girls' consequent lack of skills and, most likely, interest, in sports they have been barred from learning leaves them easy targets for continued deprivation beyond physical education in the athletics arena by claims that "girls just don't want to play rough sports so there is no need to offer them opportunities." This assertion is much like saying that Susie, who has never been allowed to sit in the front of the bus, prefers riding in the back of the bus. The contact sport exclusion may have outlived whatever usefulness in the cause of equity it had. Homogeneous grouping by size, weight, height, or age, where appropriate, within contact sport classes provides a better method of developing a gender-neutral and pedagogically sound contact sport experience. Even so, the law as it stands today provides for the possibility of single-sex classes in contact sports.

THE CONTINUING COEDUCATION VERSUS SINGLE-SEX DEBATE

In the realm of Title IX and athletics, proportionality is the focus of the most heated rhetoric. In the realm of Title IX and physical education, the focus is coeducational classes. Hormones and habits combine to make coeducational physical education classes full of challenges. When Title IX was enacted and its regulations adopted, a great deal of discussion focused on how to meet its challenges in athletics, but physical educators enjoyed little similar discussion. Some who were frustrated chose to find ways around the requirements of Title IX, especially those relating to coeducational classes. When complaints have been filed relating to physical education, most have focused on section 106.31 (fair treatment) or 106.33 (comparable facilities) rather than 106.34 (access to course offerings). Equitable treatment relating to quality of teachers, provision of equipment, size and suitability of facilities, and so forth (which are discussed in chapter 4) apply equally to the realm of physical education. The intent of the Office for Civil Rights to revisit the requirement for coed physical education classes may result in broader latitude for single-sex offerings. If it does, will a renewed blessing of the previously rejected notion of efficacy and equity in a doctrine of separate but equal produce an increase in Title IX complaints or lawsuits related to physical education because of separate but *un*equal realities? Stay tuned.

IN BRIEF

In brief, Title IX as applied to physical education classes requires equity in grading, testing, facilities, equipment, assignment of teachers, locker rooms, and other areas of support and application of the curriculum. Title IX requires coeducational experiences in all activities except contact sports. When contact sports are involved, coeducational experiences are perfectly permissible, but it is also permissible (but only where contact activities are concerned) to provide single-sex experiences. It is prudent, however, to hold fast to the "equal" part of the "separate but equal" phrase if single-sex experiences are selected for contact sports activities.

Worthy pedagogy is a challenge in all circumstances, but some teachers find that goal extremely difficult to attain in coeducational physical education situations. Perhaps this is so because old habits and traditions practiced for years in a pervasive single-sex paradigm are difficult to break. Perhaps this is so because teacher-training programs have failed to provide their students with the tools they need to discover the inherent benefits of high-quality pedagogy in a single-sex environment. Whatever the cause, our daughters and sons deserve high-quality instruction and positive learning experiences whether they are in coeducational or single-sex physical education settings.[6]

Seven Questions and Seven Answers

1. **If a physical education class includes units on basketball and volleyball, is it OK for the entire semester course to be taught in a single-sex environment?**

   No. Basketball, a designated contact sport, is a unit during which the class may be taught on a single-sex basis, although it is not required to be taught in that way. Volleyball, however, is not a designated contact sport, nor does it fit into the amorphous category of a sport whose major purpose is contact. Therefore, the volleyball unit must be taught on a coeducational basis.

2. **If a school's grading policy is different for boys and girls, is the policy a potential violation of Title IX?**

Yes. Grading policies or class requirements that are determined by a student's gender rather than by a neutral factor such as skill, experience, progress, or height and weight are not permitted under Title IX.

3. **Is it OK to teach girls and boys separately (even in noncontact classes) as long as their names all appear on one roster and we take roll and do warm-ups together?**

   No. Dummy rolls are not acceptable under Title IX. The reality of a coeducational experience, not the appearance, is significant to a determination of compliance.

4. **If a facility is old and has a girls' gym (which is smaller and less suitable but near the girls' locker room) and a boys' gym (which is bigger and better and near the boys' locker room), can the school continue to schedule the girls' contact sport, single-sex classes in the girls' gym without violating Title IX?**

   No. If a school has only two teaching stations, one of which is better than the other, single-sex classes (acceptable for contact sports) should be scheduled on an equal basis in the better gym. A formula that might achieve equity of scheduling is for the girls' class to use the better gym one semester and the boys' class to use it the next semester.

5. **Assume that a school has two elective physical education classes each hour. The school thinks that if students select their courses and just happen to register by gender, then the school has no Title IX problem. So the school offers football opposite modern dance for the first hour and weightlifting opposite aerobic dance for the second hour. Does the school have a Title IX problem?**

   Yes. Although football is a contact sport and thus may be offered as a single-sex class, the disingenuous scheduling of classes with the hope that students will self-select by gender is suspect under Title IX. During the second hour (aerobics and weightlifting) neither class has an exemption from being offered on a coeducational basis. But if the school's intent is to encourage girls to register for aerobics and boys to register for weight training, Title IX issues arise.

6. **If a school has an experienced, talented teacher who also happens to coach football and a mediocre, uncertified, poorly prepared teacher, does it matter who teaches which classes?**

   Yes. If the talented teacher is consistently assigned to teach classes in which it is anticipated that most of the students will be males or if the permissibly offered single-sex classes are assigned so that the male students have the talented teacher and the female students have the mediocre teacher, the students are not being treated equally and the inequality is gender based. Therefore, Title IX problems are present.

7. **Is it true that what guidance exists about compliance with Title IX in a physical education setting is found in the regulations rather than in the policy interpretations?**

Yes. The policy interpretations do not address physical education issues. Instead, they address athletics and, by extension, intramural programs but not physical education programs. But the tenor of the information found in the policy interpretations can, in practice, be useful to the physical educator who is trying to see areas in which inequity might exist in the physical education program. For instance, the policy interpretations explain how to measure compliance with the requirement of equal access to coaching. Extrapolation of such explanations can provide useful, if not official, guidance to the assignment of physical education teachers.

NOTES

[1] "Guidelines on Title IX Requirements" presents the current state of the regulations rather than proposing changes. See *Federal Register* vol. 67, no. 89, pages 31102-31103, May 8, 2002. Web site: www.ed.gov/about/offices/list/ocr/t9-guidelines-ss.html?exp=0.

[2] "Nondiscrimination on the Basis of Sex in Education Programs or Activities Receiving Federal Financial Assistance; Proposed Rule," *Federal Register* vol. 67, no. 89, pages 31098-31099, May 8, 2002 (was entered into the Federal Record the same day as the "Guideline" referred to in note 1). Regardless of the title, the statement does not propose changes; it only invites comments about the issue of single-sex classes and schools concerning the broad topic of increasing the latitude for offering single-sex classes and schools. Web site: www.ed.gov/legislation/FedRegister/proprule/2002-2/050802a.html. The proposed redrafted guidelines include NO suggested changes for the single sex/coed rules as they relate to physical education although changes are proposed for other subject areas.

[3] *Equity in the Gymnasium: Coed Physical Education: Finding Solutions and Meeting the Challenges*, 2000 (partially funded by a grant from the American Association of University Women), available from the National Association for Girls and Women in Sport, provides useful and effective ideas about developing coed physical education programs that benefit all. Web site: www.nagws.org.

[4] See *Williams v School Dist. of Bethlehem*, 998 F. 2d 168 (3d Cir. 1993) and *Kleczek v Rhode Island Interscholastic League, Inc.*, 768 F. Supp. 951 (D.R.I. 1991) for two courts' discussions of the basis of the contact sport exception. The points of view

of rules versus reality as a basis for determining contact, although divergent and thus not at all controlling, provide insight into the issue and effect of the contact sport exemption.

[5]Suzanne Sangree argues concisely and cogently for the removal of the contact sports exception in "Title IX and the Contact Sports Exemption: Gender Stereotypes in a Civil Rights Statute," *Connecticut Law Review* 32 (winter 2000): 381. In sum, she makes the following point: "The historic exclusion of females from athletics generally, and particularly from contact sports, combined with cultural taboos for women against developing 'male' qualities of physical stamina and strength, muscle mass, and overt aggressive competitiveness, have surely been central components of female dependence and vulnerability to violence. Moreover, benefits touted to justify large expenditures on male athletic opportunities—the emphasis on character building, leadership development, learning team work, learning to excel in highly competitive environments—would equally advantage female citizens in this competitive market economy. Unfettered participation in athletics [and physical education] for women, . . . as full status athletes [and physical education students] entitled to the respect and political and economic opportunities showered upon male athletes would have wide cultural repercussions" at 383.

[6]Helpful information and publications concerning positive teaching techniques in coeducational physical education settings are available from the National Association for Girls and Women in Sport (Web site: www.nagws.org).

3

The Law As Applied to Intramural, Club, and Recreation Sport Activities

Intramural programs (within the school) are often more relaxed and of shorter duration than interscholastic or intercollegiate programs (between schools). Intramural programs generally involve no coaching, and the competition is between teams of only one institution. Intramurals include no off-campus recruitment, no travel to other institutions, no financial aid, and no uniforms other than the pennies[1] or some other informal, use-for-the-day method of delineating team membership.

Club sports can be sports on campus with formal and continuing membership, and they sometimes have a coach. School-based sport clubs often compete with other schools but do so without rising to the level of a full intercollegiate or interscholastic team. Participants often fund club sports themselves or raise the necessary resources through fund-raising or donations from outside sources. The term "club sports," however, can also apply to teams that compete with each other in leagues not aligned with any educational institution. Some club sports are also known as recreational leagues. Sports such as soccer, field hockey, flag football, and softball often have strong club associations.

"Recreation" is a generic term that can include noninstitutional club sports as well as a pickup basketball game at a local park or a round of golf at a nearby municipal course. The terms "intramural," "club," and "recreation" have no age-based significance. Rather, the terms apply to the structure of the participation paradigm and the degree of relationship to an institution or community.

This chapter considers the applicability of Title IX to sport or physical activity outside the environs of intercollegiate or interscholastic athletic or physical education programs.

Intramural sport has a long history. Here, college women in 1933 play intramural football.

JURISDICTIONAL CONSIDERATIONS

Although intramural, club, and recreation sports are less clearly defined than physical education or interscholastic or intercollegiate athletics, whenever the three required elements of Title IX jurisdiction exist, intramural, club, and recreational sports programs need to live up to their Title IX obligations. With intramural, club, and recreational sport, determining whether all three required elements of Title IX jurisdiction exist can be difficult.

Three elements are required for Title IX jurisdiction:

1. allegation of discrimination based on *sex* within an
2. *education* program that receives
3. *federal* financial assistance.

In a discussion about Title IX jurisdiction, the first element, allegation of discrimination based on sex, is a given. Without such an allegation we wouldn't even be talking about Title IX jurisdiction.

The second element, education program, is also not a major issue, even in recreation sport programs not attached to a school. In a debate of the issue, evidence of educational content is usually forthcoming, if by no other source than elementary instruction or miniworkshops. Elementary instruction and miniworkshops are typical components of intramural, club, and recreation sport experiences.

The third component, federal financial assistance, is easily shown in intramural, club, and recreation programs found on campuses, but its absence is often a barrier to Title IX jurisdiction when non-school-based entities run such programs. The facts in *Baca v City of Los Angeles*[2] illustrate the difficulties of obtaining Title IX jurisdiction over non-school-based programs.

In the *Baca* situation, each year over 400 girls learned and competed in softball as members of the private, not-for-profit, community-based recreation program known as West Valley Girls' Softball (WVGS). Although the City of Los Angeles owned numerous softball and baseball fields, the 30-year-old WVGS had never been able to obtain a permit for a home field. Boys' baseball groups were able to enjoy home fields to the exclusion of the girls because of the "perpetual" permit advantage. Teams that had occupied a field the previous year received first choice on the field. Thus, the girls' teams never had access. The girls experienced the first element, discrimination based on sex. The sport program included

A recreation league in which children learn softball skills (including swinging a bat properly) may or may not fall under the jurisdiction of Title IX, usually depending on presence or absence of federal financial assistance.

facets that would provide the second element, education program. The presence of federal financial aid within the city's recreation and parks program, however, was doubtful. Rather than using Title IX as a tool to pursue access to the city's fields, the WVGS chose to use the legal tool of the 14th Amendment's equal protection clause. By choosing the 14th Amendment instead of Title IX, the WVGS avoided the thorny issue of whether federal financial aid was present.

The 14th Amendment, as with all constitutional-based challenges to discrimination, requires that the defendant be a "state actor" but unlike Title IX does not require the presence of federal financial aid. A state actor is an entity that is either an agency of government (such as a public school) or an entity that functions in governmental ways. The City of Los Angeles is, without doubt, a state actor, and thus the WVGS's 14th Amendment challenge to the field-permitting process could advance.[3] A home-field advantage is now possible for the softball players.

Several other noteworthy cases have challenged sex discrimination by athletic associations on constitutional rather than Title IX grounds. The plaintiffs had to take that approach because of the lack of federal funding. Using the Constitution rather than Title IX is unremarkable when the defendant is obviously a state actor. But several recent cases have involved private athletic associations that to the casual observer do not appear to fit into a classification of state actor. Among these are *Brentwood Academy v Tennessee Secondary School Athletic Association* (TSSAA), wherein the U.S. Supreme Court found that the statewide TSSAA, which regulated competition between both public and private schools, was in fact a state actor. The court used an "entwinement" theory to do so. The nature of TSSAA's activities, the makeup of the personnel on its board (which included public school principals), and the fact that 84 percent of its membership was made up of public schools (state actors themselves) were all so closely entwined with governmental policies that the TSSAA was transformed from its claims of being a private organizational status into being defined as a state actor.[4]

> "[T]he obligation to comply with [Title IX] is not obviated or alleviated by any rule or regulation of any . . . athletic or other . . . association."
>
> *34 CFR sec 106.6 (c) 1992*

THE JURISDICTIONAL DEBATE

Jurisdiction is the issue of debate within the realm of applying Title IX to intramural, club, and recreation sports programs. In many situations the potential defendant is not a state actor, even under the entwinement doctrine, and the only possible avenue to challenge sex discrimination resides in Title IX. Among those situations are private schools, the NCAA, and athletic leagues and conferences that often try to character-ize themselves as nonstate actors. Thus, finding a connection to federal financial assistance is sometimes critical.

Many parties have suggested creative methods for finding the pres-ence of federal financial assistance and thus Title IX jurisdiction, but few have yet been tested in the courts. Here are a few of the theories being discussed:

- Can federal financial aid, which is in the hands of a legally sepa-rate but related organization, trigger Title IX jurisdiction over the related organization? For example, can Title IX jurisdiction be extended to the NCAA because of the presence of federal finan-cial aid within the coffers of the legally separate NCAA's National Youth Sport Grants Program?
- Does tax-exempt status serve as a form of federal financial assis-tance to the tax-exempt organization, thereby bringing the orga-nization under Title IX (if the other two elements exist)?
- When federal financial aid comes to the hands of facilities owners rather than the sports program administrators who use those facili-ties, can the owners be brought under the jurisdiction of Title IX?

Answers to these questions do not yet exist. The issues are debated in law reviews, lawyer's offices, and school counsel conference rooms. What is certain is that potential complainants and plaintiffs are seeking to extend the length of the jurisdictional reach of Title IX. Let's look at the issues reflected by each question.

A Friend's Federal Financial Assistance

The most likely of the previously discussed methods to be successful is the first, so let's look at a leading case on the topic. *R.M. Smith v National Collegiate Athletic Association*[5] is still working its way through the judicial system, but it will most likely produce a definitive discussion of the issue when it concludes. Smith did not use up her entire athletic eligibility while an undergraduate at St. Bonaventure University. In pursuit of the appropriate graduate program in her field, one not offered by St. Bonaventure, she enrolled at Hofstra and then later at the University of Pittsburgh. Smith wanted to complete her eligibility at each of her graduate schools, but the NCAA declined to grant her a waiver to do so. Smith filed a Title IX lawsuit against the NCAA claiming, among other things, that the NCAA granted such waivers more frequently to males than to females. Smith's first attempt was dismissed.[6] Smith filed several motions and appeals. After considerable legal maneuvering had occurred, the U.S. Court of Appeals for the Third Circuit allowed Smith to amend her originally flawed complaint. The court of appeals decided that the receipt by the NCAA of dues from institutions who themselves receive federal financial assistance was sufficient to trigger Title IX jurisdiction.

The *Smith* case then went to the U.S. Supreme Court, which ruled that the presence of dues was insufficient to trigger jurisdiction, thereby overturning the court of appeals. But the Supreme Court saw the potential for other sources of federal financial assistance, as it vacated the decision of the court of appeals, and remanded the case (returned the case for further decision) to the court of appeals. The Supreme Court suggested that the court of appeals might consider either or both of the following as possible methods of showing the presence of federal financial aid within the NCAA:

1. Federal financial assistance comes to the National Youth Sports Program (NYSP) and the National Youth Sports Program Fund (NYSPF). The NCAA administers both.
2. The NCAA is the "controlling authority" over the NYSP and NYSPF even though they are, on their faces, separate and distinct entities from the NCAA.

In August 2001 the court of appeals, to which the Supreme Court had remanded the case, in turn sent the case down to the original district court for further consideration with the concurring opinion that both of the theories for triggering Title IX jurisdiction against the NCAA were worthy of consideration.

Because some courts in unrelated cases have found the "controlling authority" argument persuasive when used in Title IX cases and other courts have not, it is difficult to predict whether the argument will carry the day against the NCAA. Only time will tell.

The first argument, that federal financial assistance to the NYSP or the NYSPF triggers jurisdiction over the NCAA, may not be viable in the absence of the second line of reasoning, "controlling authority." Again, we'll have to wait for the outcome.

Tax-Exempt Status as Federal Financial Assistance

The second creative method for meeting the requirement that the Title IX defendant must be a recipient of federal financial assistance is to redefine[7] more broadly the accepted meaning of federal financial assistance to include tax-exempt status. The argument proceeds this way: "If an organization is relieved of its burden to submit taxes to the federal government, the money maintained in the organization's budget effectively came from the federal government and other taxpayers who made up the difference."[8] The courts have seldom addressed the issue and even less frequently found unanimity in their points of view. Using tax exemption as a method of gaining Title IX jurisdiction is certainly a stretch, but again, only time will tell.

A Facility Owner's Federal Financial Assistance

Sometimes the program operator is the discriminator, but the operator does not receive federal financial assistance. In the absence of federal financial assistance, Title IX jurisdiction fails. But what if the owner of the facilities used by the program operator receives federal money? Would Title IX jurisdiction apply to the owner and thereby encourage the owner to let only nondiscriminating program operators use the facilities? The law is still evolving on this topic, but that is the basis for the third creative method for gaining jurisdiction. Let's look at an example. A community recreation league rents field space owned by the local public school. The community recreation league does not allow girls to participate. In effect, the school's provision of field space abets the discriminating community recreation program. This method of gaining jurisdiction may be a reach, but the supporters of the method would argue that the program operators should be held to the same standard of nondiscrimination as the entity that is aiding the program by providing the fields. When the argument has been used in court, the courts have agreed with the argument.

PROGRAMMATIC CONSIDERATIONS

Although intramural, club, and recreation sports are less clearly defined than physical education or interscholastic or intercollegiate athletics, the provisions of Title IX and its regulations apply equally once jurisdiction has been established. Insight into what is required of such programs is available from all the usual sources, such as the regulations and the policy interpretations, even though none of those sources specifically addresses intramural, club, or recreation sports. Instead, the program operator is expected to take and comply with what applies and ignore the rest. For example, the portion of the policy interpretations that talks about scholarships does not apply to intramurals, club, or recreation sports because scholarships are not part of the programs. But when the policy interpretations instruct the program operator to provide equal facilities, the program operator of an intramural, club, or recreation program must comply just as the athletic director at a college or high school would have to comply in administering an interscholastic or intercollegiate athletic program.

If it is established that a soccer club, for example, falls under the jurisdiction of Title IX, then the club must comply with the law.

If a community youth sports league provides new uniforms to its male baseball and basketball teams with booster club money but does not provide uniforms for its female softball and basketball teams, a Title IX compliance issue arises. Booster money, whether raised at boys' games or girls' games is, in effect, a contribution to the general fund, regardless of how the boosters might be related to a particular team. If the booster money provides benefits to one sex, the league operators must find a way to provide equal benefits to the other (assuming Title IX jurisdiction).

Few lawsuits have been lodged against operators of intramural, club, or recreation sports. School intramural programs do not share the difficulty of proving federal financial assistance often found by plaintiffs in cases involving community-based club and recreation programs, and thus the plaintiff or complainant has no difficult jurisdictional hurdles to surmount. The dearth of complaints may simply be because they haven't been filed yet or because discrimination in such programs is still taken for granted in its somewhat informal participation climate.

On the other hand, the reasons for there being only a few complaints or lawsuits against community-based programs may be more complex. Although the it-just-hasn't-happened-yet and taken-for-granted categories may apply here as well, the dearth of community-based club and recreation complaints or lawsuits is most likely due in part to the difficulty in finding a method of proving the presence of the third element required for Title IX jurisdiction, federal financial assistance. Whatever the reason, program operators of club and recreation programs might find it prudent, as well as ethical, to understand the full range of requirements under Title IX.

IN BRIEF

Sport activities, even though they are outside the scope of interscholastic and intercollegiate athletic programs, must also comply with the applicable sections of Title IX where Title IX jurisdiction exists. The main issue is whether jurisdiction can be applied. Intramural programs are within the jurisdiction of Title IX if the institution that hosts them is. Community club and recreation programs, however, pose a greater jurisdictional challenge. Of the three elements required to find Title IX jurisdiction (allegations of sex discrimination, education program, and federal financial assistance), the one that poses the greatest hurdle is establishing the connection to federal financial assistance.

Creative methods for establishing a connection to federal financial assistance are currently being litigated. Several methods may be found to confer jurisdiction:

- Federal financial aid finding its way to a related, although legally separate, entity, such as NCAA and NCAA's National Youth Sports Grants Program and organizations that are under the controlling authority of entities that receive federal financial assistance
- Tax-exempt status as a form of federal financial assistance, such as NCAA and NCAA's National Youth Sports Grants Program
- Federal financial aid in the hands of the facilities owners rather than in the hands of sports program administrators who use those facilities

Seven Questions and Seven Answers

All of the following questions make the assumption that Title IX jurisdiction of the specific sport program has been obtained. Remember, Title IX jurisdiction over club and recreation sport is an evolving area of the law, and thus one should not assume that answers to the following questions are universally applicable to all club and recreation sport programs.

1. **Is football, such as a Pop Warner Football program, excluded from the requirements of Title IX?**

   Football, in any forum, does not carry with it an exclusion from the requirements of Title IX. What triggers exclusion of any program (not a specific sport) is simply the inability to obtain jurisdiction because one or more of the three required elements of Title IX cannot be found. For instance, if the plaintiff or complainant is unable to establish a suitably strong connection to federal financial assistance, no jurisdiction can be obtained. An interesting fact is that several thousand high school girls play football on their school's varsity teams.

2. **Our youth sport program offers the same number of teams for boys and girls. Therefore, are we justified in feeling that it complies with Title IX participation requirements?**

   No. Access to participation opportunities is never evaluated based on the number of teams. The evaluation assesses actual participation slots. If one sex has a large rostered team and the other does not, the second group may need to have a larger number of teams to have an equitable number of participants.

3. **Booster clubs give money and equipment to some of our Police Athletic League's boys' teams but not to our girls' teams. Because the funding is voluntary and not provided by the league or town, is the imbalance in equipment and funds a Title IX issue?**

   Yes, it may be. The source of the funding is irrelevant. The provision of equal benefits is the yardstick.

4. **Our town has a girls' lacrosse league and a boys' soccer league. We spend the same amount of money on each league. Can we be confident that there are no Title IX issues?**

   The amount of money is irrelevant. The provision of equal benefits is the yardstick. For example, if uniforms are provided, they must be of the same quality and must be replaced with the same appropriateness of timing.

5. **Our youth sports league includes a cheerleading group. We let the cheerleaders decide which games they want to perform at. They like the larger crowds that attend the boys' basketball games, so they attend and perform at the boys' basketball games but not the girls' basketball games. We don't think there would be any Title IX issue because, as leaders, we were not involved in the selection of events at which the cheerleaders would perform. Are we correct?**

No. Title IX requires equal support. Cheer squads are a form of support. The cheerleaders need to be provided equally to the boys' and girls' programs. Most administrators find it best, if they want to include student choice, to require an equal number of boys' events and girls' events at which the cheerleaders will perform and then let the cheerleaders decide which events within that parameter they will schedule.

6. **Parents like to see their kids play. Our biggest attendance is at the boys' basketball games, so we schedule the games after the workday is over so that more parents can attend. We use the girls' basketball games as the warm-up game earlier in the day. Are we correct in thinking that we have no Title IX problem?**

No. Access to prime time is a benefit that you need to provide equally. The opportunity to have parents see their children play is important to kids. The boys shouldn't be the only ones who have that opportunity. Prime time should be alternated or at least equally shared.

7. **When a girl insists on playing on a boys' football team within our youth sports program, she must first complete a battery of fitness tests and a medical exam to determine her level of sexual maturation. Although this process often discourages the girls from going forward with playing football, we think that we are doing the right thing because football is a boys' game and we want to make sure that the girl can compete safely without endangering herself or those around her.**

If the test is also applied to boys who want to play football, or if the test is applied by a gender-neutral factor such requiring that anyone who weighs less than X pounds must take the test and the test measures skills or characteristics that directly relate to football, the test would not run afoul of Title IX. But it would be difficult to justify that sexual maturation[9] is a test relating to football. Similarly, imposing the test solely on females would trigger Title IX issues.

NOTES

[1]Pennies (perhaps short for pinafores) were widely used by female athletes in the pre–Title IX era to denote membership on a team. Pennies are two rectangles of colored fabric with straps connecting the two. One panel would be on the athlete's back and the other on the front, with straps over the shoulders and other straps tied at the sides. Each team's pennies were of a different color. When female athletes were afforded uniforms, the use of pennies fell away except for their use in intramurals, where both genders now use them.

[2]See Rocio De Lourdes Cordoba, "In Search of a Level Playing Field: *Baca v City of Los Angeles* as a Step Toward Gender Equity in Girls' Sports Beyond Title IX," *Harvard Women's Law Journal* 24 (spring 2001): 139. See also "Amateur Hockey Association of Illinois Is Not Subject to Title IX Because It Doesn't Receive Federal Funding," *Entertainment Law Reporter* 23, no. 5 (October 2001).

[3]Several other cases of note have challenged sex discrimination by athletic associations on constitutional rather than Title IX grounds. Constitutional grounds were selected to avoid issues raised by the lack of federal funding. Using the Constitution rather than Title IX is unremarkable and without great significance in the fight against discrimination when the defendant is obviously a state actor. But several recent cases have involved private athletic associations that to the casual observer do not appear to fit into a classification of state actor. Among these are *Brentwood Academy v Tennessee Secondary School Athletic Association*, 121 S. Ct. 924 (2001), which found that the statewide TSSAA that regulated competition between both public and private schools was in fact a state actor. TSSAA was deemed a state actor because its structure was entwined with public schools and their officials and because its functions were paragovernmental in nature. In the *Brentwood Academy* case the Supreme Court cited two lower court cases of the same ilk, thus giving support to the principle of the "entwinement" doctrine for finding an entity to be a state actor (*Clark v Arizona Interscholastic Association*, 695 F. 2d 1126 [1982], cert. denied at 46 U.S. 818 [1983], and a race-based case, *Louisiana High School Athletic Association v St. Augustine High School*, 396 F. 2d 224 [1968]). Discussion of the logic in the *Brentwood* case is found in "Sixth Circuit Dropped the Ball: An Analysis of *Brentwood Academy v Tennessee Secondary School Athletic Ass'n* in Light of the Supreme Court's Recent Trends in State Action Jurisprudence," *2001 Brigham Young University Law Review* 1313 (2001).

[4]Would the same logic apply to the NCAA, thus bringing it under the strictures of the Constitution in its dealings? It is difficult to predict. The NCAA has been the defendant in a variety of cases from drug testing to having a hand in the firing of Jerry Tarkanian, a former basketball coach at the University of Nevada, Las Vegas. At various times, the NCAA has been proclaimed a state actor, although most instances have found the NCAA not to be a state actor. The designation, state actor, is not a

permanent cloak, worn forevermore by an association. Rather, its designation relates to the particular activity involved in the case. Although the U.S. Supreme Court found the NCAA not to be a state actor in one of the long line of Tarkanian cases (*National Collegiate Athletic Association v Tarkanian*, 488 U.S. 179 [1988]), it referred to *Tarkanian* in the *TSSAA* case and noted that even in *Tarkanian*, the outcome might have been different under the entwinement doctrine if it had involved an NCAA membership limited to one state.

[5]The *Smith* case has traveled up and down the judicial ladder, and in its travels has altered its theories of jurisdiction, in part, with the suggestions of the U.S. Supreme Court.

[6]The district court agreed with the NCAA that Smith had failed to allege that the NCAA was a recipient of federal funding. The failure is more understandable when we realize that Smith filed her original lawsuit on a pro se basis (without representation) and had as her opponent a well-represented NCAA.

[7]The regulations for Title IX at 34 C.F.R. section 106.2 (g) propose a definition of federal financial assistance. See appendix A for the full definition, and consider how it might be used to draw organizations under the Title IX jurisdictional rubric.

[8]See "Tax Expenditures, Social Justice, and Civil Rights: Expanding the Scope of Civil Rights Laws to Apply to Tax-Exempt Charities," 2001 *Brigham Young University Law Review* 167 (2001) for a cogent discussion of the arguments to extend the definition of federal financial assistance to include tax exemption.

[9]New York State imposes such a test on its female students who wish to participate on boys' teams such as football. Besides requiring skills tests that boys who play on the team do not need to meet, the New York test requires a medical examination that includes determination of the sexual maturation of the girl evaluated by, among other means, a review of the amount of pubic hair. Such tests, even if introduced with well-intended but misguided motivation, are extraordinarily off-putting for young women who want to exercise their right to participate. The test continues to exist primarily because of a lack of challenge, but one can hope that the test will either be withdrawn voluntarily or, failing that, be successfully challenged in court.

4

The Law As Applied
to Athletics

The application of Title IX to athletics has made a 1972 piece of federal statute a household word. Parents know that Title IX means that their eighth-grade daughter's basketball team should have access to the big gym equal to her twin brother's team. The members of the middle school girls' soccer team competing at the state championships at least know that they are able to participate because of "some law passed years ago." Architects of new schools know that locker rooms and training facilities need to be equal for both sexes. Athletic directors know that the requirements of Title IX are not something of the past but are central to all their planning.

The application of Title IX to athletics has commanded more intense judicial, legislative, and executive branch attention than any other endeavor under its jurisdiction. Two factors have brought this about. First, athletics involves a mainly sex-segregated construct and thus discrimination is readily apparent. Second, athletics involves a historically male-centered domain, and opening the door to new participants means having to share resources previously thought to be for males alone. Change is difficult. Sharing is even more difficult, as any parent who has tried to teach the principle to a young son or daughter knows. But learning to share is vital to maturation and to gaining a clear sense of the broader world.

Let's look at what Title IX requires of athletics programs. These requirements[1] apply to all ages and levels of participation, including Division I, Division II, Division III, high school, college, NAIA, and NCAA. As we discussed in chapter 1, the regulations carry the basics, and the policy interpretations provide details. We'll refer to the policy interpretations only when they add to or more specifically define a particular point. Otherwise, we'll stick to the regulations (which, you'll remember, have the force of law).

FINANCIAL AID

Financial aid is the first issue tackled in the regulations that applies directly to athletics. Let's look at the fine print.

Section 106.37 Financial assistance.

(a) *General.* Except as provided in paragraphs (b) and (c) of this section, in providing financial assistance to any of its students, a recipient shall not:

(1) On the basis of sex, provide different amount or types of such assistance, limit eligibility for such assistance which is of any particular type or source, apply different criteria, or otherwise discriminate;

(2) Through solicitation, listing, approval, provision of facilities or other services, assist any foundation, trust, agency, organization, or person which provides assistance to any of such recipient's students in a manner which discriminates on the basis of sex; or

(3) Apply any rule or assist in application of any rule concerning eligibility for such assistance which treats persons of one sex differently from persons of the other sex with regard to marital or parental status.

(b) *Financial aid established by certain legal instruments.*

(1) A recipient may administer or assist in the administration of scholarships, fellowships, or other forms of financial assistance established pursuant to domestic or foreign wills, trusts, bequests, or similar legal instruments or by acts of a foreign government which requires that awards be made to members of a particular sex specified therein; *Provided,* That the overall effect of the award of such sex-restricted scholarships, fellowships, and other forms of financial assistance does not discriminate on the basis of sex.

(2) To ensure nondiscriminatory awards of assistance as required in paragraph (b)(1) of this section, recipients shall develop and use procedures under which:

(i) Students are selected for award of financial assistance on the basis of nondiscriminatory criteria and not on the basis of availability of funds restricted to members of a particular sex;

(ii) An appropriate sex-restricted scholarship, fellowship, or other form of financial assistance is allocated to each student selected under paragraph (b)(2)(i) of this section; and

(iii) No student is denied the award for which he or she was selected under paragraph (b)(2)(i) of this section because of the absence of a scholarship, fellowship, or other form of financial assistance designated for a member of that student's sex.

Two issues, then, are the focus of section 106.37:

1. distributing financial aid fairly and
2. avoiding giving assistance to outside groups that discriminate.

Looking at some examples of these issues might help us understand their purpose. First, let's take the distribution of financial assistance. Assume that a school sets SAT criteria lower for males than for females as a requirement for obtaining financial aid. Doing so would be in direct violation of section 106.37 (a)(1), which says, essentially, "Don't do it."

A more typical example is an admission process that provides particularly gifted athletes in high-profile sports with admission and financial aid to an institution that generally requires higher academic standards than the athletes can meet. Whether the practice of favored admission is academically sound is a question for another book, but when the favored admission process benefits male athletes rather than female athletes, a Title IX question arises. Because the favored admission process and its concomitant financial aid are used to assist football players more than other athletes, on many campuses it is likely that violations of Title IX prohibitions against having either different criteria or providing different levels of benefits based on sex are occurring.

Let's look at an example of the second issue: assisting outside, discriminating groups. In an effort to circumvent the requirements of Title IX and in ignorance of the requirements of section 106.37 of the regulations, some schools in the early years of Title IX allowed their facilities or mailing lists to be used to assist booster clubs and other outside fundraising groups that planned to discriminate as they gave funds raised for the college's athletics program. The college planned to accept the funds for use as financial aid and to honor the discriminatory restrictions placed on the use of the funds by the outside group. As a hypothetical example, let's say that as an aid to fund-raising efforts, a college shared its mailing list of football alumni with Discriminators Anonymous (DA), an outside booster group whose motto was "Athletics for Men Only." Because DA restricted the use of its funds to male students, the college is violating Title IX even if DA is beyond the reach of Title IX and even if the school did nothing more than provide a mailing list to DA and then receive its money.

Booster clubs, on both the college and the high school level, can provide great assistance to athletics programs. But an athletic director should not provide access to facilities or other assistance to such groups until determining that the group is not itself setting discriminatory limits on the use of its gifts. Even if the school is not discriminating, the school can be drawn into a Title IX violation by assisting an outside group that is.

After prohibiting discrimination in the granting of financial aid and prohibiting provision of assistance to outside groups that discriminate (106.37 (a)(1-3)), the regulations continue by providing directions for the nondiscriminatory use of financial aid money that arrives with strings attached (106.37 (b)(1-2)). "Strings attached" could be in the form of limiting the financial aid to members of the baseball team (baseball teams are made up of males rather than females), athletes who have played high school football (unlikely to include females), athletes who are Eagle Scouts (males only), and other narrowly construed groups that would typically include only males. Institutions must set nondiscriminatory criteria for selecting students who are to receive financial aid. Then, after selecting recipients, institutions may use financial aid funds that have arrived with restrictive strings attached to fund grants to the restricted group for which the funds have been limited, but only if the institutions find other funding to provide similar financial aid to those students who have met the selection criteria but do not fall into the restricted class. In the words of 106.37(b)(2), restricted money may be used only if "the overall effect of the award of such sex-restricted scholarships, fellowships, and other forms of financial assistance does not discriminate on the basis of sex." Because of this requirement, athletics directors need to be sure that they can find nonrestricted funds equal to the task before accepting restricted funds.

Subsections (a) and (b) of section 106.37 tell us that we must distribute financial aid fairly and must not aid outside groups who discriminate, but we still need to know how compliance with these two requirements will be measured. Subsection (c) of the regulations addresses that issue (see appendix A for the full text of this section). Section 106.37 (c)(1) of the regulations tells us that the distribution of scholarships must "provide reasonable opportunities for such awards for members of each sex in proportion to the number of students of each sex participating in interscholastic or intercollegiate athletics." The key wording is "reasonable opportunities," but defining "reasonable" is difficult. The policy interpretations put flesh on the bones of what the regulations tell us.

The policy interpretations are where we learn the details of how to measure the equitable nature of financial aid. We do so by comparing the ratio of the dollars of financial aid given to men and women to the ratio of their participation in the athletic program. For example, if $100,000 of financial assistance is given to athletes and 47 percent of the participants in the athletics program are females (whether financial assistance recipients or not), $47,000 of the $100,000 must be given to female recipients. Financial aid is the only place where actual expenditure rather than a comparison of benefits is used as the measuring stick. Benefits are purchased with dollars, of course, but other than in the area of financial aid, the equitable nature of the benefit (new shoes, experienced coach, bus transportation versus airplane transportation, and so forth) is the yardstick to be used, not the dollar price tag for those benefits.

The policy interpretations tell us that financial aid dollars need to be distributed in "substantially equal amounts." "Substantially equal" is a bit more helpful than the guidance of the regulations to be "reasonable." "Substantially equal" does not mean that a female's financial aid package has to be equal to a male's financial aid package but that the ratio of the total amount expended for the males in the program compared with the total for the women's program must be "substantially equal" to the ratio of males to females in the athletics program (not in the student body, as is the yardstick for participation). So the policy interpretations have at least told us how to count the dollars: We need to be counting the total dollars spent on men's program versus the dollars spent on women's programs rather than the dollars provided to one athlete. But what does "substantially equal" really mean?

The Office for Civil Rights of the United States Department of Education defined the term "substantially equal" in 1998, exactly a month after the 26th birthday of Title IX.[2] The 1998 letter clarifying the meaning of "substantially equal" was sent to Bowling Green University in response to a specific request from Bowling Green for guidance (see appendix D for the text of the 1998 letter). According to the 1998 Bowling Green letter, a 1 percent disparity in the ratio of financial aid dollars compared with the ratio of male to female athletes is the maximum allowable by OCR unless an acceptable nondiscriminatory reason for greater disparity exists. The letter superseded whatever percentages had been previously rumored to be acceptable ranges for either financial aid or participation disparities. In addition, the letter noted that measures for acceptable disparities were not the same for financial aid as for participation rates. The measurement of participation rates (ratio between male and female membership in the student body) was based on a questionable statistical test found in the 1990 *Investigator's Manual*. The measurement of financial aid (ratio between male and female membership in the athletics program) is to be measured not by a statistical test found

A female basketball player and a male basketball player need not have equal scholarship packages, but the amount of scholarship money for men's teams and for women's teams must be proportional to the number of male and female athletes.

in the *Investigator's Manual* but by adherence to the 1998 articulation of the 1 percent rule.

Frustration increased at many colleges when administrators read the 1998 Bowling Green letter because they had thought they were "doing enough" based on previous assumptions, rumors, or even agreements with the OCR[3]. OCR, perhaps rightly so, was asking them to lengthen their stride. Understandably, the colleges were frustrated by the lack of opportunity to comment and the shortness of the notice about a stringent definition that they had previously assumed to be more flexible. In any case, as the years passed, colleges have realized that the provision of financial aid is an enticement to participate; the provision of enticements to participate in a fair manner affects the ultimate fairness of the opportunity to participate. In other words, athletes, both male and female, are more likely to attend a particular school if financial aid is provided to them. Therefore, if financial aid is provided on an equitable basis, financial aid will serve as an enticement on an equitable basis and opportunities both for a college education and athletic participation will be more likely available on an equitable basis. It all starts with financial aid.

The policy interpretations graciously provide two acceptable excuses for not meeting the "substantially equal" yardstick: (1) imbalances created by nondiscriminatory grants of in-state versus out-of-state fees and (2) when not all financial aid available in a given year is distributed so that a new team is able to stagger grants over the first few years of the team's existence. (See appendix B for the exact wording of the policy interpretations on this topic.)

One method an administrator of ill will might use to circumvent the financial aid requirements of Title IX is to count money given to nonathletes such as training-room assistants as though it were given to athletes. To such an administrator's chagrin, the OCR will not count it that way. The policy interpretations define who is to be counted. See the following section of the policy interpretations for that definition.

> (4) Definition: For purposes of examining compliance with this Section, the participants will be defined as those athletes:
>
> a. Who are receiving the institutionally-sponsored support normally provided to athletes competing at the institution involved, e.g., coaching, equipment, medical and training room services, on a regular basis during a sport's season; and
>
> b. Who are participating in organized practice sessions and other team meetings and activities on a regular basis during a sport's season; and
>
> c. Who are listed on the eligibility or squad lists maintained for each sport; or
>
> d. Who, because of injury, cannot meet a, b, or c above but continue to receive financial aid on the basis of athletic ability.

Another strategy that an administrator of ill will might pursue is to provide nonfinancial assistance such as work-related aid or loans on a discriminatory basis. The policy interpretations make it clear however, that doing so could constitute a violation of Title IX.

The regulations and policy interpretations, when taken together, make it clear that financial aid is fully under the jurisdiction of Title IX.

We have learned that the requirement of "reasonableness" found in the regulation is more narrowly construed in the policy interpretations to mean "substantially equal." We've learned that where financial aid is concerned, the key for evaluating compliance is the amount of financial aid given to female athletes and male athletes compared to their ratio of representation among the athlete population, not the student body. We've also learned that nondiscriminatory professional decisions such as those related to spreading out financial aid over several years for new teams or the vicissitudes of in-state and out-of-state tuition may allow for some degree of variance in the ratio of financial aid given to each sex. Furthermore, funds for financial aid given to the school with "discriminatory strings attached" can evade Title IX problems only if (a) the decisions about granting financial aid are nondiscriminatory and (b) funds are found to provide for those eligible students who are not included in the "strings attached" funding.

PARTICIPATION

If you are not in the game, you don't need a uniform. The opportunity to participate is central to the overall fairness required by Title IX and similar legislation. The regulations discuss the quality and support for team members but do so only after talking about access to participation opportunities. We'll talk about when females must be allowed to try out for a males' team, the differences between contact and noncontact sports, and finally, how compliance with the need to provide access to participation is measured.

Separate Teams

You'll remember from chapter 2, "The Law As Applied to Physical Education," that separate classes are not required but are allowed when the activity is defined as a contact sport. Within the interscholastic, intercollegiate, club, or intramural athletics context, separate teams are also allowed under two circumstances:

1. when competitive skill determines membership on the team (those of us who are clumsy, unskilled, or just plain klutzy wouldn't be invited to join the team) or

2. when the activity is a contact sport.

Membership on teams falling within the rubric of interscholastic, intercollegiate, club, and, to some lesser extent, intramural athletics, is most often determined by competitive skill rather than social or other non-skill-oriented group adhesion. So separate teams for males and females are generally permissible. Basketball, for example, is a permissible sport in which to have separate teams. Varsity basketball meets both of the two circumstances even though it only needs to meet one; competitive skill is the primary selection criteria for varsity basketball teams, and varsity basketball is a contact sport.

When a particular sport is offered for one sex but not the other, something more than merely the separateness issue is raised. Athletics programs for males do not need to mirror athletics programs for females in the type of sports offered. But when a female wants to try out for a male team, other than one defined as a contact sport,[4] she must be allowed to do so.

> "My mindset is preserve opportunities and increase them, not cut them in the name of paper compliance. That creates hard feelings and it causes people to assess blame, and that's always bad."
>
> *Lynette Labinger, attorney, in* NCAA News, *November 9, 1998*

If a high school offers a volleyball team for its boys but has no girls' volleyball team, Susie, who wants to be on a volleyball team, must be allowed to try out for the boys' team. If the high school athletic association to which the school belongs will not allow any school that has a coed volleyball team to play in the state championship, the high school must adhere more loyally to the requirements of Title IX than to the regulations of the association. Thus, regardless of the rules of any outside organization, Susie's high school must let her try out for the boys' team and cannot place in her way any requirements or standards not placed in the way of boys who would try out for the same team.[5]

Interest and Ability

We've been talking about the requirement to permit females to try out for males' noncontact sport teams when there is no offering of the same sport on the females' side of the program and the option to allow females to try out for contact sport teams when there is no offering of the same sport on the females' side of the program. In addition to the requirements concerning tryouts, there is an overarching requirement to "accommodate effectively" the interests and abilities of students, which is most fully illuminated by the policy interpretations.

In the policy interpretations we read the following:

> a. Contact Sports: Effective accommodation means that if an institution sponsors a team for members of one sex in a contact sport, it must do so for members of the other sex under the following circumstances:
>
> (1) The opportunities for members of the excluded sex have historically been limited; and

(2) There is sufficient interest and ability among the members of the excluded sex to sustain a viable team and a reasonable expectation of intercollegiate competition for that team.

b. Non-Contact Sports: Effective accommodation means that if an institution sponsors a team for members of one sex in a non-contact sport, it must do so for members of the other sex under the following circumstances:

(1) The opportunities for members of the excluded sex have historically been limited;

(2) There is sufficient interest and ability among the members of the excluded sex to sustain a viable team and a reasonable expectation of intercollegiate competition for that team; and

(3) Members of the excluded sex do not possess sufficient skill to be selected for a single integrated team, or to compete actively on such a team if selected.

The policy interpretations set out under what circumstances a school would be required to start a team in a specific sport for females. A school must do more than merely allow females to try out for males' teams. In contact sports only two elements must be present to require a school to offer a new team for females:

- the sex of those wanting the new team has been underrepresented and
- sufficient interest and ability are present so that the team, when formed, would be sustainable and would have people to compete against from other venues.

The two elements needed to form a contact sport team seem simple. But the second element contains some of the nature of the question "Which came first, the chicken or the egg?" Where females have been kept out of certain sports, such as football, even in their physical education experience, it is difficult to imagine a situation in which a number of new female football teams would spring onto the field at the same time, thereby meeting the need for competition as required by the second element.

The regulations allow a school's physical education program to hide from its female students knowledge and skill development about contact sports such as football. If a school's female students later have interest in participating in football, they have had no opportunity available to add ability to their interest. In effect, a committed discriminator could read the contact sport team requirements as saying, "Females in football—never!" Although this reading may seem drastic, ice hockey, also considered a contact sport, is a fast-growing sport among the nation's collegiate women. The committed discriminator could make the same interpretation: "Females in ice hockey—never!" Fortunately for those pioneering women who brought ice hockey to a college near you, many non-school-based locations were available for females to learn ice hockey skills, and administrators were willing to give teams a chance to find competition in an emerging sport.

Where a noncontact sport is concerned, a third element is added. Remember, Title IX requires a school to allow a female to try out for a noncontact sport team if a separate team does not exist. But when a female is not sufficiently skilled or otherwise physically prepared to be selected for the males' team, she may request the formation of such a noncontact sport team for females only. Assuming that a sufficient number of other female students have the interest and ability and that the new team would have competition available,[6] the school must form the new team.

The third element found in the noncontact category recognizes that simply requiring a school to permit a tryout may in some cases be a sham and a hollow victory for the female interested in playing a particular sport.

Confused? Table 4.1 presents the guidelines for contact and noncontact sport schematically.

Have We Outgrown the Contact Sports Restriction?

Females were not permitted to run a marathon in the Olympics until 1984, only 20 years ago. Perceptions of the capability and interest of females in sport participation have changed quickly. When restrictions have been removed, females have universally filled the newly opened fields, tracks, and gymnasia of participation opportunities.[7] But more

Table 4.1

	Noncontact sport	Contact sport
Must have two teams if . . .	females are underrepresented. females have interest and ability. females would be left out if they tried out.	females are underrepresented. females have interest and ability.
Must allow females to try out if . . .	females are underrepresented.	allowing tryouts is not required.

than 30 years after the enactment of Title IX, the definition of contact sport still restricts females from being allowed to try out for teams in which they may have both the interest and skill to participate. Several thousand females play high school football on boys' teams at forward-looking schools that allowed them to try out. Thousands of other girls may want to try out, but their schools bar them because of the contact sport exclusion. Over 3,000 female high school wrestlers participate on boys' teams at schools that allowed them to try out. Thousands more have the interest and ability, but their schools have barred their participation.

These female football players and wrestlers are facing much of the same stereotyping that female marathoners received a quarter of a century ago. Still widely held is the unfounded assumption that women are too frail for certain physical activities. Is it time to remove the contact sports exclusion? As was probably part of the motivation for its inclusion in the regulations years ago, today the main function of the contact sport exemption may still be to carve out a protected, all-male, females-need-not-apply domain for one sex that goes directly against the spirit and purpose of Title IX. Would as many wrestling teams have been terminated in past years if females had been allowed to try out? Would the excesses of football have remained unfettered if females had been allowed to try out or if female football teams had been created (if opportunities had been available to learn skills in females' physical education experiences)? These questions offer interesting, valuable material to debate around the old woodstove[8] and to discuss as we move forward into the 21st century.

Let's move on to another hotly debated topic relating to participation: How should compliance be measured?

Three-Prong Test

As we mentioned briefly in chapter 1, the policy interpretations presented the three-prong test for measuring compliance with the requirement to effectively accommodate the interests and abilities of the under-represented sex. The regulations do not include the test. A school must meet only one of the three prongs to achieve compliance. This is one area of Title IX that has either been confusing or been subject to efforts of people to obfuscate it. A school has to meet only one of the three prongs, and it doesn't matter which prong the school meets. A school must select one of the following:

1. Participation opportunities for male and female students are provided in numbers substantially proportionate to their respective enrollments.

2. The school can show a history and continuing practice of program expansion that is demonstrably responsive to the developing interest and abilities of the members of that sex.

3. The school can demonstrate that the present program fully and effectively accommodates the interests and abilities of the members of that sex.

The three-prong test sounds simple enough, but 8 of the 12 federal circuit courts of appeal have been asked to decide whether the list is an appropriate one from which to have an institution choose. Congress has held hearings on the same question, and the federal government has been sued over the list. (See chapter 9 for a more complete discussion of the life and times of the three-prong test.) The debate has been long and emotional, but it has been determined that the list of choices is an appropriate compliance assessment tool (see figure 4.1).

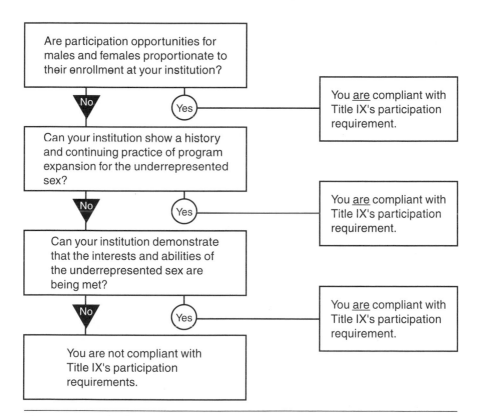

Figure 4.1 Methods of complying with the Title IX participation requirement known as the three-prong test.

THIRTEEN PROGRAM AREAS

The three-prong test is an umbrella assessment tool with which to measure compliance for providing equitable *participation* opportunities. Although the regulations don't mention the three-prong test, section 106.41(c) of the regulations provides a few, more specific indices of equitable *treatment* within an athletic program. They are specific places to start looking for compliance with the requirement to provide equal athletic experiences and support to both males and females. The section of the regulations lists 10 areas, but the policy interpretations add 2 more (recruitment and support services), and, when referred to generally, a 13th, financial assistance, is added from section 106.37 of the regulations. The entire group, providing places to start evaluating compliance, is frequently referred to as the 13 program areas, presented here in their composite nature:

1. Whether the selection of sports and levels of competition effectively accommodate the interests and abilities of members of both sexes
2. The provision of equipment and supplies
3. Scheduling of games and practice time
4. Travel and per diem allowance
5. Opportunity to receive coaching and academic tutoring
6. Assignment and compensation of coaches and tutors
7. Provision of locker rooms, practice and competitive facilities
8. Provision of medical and training facilities and services
9. Provision of housing and dining facilities and services
10. Publicity
11. Recruitment
12. Support services
13. Financial assistance

All of the 13 program areas except financial assistance are evaluated on the basis of benefit received rather than dollar expenditures. Sports differ in the expense of uniforms and equipment, number and cost of officials, travel requirements, and number of coaches needed. For an institution to be in compliance, the participants of the females' program must receive equal benefit, such as the same quality of uniforms replaced at the same degree of wear as those of their male counterparts. Female participants do not need to receive $1,000 each for uniforms just because football uniforms might cost $1,000 per participant. Similarly, if providing security guards at competitive events involved greater cost for a men's basketball event compared with a women's basketball event, no Title IX problem would be present if the disparity was based on the nature, size, or demeanor of the crowd for the men's game, as long as each event, men's and women's, received the appropriate level of security support in relation to the crowd.

Evaluating Equity of Scheduling

The policy interpretations expand the details within many of the 13 program areas. For instance, within the program area of scheduling of games and practice, the policy interpretations add the following:

> Compliance will be assessed by examining, among other factors, the equivalence for men and women of:
>
> (1) The number of competitive events per sport;
>
> (2) The number and length of practice opportunities;
>
> (3) The time of day competitive events are scheduled;
>
> (4) The time of day practice opportunities are scheduled; and
>
> (5) The opportunities to engage in available pre-season and post-season competition.

So, through the clarifications found in the policy interpretations we learn that scheduling practice for teams in the females' program in the hours left over after the males' program has been scheduled is not likely to meet compliance requirements. To fund boys' teams that make it to the state championships, either out of the general budget or out of booster-provided funds, but to require members of girls' teams to raise their own funds to compete at the state championships violates Title IX. The specifics found in the policy interpretations add meat to the bones of the regulations and help us evaluate our own circumstances for compliance.

Evaluating Equity of Equipment and Travel

The policy interpretations also provide details in the areas of equipment, travel, locker rooms, coaching, medical support, hiring, recruitment, and support services by which to judge compliance.

Let's look at the details provided by the policy interpretations in the areas of (1) equipment and supplies, and (2) travel and per diem allowances.

a. Equipment and Supplies (Section 86.41(c)(2)). Equipment and supplies include but are not limited to uniforms, other apparel, sport-specific equipment and supplies, general equipment and supplies, instructional devices, and conditioning and weight training equipment.

Compliance will be assessed by examining, among other factors, the equivalence for men and women of:

(1) The quality of equipment and supplies;

(2) The amount of equipment and supplies;

(3) The suitability of equipment and supplies;

(4) The maintenance and replacement of the equipment and supplies; and

(5) The availability of equipment and supplies.

c. Travel and Per Diem Allowances (Section 86.41(c)(4)).

(1) Modes of transportation;

(2) Housing furnished during travel;

(3) Length of stay before and after competitive events;

(4) Per diem allowances; and

(5) Dining arrangements.

Evaluating Personnel Equity

Title IX also covers personnel in the form of coaches and tutors as one of the 13 program areas, and the policy interpretations provide details to help evaluate compliance (see appendix B). As cryptic as the details are, at least they give some direction about where to look for equity versus inequity.

d. Opportunity to Receive Coaching and Academic Tutoring (Section 86.41(c)(5)).

[Coaching] . . .

(a) Relative availability of full-time coaches;

(b) Relative availability of part-time and assistant coaches; and

(c) Relative availability of graduate assistants.

[Tutoring] . . .

(a) The availability of tutoring; and

(b) Procedures and criteria for obtaining tutorial assistance.

The application of Title IX to employees has been increasingly limited because Title IX provides a parallel set of protections already granted to some extent by prior federal legislation such as Title VII and the Equal Pay Act (EPA). Having a double layer of protections is not consistent with the need for legislative or judicial economy. Thus, the protections of Title IX have, through case law, been transferred more to other statutes.[9] Although an aggrieved employee is directed to pursue her rights under Title VII or the Equal Pay Act[10] rather than Title IX, gender-based disparity in salaries is still actionable under Title IX. That right, however, belongs to the student-athlete, not the coach. The requirement of Title IX relating to the compensation of coaches is enforceable by the student-athlete rather than the coach if the disparity in salary must affect the quality of coaching received by the athlete. Disparity causing an effect solely in the pocketbook of the coach is not actionable under Title IX. Instead, Title VII and the Equal Pay Act may provide remedies for the coach.

The policy interpretations list a few of the items to consider when evaluating whether the female athlete is receiving equitable coaching benefits. Remember, salary disparities are actionable under Title IX only if they produce a disparity in the level of coaching received by the athlete.

> e. Assignment and Compensation of Coaches and Tutors (Section 86.41(c)(6)).
>
> In general, a violation of Section 86.41(c)(6) will be found only where compensation or assignment policies or practices deny male and female athletes coaching of equivalent quality, nature, or availability. . . .
>
> (1) Assignment of Coaches . . .
>
> (a) Training, experience, and other professional qualifications;
>
> (b) Professional standing.
>
> (2) Assignment of Tutors . . .
>
> (3) Compensation of Coaches . . .
>
> (a) Rate of compensation (per sport, per season);
>
> (b) Duration of contracts;
>
> (c) Conditions relating to contract renewal;
>
> (d) Experience;
>
> (e) Nature of coaching duties performed;

(f) Working conditions; and

(g) Other terms and conditions of employment.

One of the issues for determining compliance within the area of coaches' compensation is the length of contract (item 3b in the previous list). Many female coaches receive only a one-year contract, whereas their male counterparts receive multiyear contracts. If the imposition of one-year contracts for coaches of female teams[11] diminishes the quality of coaching received by female athletes, the female athletes could pursue a Title IX claim but the coach could not. The coach would instead need to pursue a Title VII claim.

Evaluating Facilities Equity

The policy interpretations include physical plant considerations in the 13 program areas. For instance, the policy interpretations offer places to look for equity versus inequity. Among the places to look for issues of equity or inequity are locker rooms; practice facilities; competition facilities; and preparation, maintenance, and quality of the facilities.

Correcting architectural barriers to Title IX compliance in older, pre–Title IX facilities often involves a great deal of money. Many schools with older facilities but without awareness of Title IX have found visiting team locker space by moving their own female teams into the locker room used by the general student body and then inviting the visiting team to use the home team's locker room. Male students at the same schools often have both a team locker room and a visiting team locker room because, when the building was built, only males were thought of as athletes. The expense of retrofitting facilities is irrelevant to the force of the requirement. If retrofitting the facilities is not possible or if the school finds the expense too onerous, then the school must employ other methods; the requirement for equal locker rooms stands. For instance, a school might meet the requirement by alternating the use of the formerly male visiting team locker room between its female teams and its male teams, with the home teams alternately having to use the locker room of the general student body.

The same type of interim solution can be found for sharing competitive and practice facilities on a rotating basis. Past generations of girls and women often never experienced facilities other than the "Women's (or Girls') Gym," which meant the old gym. Having the males play and practice half the time in the old gym while the females use the new gym half the time is an equitable method for overcoming expensive facilities problems. A bit of creativity and goodwill can solve many Title IX compliance problems. In addition, sharing helps the favored group to have greater empathy for the effects of discrimination on the nonfavored group.

Evaluating Overall Equity and Compliance With the Requirements of Title IX

The policy interpretations contain similar details for the remaining 13 program areas. Besides reviewing compliance on each of the individual 13 program areas, OCR also takes an overall view of the program as noted in the policy interpretations:

> 5. Overall Determination of Compliance.
>
> The Department will base its compliance determination . . . upon an examination of the following:
>
> a. Whether the policies of an institution are discriminatory in language or effect; or
>
> b. Whether disparities of a substantial and unjustified nature exist in the benefits, treatment, services, or opportunities afforded male and female athletes in the institution's program as a whole; or
>
> c. Whether disparities in benefits, treatment, services, or opportunities in individual segments of the program are substantial enough in and of themselves to deny equality of athletic opportunity.

It is tempting to look at Title IX compliance on a team-versus-team basis: baseball versus softball, basketball versus basketball. But Title IX compliance is mainly judged on a programwide basis, not a team-by-team basis. If an institution divides its program using a tier[12] system, with teams in the second level being deprived of some of the benefits granted to the first-tier teams, the disparity between the first and second tiers may not be a violation of Title IX. The program is reviewed as a whole, not on a team-by-team or tier-by-tier basis. But if the females in the total program are receiving benefits unequal to those of the males in the total program, Title IX issues may swiftly arise.

> "Title IX is not an affirmative action statute; it is an anti-discrimination statute . . ."
>
> Cohen v Brown University, *991 F 2d 888*

IN BRIEF

The most publicized effect of Title IX relates to interscholastic and inter-collegiate athletic programs. The policy interpretations, 1996 clarification letter (three-prong test), 1998 clarification letter (financial assistance), and the 2003 further clarification letter (three-prong test) add details to the application of the regulations to athletics.

Compliance with the requirement to provide equal participation access is measured by one of three methods: history of upgrading, meeting interests and abilities, or proportional representation of male and female athletes relating to the ratio in the student body. Compliance with the requirement to provide "substantially equal" financial assistance is measured by a comparison to the ratio of male and female athletes in the athletics program, not in the student body. Dollars spent are the measure only in financial assistance considerations.

> Investigation by NWLC (National Women's Law Center) Finds $6.5 Million Athletic Scholarship Gap for Women at 30 Colleges and Universities
>
> National Women's Law Center *Press Release, June 18, 2002*

The source of funds is irrelevant. The benefit provided is the measure (except in the area of financial aid, where the expenditures are the measure); booster funds or funds designated for a particular purpose or team do not relieve the obligation to provide equal benefit.

Assessments of compliance focus on 13 program areas. The policy interpretations include details of compliance requirements for each of the 13 program areas.

Thirteen Questions and Thirteen Answers

1. **Your high school boys' badminton team has a well-developed parents' booster club called the Racqueteers. The Racqueteers have raised over $3,000 by selling birdhouses at each of the team's matches. You are the athletic director. The head Racqueteer has come to you offering to use the $3,000 to fund a week for the entire boys' team at Birdland International Badminton Camp. What should you do?**

   If you can find funds elsewhere, either from outside sources or from your program's budget, to purchase equal camp opportunities for your girls' program, you can feel free to accept the head Racqueteer's offer. But if you cannot provide the girls' program with equal benefits, you should accept the funds only if you are successful in convincing the head Racqueteer that the funds should be used for both the boys and girls. Otherwise, you should say, "Thanks but no thanks" to the offer. Title IX is not a respecter of the source of funds; it cares only about the provision of equal benefits.

2. **Is the proportionality prong of the three-prong test legally valid?**

Yes. Judicial, administrative, and legislative support has been consistent. All portions of the three-part test are valid, and none is favored over any other. Meeting one of the three is sufficient. Roster management (limiting the size of males' teams and providing open unused slots for females' teams) is not a favored method of meeting the proportionality prong.

Eight of the 12 circuit courts of appeal have heard cases on the issue. All eight have found that the proportionality prong is a valid member of the three-prong test.

Both the 1996 clarification letter and the 2003 further clarification letter are formal reaffirmations of the appropriateness of the proportionality prong.

Hearings of many sorts have left the proportionality prong intact. The proportionality prong is a legally valid member of the three-part test. See chapter 9 for a fuller discussion of the hearings.

3. **May a state high school athletic association impose rules that require tests or skill requirements for girls who want to participate on boys' teams when the boys do not have to meet the same standards to participate on boys' teams?**

No. Such tests were often created during an era of paternalism and remain on the books out of habit. Requiring girls to overcome barriers that are not placed in the way of boys is difficult to rationalize in today's world. A state high school athletic association that is still using such tests is walking on thin ice in relation to Title IX, especially following the decision in *Brentwood Academy* (see the discussion about jurisdiction of Title IX over associations as well as a discussion of the *Brentwood Academy* decision in chapter 3).

4. **Our female coach of the women's tennis team has the same resume as the male coach of the men's team, yet she is paid less. Is this OK?**

No, but it is not actionable by the female coach under Title IX. Instead, the female coach should look at using Title VII or the

Equal Pay Act if change cannot be effected through nonadversarial methods.

5. **If high-quality shoes for our men's basketball team cost $150 per pair and shoes of the same quality for our women's team cost only $100 per pair, are we in violation of Title IX?**

   No. The benefit is the measure, not the cost of the benefit. If the benefit is the provision of high-quality shoes, the benefit in this scenario is equal regardless of the cost.

6. **Are both financial assistance and the proportionality prong measured against the ratio of males and females in the student body?**

   No. Financial assistance is measured against the ratio of males and females in the athletics program, not in the student body. On the other hand, proportionality is measured in relation to the student-body ratio.

7. **Our school was built in the 1940s and has a large boys' gym and a smaller girls' gym. The boys' gym has bleachers, and the girls' gym does not. We have no money and no space to build any new gyms. How do we comply with Title IX?**

   Lack of money or the presence of architectural barriers is not a justification for noncompliance to Title IX. Therefore, you will need to develop creative measures such as alternating use of the gyms between the boys' and girls' teams so that each has equal access to the larger gym.

8. **When our football team travels to Neighbor University, they ride in a chauffeured coach. Our women's soccer team takes the two college vans driven by the coach and assistant coach when they travel to Neighbor University. Is this a problem?**

   Yes. Your arrangement confers benefits on the football players that you do not provide to the women's soccer team. For instance, the coaches of the soccer team will arrive tired and less able to coach effectively on arrival at Neighbor University. In addition, the safety of the athletes is in greater jeopardy as a fatigued coach drives home.

9. **Our men's fencing team has an outstanding coach. He is a past Olympic athlete and a member of the Fencing Coaches Hall of Fame. He has 15 years of coaching experience. Our women's fencing coach moved away during the summer, and we are look-**

ing for a replacement. Because of budget constraints, we don't think that we can afford to pay for a well-experienced coach for the women, so we have advertised the job as "No experience required." Is this OK?

No. Besides not subjecting your athletes to the obvious danger of having an inexperienced person trying to coach a fencing team, you must provide members of the women's team their Title IX right to access to a level of coaching skill equal to that of their male counterparts. (Note that comparisons are actually made on a programwide basis, but for the sake of illustration we are assuming that no such abuses of male students are occurring.)

10. **Our athletic trainer likes basketball, so he assigns himself as the trainer for the events of the men's basketball team. He assigns student trainers to all other games, both men's and women's. Is this a problem?**

Yes. Although some men's teams and all women's teams are receiving a diminished level of medical care, some men are receiving favorable treatment by having access to an experienced athletic trainer. Thus, in a programwide comparison the women are receiving a diminished benefit when compared with the overall athletic training benefit received by the men in the program.

11. **Do all 13 program areas come from the regulations?**

No. Some come from the regulations, but the topics of support services and recruitment come from the policy interpretations. But regardless of source, the 13 program areas are applied similarly.

12. **What takes precedence when conflict exists, Title IX or association rules?**

Title IX requirements take precedent.

13. **The females on our school's basketball team have asked us to hire an assistant coach. All of the males' teams in our program have a graduate assistant who volunteers as an assistant coach and a half-time paid assistant coach. Currently, the women's basketball team has only a head coach, but she has a resume similar to the resume of the coach of the men's team. No females' team has an assistant coach. Do we need to hire an assistant coach for the females' team?**

Access to coaching is one of the 13 program areas in which equal benefit needs to exist. The presence of additional coaching support for the females' team to bring it up to the coaching support of the males' program is appropriate. Besides finding an assistant coach for the females' basketball team, you need to ensure that other females' teams also receive benefits of coaching access equal to those of the males' teams.

NOTES

[1]The requirements for athletics are mainly found in the policy interpretations but also in more general terms in the regulations.

[2]The 1998 clarification letter directed to Bowling Green State University appears in appendix D. Bowling Green requested guidance from OCR about the topic. The responding letter from OCR, although addressed to Bowling Green, serves as clarification to all who have the same question.

[3]See Karla Haworth's article "Statement on Sports Scholarships Frustrates and Confuses Colleges," *Chronicle of Higher Education*, Sept. 4, 1998, for a discussion of the reaction by other colleges to the definition of "substantially equal."

[4]Contact sports are defined as boxing, wrestling, rugby, ice hockey, football, basketball, and other sports that involve bodily contact in their purpose or major activity (106.41 (b)). See appendix A for the exact wording.

[5]In violation of Title IX, some state high school athletic associations have imposed rules that require any student who wants to participate on a team of the opposite sex to pass physical or skill tests not required of the members of the same sex. An example of some of the extra requirements still in force in some states at the writing of this book are a medical examination that includes an assessment of the amount of pubic hair, breast development, and overall "maturation," and physical fitness tests not required of the male team members.

[6]The policy interpretations make it clear that Title IX is not a quota, but they recognize that expanding opportunities for females may take some degree of palliative effort on the part of the institution to remove the effects of past discrimination: "Institutions are not required to upgrade teams to intercollegiate status or otherwise develop intercollegiate sports absent a reasonable expectation that intercollegiate competition in that sport will be available within the institution's normal competitive regions. Institutions may be required by the Title IX regulations to actively encourage the development of such competition, however, when overall athletic opportunities within that region have been historically limited for the members of one sex."

[7]See Acosta and Carpenter, *Women in Intercollegiate Sport—Twenty Seven Year Update,* available at the following Web site: webpages.charter.net/womeninsport, as well as chapter 9 for data about increasing participation numbers.

[8]The authors, rocking back and forth in their rockers around the old woodstove, might be heard to propose dropping the contact sport exemption for physical education (see chapter 3) so that females might have greater access to learning experiences in contact sports. Then, if females have the interest and the newly gained ability through their physical education experiences, they could more realistically take advantage of the potential for adding new all-female contact sport teams in the athletic programs. The authors would also argue the need to maintain the third

element under the noncontact sport heading, which takes into account that simply allowing a female to try out for a males' team may be an ineffective method of increasing opportunities.

[9]See the discussion of the *Lowrey* case in chapter 7 for a fuller understanding of the transfer and its effect.

[10]The Equal Employment Opportunities Commission (EEOC), which is the administrative enforcement agency for both the EPA and Title VII, has developed a helpful discussion of the interrelation and applicability of the Equal Pay Act and Title VII as it affects coaching salaries. The material, in the form of an official "guidance," is available online at www.eeoc.gov/press/10-31-97.html or by writing EEOC's Office of Communications and Legislative Affairs at 1801 L Street, N.W., Washington, DC 20507 and requesting *Enforcement Guidance on Sex Discrimination in the Compensation of Sports Coaches in Educational Institutions.*

[11]Only 2 percent of males' intercollegiate teams are coached by females, whereas 46 percent of females' intercollegiate teams are coached by females. See Acosta and Carpenter, *Women in Intercollegiate Sport—Twenty Seven Year Update,* available at the following Web site: webpages.charter.net/womeninsport.

[12]The tier system divides teams into two or more groups. The institution considers one tier or group of teams as its premier or favored teams and funds them accordingly. Another tier may include teams that play what the institution considers minor sports, and thus those teams receive less financial support.

PART II

Title IX in Society and in the Courts

(Social, Legislative, and Judicial History of Title IX)

After reviewing the specific requirements of the law by reading part I (chapters 1 through 4), we will look at the place of Title IX in society. Reviewing the various philosophical, moral, judicial, and political underpinnings of Title IX will help you understand the contexts, concepts, and concrete legal principles and their nexus with one another.

First, we look at what was going on in society, Congress, and the nation's schools in the years preceding, surrounding, and following the birth of Title IX. Then we track the experience of Title IX in the courts, noting the refinements that each significant case has brought to the understanding of Title IX.

Chapter 5   Title IX in Social and Legislative Context

Chapter 6   Title IX in the Courts, 1972 to 1992

Chapter 7   Title IX in the Courts After *Franklin v Gwinnett,* 1992 to 2004

5

Title IX in Social and Legislative Context

Sports and physical education for females did not sprout full grown into America's schools, colleges, and communities when the vote counting was completed on Title IX in 1972, nor was the physical education and sport experience of females in those pre–Title IX days the same as it is now.

Legislation sometimes leads and sometimes follows the rambling of society toward its future. Seldom is legislation more than a step ahead or two behind. Title IX would not have been brought to a vote by Congress a decade earlier simply because society was not ready for legislation concerning the civil rights of females.[1] Not until 1964 did President Lyndon Johnson sign the landmark Civil Rights Act after a lot of skillful arm twisting and politicking in the halls of Congress. But the absence of legislative encouragement did not stop girls and women from finding every avenue open to them to participate; the problem was that many avenues had "One way" (males only) and "Do not enter" signs posted on them. We, the authors, gray haired though we are, remember facing such signs posted on our high school physics course, outside the only gymnasium in our middle school, and at the registration line for our college's athletics training course. We also recall our college yearbooks—two inches thick with not a single photo of a female participating in any sport-related activity except being a cheerleader for males. Yet in spite of the "One way" and "Do not enter" road signs, pre–Title IX history of females in sport and physical education has a cherished richness and flavor different from the conditions today. Although severely limited in its breadth by forces and circumstances from without, the heart within was earnest and strong.[2]

BUILDING A FRAMEWORK

When Mom was a youngster in the 1910s and 1920s, several organizations that were to have an influence on sports opportunities for her and her daughters were also in their youth. In 1885 the Association for the Advancement of Physical Education was formed. Although the organization went through several name changes[3] before attaining its current name, the American Alliance for Health, Physical Education, Recreation and Dance (AAHPERD), it has served as the home for the current National Association for Girls and Women in Sport (NAGWS) for over a century. NAGWS, the longest functioning association focusing on sport for females, started in 1899 as the Women's Basketball Committee (WBC).

James Naismith invented basketball in 1891. Within a year, Senda Berenson took the new game to the women of Smith College. Within a few years, it became apparent that women should have their own rules, so in 1899 the WBC was formed as part of AAPERD. Berenson followed Alice Foster and Alice Snyder as the third leader of the WBC, an office Berenson held from 1901 to 1917. In 1917 the WBC, essentially a rules committee, became a subcommittee of the newly formed Committee on Women's Athletics (CWA). The CWA's purpose was to develop standards for participation by women, not just in basketball but also in other athletic endeavors. Elizabeth Burchenal led the CWA for four years, followed by Blanche Trilling for the next three. In 1925 the organization changed its name to reflect its expanding horizon; the new name was National Section on Women's Athletics (NSWA). In 26 years the organization had grown from a rules committee for a brand new sport to a national organization dealing with all aspects of women's athletics. The organization had maintained the name NSWA for more than a quarter century as it published the first stand-alone *Standards in Athletics for Girls and Women* in 1937.

In 1952, to describe the constituency it served more fully, the organization's name was changed to National Section on Girls' and Women's Athletics (NSGWA), a name it carried for six years under the leadership of women such as Josephine Fiasco, Aileen Lockhart, Grace Fox, and Mabel Locke.

Names, names, names. Sometimes name changes have reflected a change in focus, and sometimes the changes were merely expedient. In 1958 another new name was adopted; the organization became the Division for Girls' and Women's Sports (DGWS). Because the organization was under the umbrella of AAPERD, which changed its organizational structure many times over the century-plus of its existence, organizations

© Smith College archives

Senda Berenson, pictured here in 1895, was leader of the Women's Basketball Committee for 16 years.

within it sometimes also needed to alter their names without altering their missions. But the change from NSGWA was related to mission. The replacement of "athletics" in NSGWA with "sports" in DGWS signaled an expansion of participation opportunities for females, along with a broadening of the focus of the organization so that it would include instructional and intramural sport along with athletics.[4]

DGWS remained the name through the enactment of Title IX and now bears a slight variation adopted in 1974: the National Association for Girls and Women in Sport (NAGWS). The additional preposition "in" signifies a focus on the participant rather than the sport. NAGWS celebrated its 100th anniversary in 1999 and could rightfully add to the commemoration of longevity a celebration for playing a continuing and vital role in the expansion and formation of sports opportunities for the nation's girls and women.

Earlier, we listed the names of specific women who worked within the organization because history often refers to the women who formed and over the years shaped NAGWS as a "group of women" rather than as individuals with names, personalities, and struggles of their own. Not recognizing those women individually does a disservice to their courage, foresight, and dedication. The fact that so frequently sport histories do just that illustrates the way pre–Title IX society perceived females who were active in sport. Their accomplishments were devalued, and their efforts were often demeaned.

EARLY ATHLETES

School athletic letters were not thought of as something a female could earn, even though she was as valiant a competitor as her male counterpart. Even though she practiced in substandard facilities, wore sneakers bought with her lunch money, or received coaching from highly skilled but unpaid and frequently disrespected volunteer physical educators, a letter was not hers. In fact, most believed her to be physiologically incapable of dribbling a basketball more than three times[5] or running a marathon.[6]

Along with being denied the award of a letter, she received no medical treatment or athletic training for her injuries, except through her own doctor. She was not considered for scholarships and was denied access to team locker rooms and the weight room. The assertiveness, aggressiveness, confidence, and skill necessary to participate in sport, especially in the face of the barriers placed before her, were traits denounced as unfeminine. No mention of her successes was hers as she found that if she carried the traits needed for athletic success beyond the gym floor or outside the boundaries of the hockey field, they would be viewed as tomboyishness at best and as evidence of perversion at worst. No letter would be hers, nor would her name appear in the school yearbook for her athletics participation, even though she was at the softball field before sunup because that was the only time available for the women's team to have access.

Yet females found ways to participate in sport. The commitment against great odds of female athletes to find ways to participate is worthy of acknowledgment. A few institutions have sought out their early female athletes and have awarded letters surely earned but not previously acknowledged. Other institutions have tried to do so but have found that although the names of their male athletes are remembered, the names of their valiant female athletes were never deemed worthy of inscription and are lost to history. But these female athletes were more than a "group of women," faceless and unvalued.

Former NAGWS leaders and "faceless" women Rachel Bryant and Aileen Lockhart.

In the 1920s, 1930s, and 1940s, girls and women formed archery and rifle teams and competed with teams from other schools through postal tournaments. Because institutional support, funds for travel, and facility access were denied, females competed in sports in which competitors didn't absolutely have to face each other to determine a winner. Such teams often employed postal tournaments. Each team would shoot the requisite number of bullets or arrows or bowl the required number of frames and then mail their scores to the school with whom they were competing. Someone would be designated to compare the scores and declare a winner. Honesty was a matter of honor. Postal tournaments seem laughable today, but they reflected not reduced competitiveness among their participants but overwhelming desire to find a way to compete even when doors were closed against females.

ROLES OF WOMEN IN FLUX

Although their goals were different, the NAGWS and the NCAA each played vital roles in fulfilling the need for a national system of governance for sport participation. NAGWS served all ages of females participating in sport and physical education and sought to assist in building healthful, safe, and appropriate programs. Appropriateness is, by definition, tied to society's views at any given time, so for the first 75 years of its existence, NAGWS focused on the healthful, safe, a-girl-for-every-sport-and-a-sport-for-every-girl (broad-based participation) model.

The NCAA, born in 1906, seven years after the formation of the Women's Basketball Committee (the precursor for NAGWS) and two years after the invention of the sports bra,[7] was formed at the urging of President Theodore Roosevelt to find a way to reduce the injuries, fatalities, out-of-hand gambling, and other unethical competitive practices associated with college football at the turn of the century.[8] Although created ostensibly to do what the Women's Basketball Committee was created to do, the NCAA, reflecting society's views of male sport participation, instantly adopted a major tenet of its existence: the governance of high-level competition among the male students of its member schools. The new organization never gave a second thought to whether high-level competition was appropriate for males; it was concerned only with how to organize and govern that competition. Such was not the case for females, who were deeply mired in society's restrictions against the female competitive spirit. The massive difference in the views of what was appropriate for males and females is not difficult to comprehend when we recall that women were not allowed to vote when the NCAA was born in 1906. Women were viewed as not having sufficient sense to make logical decisions in the voting booths of America. How could a society that denied women suffrage view them as having the physical stamina or desire to participate in highly competitive sports?

World War I swept the globe, the 19th Amendment[9] to the Constitution was ratified, the Great Depression came and went, and athletics for females progressed to "play days." The gymnasium doors were still locked, but school-aged girls were now meeting for one-day events at which they joined girls from other schools and played sports on mixed teams not identified by school. The mixing of athletes from several schools on each team was designed to prevent the elevation of competition over camaraderie. But the absence of school identity did not greatly lessen the level of competition in the events. Play days also had the perceived advantage of involving a greater number of students than could be accommodated on a single "varsity" team.

"Sports days" were also single-day events, but unlike play days, students arrived and played as teams representing their schools. Coaching, if any, was in the form of a dedicated volunteer female physical educator who gave up her day so that her students could have a competitive and socializing experience with students from other institutions. Females were still struggling to find a way to express their athletic talents.

Smith College class of 1895 basketball team and an intramural college game circa 1904. Though some women were playing and watching basketball at the turn of the 20th century, no women were yet allowed to vote.

Rosie the Riveter in World War II, the 1954 *Brown v Board of Education* Supreme Court decision, and the Civil Rights Act of 1964 helped change, or reflected change in, society's perspective on full access for all of America's citizens, including its mothers and daughters. On the basketball court, three-zone, three-dribble basketball for girls became a two-zone game, with players in one zone being guards and in the other forwards. Females were now deemed capable of running a few more steps on the basketball court, but they wanted much more.

© Smith College archives

Though these 1940s lacrosse players are clearly healthy and athletic, even in the 1960s women were still viewed as too frail to play full-court basketball.

In the late 1960s, almost as an experiment, the "rover" became part of girls' basketball. The rover rules meant that two players on each six-person team played full-court basketball while two of the remaining four were locked into the backcourt as guards and two played only in the forecourt as forwards. Without having to call time-out, a tired rover could, on the run, trade duties with any of the four remaining players. Females were finding ways to breach their societally imposed boundaries.

Women playing college basketball in the 1960s.

© Smith College archives

BIRTH OF THE AIAW

The women, members of a "group of women" who spent their energy and professional capital advancing the interests of girls and women in sport through the Division of Girls and Women in Sport,[10] were not blind to the pressure from the participants and their physical education teachers cum coaches for more highly competitive experiences. Where, how, and by whom that expansion might be facilitated were open questions. Would it come at the expense of broad-based opportunities for the moderately skilled? Would it follow the male model of the NCAA and carry with it the negatives of abuse and exploitation so long avoided by the women in the NAGWS?

In 1964, the year that the Civil Rights Act was enacted, the NCAA convention included a visit from two of the leaders of DGWS.[11] The women were seeking to ascertain the intentions of the NCAA regarding women's athletics. A special session at the NCAA convention was arranged for them to do so. The introduction of the two women by the supportive Richard Larkins[12] provides insight about the direction in which the NCAA thought it was going. The rhetorical stance of Larkins' introduction provides a flavor of the times and perhaps an inkling about society's somewhat patronizing, although publicly genteel and polite, detachment in relation to females' sports participation:

> Ladies and gentlemen, in introducing this subject, I will make it as brief as possible. There has been an increasing amount of interest within the NCAA, particularly the Executive Committee and the Council, in the progress and development of women athletes.
>
> I would like to point out clearly that there is no attempt to move into the activities which are very well handled by competent leadership. I think our purpose today is merely to understand what the women are doing. I think we have enough to do in solving some of our own problems without attempting to solve the problems of women.
>
> We have here today two lovely people, eminently qualified to at least explain to us the problems that they confront, the help that they need, and whatever understanding they may secure from this eminent body of men.[13]

In response to their mission to the NCAA, the women received mixed messages about the NCAA's intentions regarding women's athletics.[14] DGWS needed to know the NCAA's intentions because DGWS was about to embark on the creation of a new organization that might govern elite-level competition for women. Finally, two years later, still uncertain about the NCAA's intentions, the women of DGWS continued to seek an answer to their question. They even inquired through intermediaries such as Larkins. Ultimately, in response to their 1966 efforts, Charles Neinas, the assistant to the executive director of the NCAA, made this reply in March 1966:

> The NCAA limits its jurisdiction and authority to male student athletes. In fact, the Executive Regulations of this Association prohibit women from participating in National Collegiate Championship events. Also, the NCAA's Constitution and By-Law provisions concerning the recruitment of athletes and conduct of intercollegiate athletics relates to the programs sponsored by our member institutions for male students. Consequently, a national organization assuming responsibility for women's intercollegiate athletics would not be in conflict with this Association.
>
> Please assure the DGWS that the NCAA stands ready to be of assistance, in an advisory capacity, in formulating policies and procedures for the conduct of intercollegiate athletics for women. We wish the DGWS well in this important endeavor.[15]

Within three months of the March 1966 Neinas statement, DGWS created a Commission on Intercollegiate Athletics for Women (CIAW) and began developing the organizational framework necessary to govern intercollegiate athletics, including national championships, for women. Within 12 months, however, the NCAA appeared to be renouncing its previous statements about who should be in the governance role over women's athletics. In response to what might be characterized as a letter of protest about the change in the NCAA's point of view from CIAW chair Katherine Ley, Walter Byers, executive director of the NCAA responded,

> I don't know precisely what you mean by our "hands off" policy or who told you this was the official position of the Association [NCAA]."[16]

The days, weeks, and months went by. The women of the CIAW worked at forming a governance structure for women's athletics. The NCAA continued to deny its interest while, on the other hand, appearing to have interest in women's athletics. A battle with the Amateur Athletic Union (AAU) for the premier position as the feeder organization for the Olympic movement may have motivated the NCAA's concern. Emotions ran high; motivations became complex. Arguments were convoluted. An example is found in a February 1971 memo from Walter Byers:

> The NCAA Constitution and Bylaws do not specifically bar female athletes from participating in intercollegiate athletics although it is recognized that traditionally intercollegiate athletic competition has involved only males. Nonetheless, the NCAA was formed to administer intercollegiate athletics and the Constitution and Bylaws do not contain any legislation which would prevent the Association from adopting rules applicable to female athletic competition.
>
> Because there are numerous opportunities for female athletes to participate (e.g., the Olympic Games), they would have justification to complain that the NCAA does discriminate by preventing females from competing in events against other female athletes. (If the United States constitutional amendment for women's rights is adopted, there probably no longer would be any legally tenable grounds for disqualifying an athletically-talented female from competing in an NCAA event against males.)[17]

The women of the CIAW and its parent group, the DGWS, rightly realized that the mission of the DGWS and the to-be-formed Association for Intercollegiate Athletics for Women (AIAW) were not the same. DGWS sought more broad-based participation with a membership of individuals, whereas the AIAW would focus on elite-level competition with a membership of institutions. Although the AIAW was the creation of DGWS, it was created as a stand-alone, independent organization in recognition of the conflicts of interest and direction that might have otherwise occurred if it was part of DGWS.

By the summer of 1971, the CIAW forwarded to the NCAA a copy of the proposed operating code of the about-to-be-formed AIAW. Instead of responding to the CIAW, the NCAA began forming its own plans for governing women's intercollegiate athletics. By the fall of 1971, the AIAW was officially open for business amidst continuing battles with the NCAA over the governance of women's athletics.

Half a year later, Title IX was enacted. Women's intercollegiate athletics began to flourish under the direction of the AIAW, but the organization, yet in its infancy, faced challenges that shook it to its core.

DGWS long believed that financial aid for athletes was a source of exploitation and abuse. The AIAW also initially turned away from the use of financial aid. AIAW polled its member institutions on whether DGWS' policy and thus AIAW's policy should change; 80 percent were in favor of change. A report on the results of the poll offers this conclusion:

> This surprisingly high affirmative vote reflects the consciousness of member institutions that the time for change has arrived.
>
> Perhaps it is an exaggeration to say that the time for change has arrived. It would be better to say that the time has come to acknowledge and bring into the open what has been going on for a long time in some places. The basic beliefs of the women in AAHPER have not changed—they do not wish to see girls exploited in school and in recruiting. They do not wish to be parties to hustling and unethical recruiting practices themselves.
>
> But there is no doubt that the consciousness of women as to their rights and privileges has been raised, and the whole theory of protecting women from exploitation, or paternalistic action "for their own good," has been a casualty of the student movement and the women's rights movement. In addition, there is another basic factor. If two children of a family both have musical ability, the boy plays a violin and the girl the piano, they may both have *talent* scholarships, but until now, if brother and sister both had athletic ability, only the male child could have a talent scholarship.[18]

In response to the poll, a special committee met in March 1973, when Title IX was less than a year old. The committee rewrote DGWS' philosophical statement concerning financial aid and created interim regulations for such awards. The revised philosophical statement tells us a great deal about the struggles surrounding financial aid. Read now, a third of a century later, the statement resonates with guidance for repairing current the ills of big-time athletics. Let's take a look.

DGWS' *Philosophical Statement* reaffirmed its concern at the same time that

> the provision of scholarships or other financial assistance specifically designated for athletes may create a potential for abuses which could prove detrimental to the development of quality programs of athletics. Specifically, the DGWS deplores

the evils of pressure recruiting and performer exploitation which frequently accompany the administration of financial aid for athletes.

The DGWS is concerned that many collegiate athletic programs as currently administered do not make available to female students benefits equivalent in nature or extent to those made available to male students. While a curtailment of programs of financial aid to female students involved in athletics does eliminate the potential for abuses inherent in any such programs, this remedy is overly broad because it operates inequitably to deny to female students benefits available to their male counterparts. Specifically, these benefits might include the recognition of athletic excellence and the opportunity for economic assistance to secure an education.

Therefore DGWS believes that the appropriate solution in our contemporary society is one directed to avoiding abuses while providing to female students, on an equitable basis, benefits comparable to those available to male students similarly situated.

Success of financial assistance programs is dependent upon the quality of administration. To foster appropriate administrative procedures, the following guidelines are recommended:

1. The enrichment of the life of the participant should be the focus and the reason for athletic programs.

2. Adequate funding for a comprehensive athletic program should receive priority over the money assigned for financial aid. A comprehensive athletic program provides adequate funding for (a) a variety of competitive sports which will serve the needs of many students; (b) travel using licensed carriers; (c) appropriate food and lodging; (d) rated officials; (e) well-trained coaches; (f) equipment and facilities which are safe and aid performance.

3. The potential contribution of the "educated" citizen to society, rather than the contribution of the student to the college offering the scholarship, should be the motive for financial aid.

4. Staff time and effort should be devoted to the comprehensive program rather than to recruiting.

5. Students should be free to choose the institution on the basis of curriculum and program rather than on the amount of financial aid offered.

6. When financial aid is to be given, participants in certain sports should not be favored over those in other sports.

7. Students should be encouraged to participate in the athletic program for reasons other than financial aid.

If the DGWS *Philosophical Statement* was followed today, would men's minor sports have served as sacrificial teams to the "premier" sports on campus? Would the headlines be as full of abuse and deceit regarding financial aid? Would high school coaches of extremely talented basketball or football players see their student-athletes enticed to forego an education in order to pursue the unrealistic dream of huge pro contracts?[19]

IN A NUTSHELL: AIAW VERSUS NCAA

In the days following enactment of Title IX, the NCAA was also struggling to find its role: Did it want to turn its back on women's sport? Did it want to control it all? The following three statements provide the short version of the next decade and the interactions between the AIAW and the NCAA:

- The NCAA lost its battles to exclude athletics from Title IX.

- The NCAA determined that it would be in its best organizational interests to control women's athletics.

- The NCAA seized universal control of women's intercollegiate athletics (except for those schools belonging to smaller organizations such as the National Association of Intercollegiate Athletics) after blocking AIAW's access to the financial resources associated with national championships, thus confirming the demise of the AIAW.[20]

Before its demise, the AIAW offered 41 national championships in 19 sports to over 6,000 teams in 960 member colleges and universities. AIAW was also a prime mover in bringing about the Amateur Sports Act of 1978, an act that ended the dispute between the AAU and the NCAA and set the United States Olympic Committee (USOC) on a course that would later increase opportunities for females.

For much of the 1970s both the NAGWS and AIAW flourished. Together with other education-based organizations focused on equity, they sought to have HEW's Title IX regulations provide an effective means of change. They did so in a climate of fear and wildly divergent rumors about the havoc or positive changes that Title IX and its regulations might bring. Would coed locker rooms be required? Would sports for males cease to exist so that females could have access? Are females anatomically and physiologically able to participate in sports activities without ending their child-bearing potential? Marjorie Blaufarb of AAHPER noted, "If one makes the effort, in good faith, toward including girls and women on a basis of equality in programs and employment opportunities, there should be no need to fear what regulations will say."[21] The issue was a matter of mind-set.

WHO HOLDS THE REINS ON CAMPUS?

Mind-set affected the merging of men's and women's departments of physical education and athletics. In the early 1970s, before the promulgation of the Title IX regulations, formerly separate departments merged. Almost without exception, the former head of the men's department became the head of the merged department, with the former head of the women's department being offered a subordinate position. The merging and the mind-set that only males had the ability to lead (at least when anyone but females might be involved in the group being led) existed so broadly across the nation that the Women's Equity Action League adopted in 1974 a resolution on the matter.

> Whereas educational institutions throughout the country are frequently merging their girls' and women's physical education and athletic programs with their boys' and men's programs under the guise of responding to the equal rights movement and, whereas in reality many of these mergers are male takeovers of the women's physical education and athletic programs, let it be resolved that where merger occurs, an affirmative action plan be written to insure that women employees are not demoted or removed and that they retain decision making authority, and that opportunities for women and girls be strengthened.[22]

Saying it does not always make it so. Female head coaches became assistant coaches. Female department chairs with doctorates became deputy chairs of merged departments[23] headed by males possessing only master's degrees. Many of the fears of women professionals about the continuation of a patronizing mind-set were realized. On the other hand, it is difficult to find fears held by their male counterparts that became reality. Locker rooms remained single sex; facilities were either shared or remained male dominated. Sport opportunities for males on every level continued to grow. Indeed, even today, the massive increase in participation by females has still brought them to a position less than that enjoyed by males when Title IX was enacted three decades ago. The push at the door is considerable, but the doors are still slow to open.

IN BRIEF

The passage of Title IX in 1972 reflected a growing awareness of prior limits on civil rights in general across the nation. The struggle for control of the governance of women's intercollegiate sport involved a male organization (NCAA) and a female organization (AIAW) as protagonists. Motivations for seeking control of women's athletics ranged from having females control programs for females to the NCAA's pursuit of strength in its governance fight with the AAU concerning its Olympic relationships.

The role of women in the social matrix of the 1970s coupled with the existing financial power of the male organization (NCAA) strongly influenced which organization would prevail. Three decades later, the NCAA, its leadership's view of Title IX, and the power of females within the organization are considerably different from what they were during the 1970s and 1980s. Women's voices are being heard (not being responded to with catcalls as they were at the first NCAA convention attended by women) and, to a greater extent, being valued. The NCAA has had a female president, Judith Sweet. The NCAA conducts Title IX workshops that focus more on compliance than on methods of avoiding compliance. In general, the years of trying to include female leaders but keep them "in their place" and away from the real power within the NCAA have ended; women now have a greater power base. Much of the increase in true respect for those voices has come because of the great courage, diligence, creativity, commitment, vigilance, and steadfastness of the women of the National Association of Collegiate Women Athletic Administrators,[24] many of whom shared in the AIAW experience.

> "I never had the opportunity to be a varsity athlete, and when I talk to the female athletes and try to put that in perspective compared to the opportunities they have now, all I get are blank stares. That's positive because they can't relate to what I'm saying."
>
> *Judith Sweet, former NCAA president, NCAA News, January 27, 1993*

This little girl has already taken advantage of and experienced the benefits of athletic opportunities her grandmother never had.

Thirteen Questions and Zero Answers

Unlike the other chapters, this one provides no answers in response to the questions. Your answers will reflect your view of history and your personally held beliefs about athletics in general and sex equity in particular. Have fun.

1. Would the current excesses and ethical issues facing NCAA-governed athletics have existed if an organization other than the NCAA had continued to govern women's intercollegiate athletics?

2. Would women's sports have followed the male model if the AIAW had continued to be the governing organization for women's athletics?

3. What do you think would have been the outcome for women's programs and men's "minor" sports programs if Title IX jurisdiction had excluded football from its reach?

4. What social changes of the 1950s and 1960s had the greatest influence on creating an era favorable to civil rights legislation? (See chapter 8 for some of the data of the era.)

5. Have you recently seen a young girl dressed in her team uniform in a store on her way home? What was your reaction to her athletic mode of dress? What would your parents' reaction have been if they had seen her in a store similarly dressed when Title IX was enacted 30 years ago? If your reaction and the reaction of your parents would be different, to what might you attribute the difference? Assuming that a girl in her team uniform in a store would meet greater acceptance today than she would have 30 years ago, to what do you attribute the change in attitude?

6. Why do you think that Title IX passed and the Equal Rights Amendment did not? Remember, Congress enacted Title IX, and the ERA faced the additional hurdle of ratification by the states.

7. In the late 1960s and early 1970s intercollegiate competition for women was characterized by short seasons and restricted funding for equipment, coaching, uniforms, and travel. Find a few positives among the negatives.

8. In 2004 intercollegiate competition for women is characterized by full seasons, paid coaches, financial aid, and more similar funding for equipment, uniforms, and travel. Find a few negatives among the positives.

9. Besides their desire to protect males' sports, what might have been the motivation of the men of the NCAA as they alternately sought to have nothing to do with women's sports and to control women's sports? Is there anything in the 1970's view of women in society that might have been influential?

10. Title IX affects the entire education endeavor, not just physical education and athletics. If you were a supporter of or lobbyist for Title IX in 1971 and were focused on nonsport applications of Title IX such as removing bars to females wanting to enter physics classes, would you have welcomed the debate to include athletics or would you have seen it as making your job more difficult as you tried to garner votes? Why?

11. Imagine yourself to be a lobbyist for Title IX. What would be your most persuasive arguments for its passage as you meet with members of Congress?

12. Would the early years of Title IX have involved less strife and conflict as it applied to athletics if it had been passed in 1982 or 1992 or 2002 rather than in 1972? If so, what would have made the difference?

13. Some have said that athletics opportunities for female athletes and fairer treatment for females in physical education classes would have increased naturally even without the prodding of Title IX. Do you agree? If so, what would have been the impetus for such expansion and would it have resulted in the massive growth in participation by females that we see today? If you disagree, discuss what societal factors would have continued to retard access to participation for the nation's daughters?

NOTES

[1]United States Representative Patsy Mink (D-Hawaii) was one of the prime movers for civil rights legislation, and her efforts were vital to the enactment of Title IX. Rep. Mink, who passed away during the summer of 2003, recollected in "Title IX at 30—Making the Grade?" by Patrice Gaines, *AAUW Outlook,* spring-summer 2002, about the struggle to include gender discrimination in civil rights legislation. Concerning adding gender to the list of categories protected by Title VII she recalled, "The Justice Department kept saying it couldn't [legally] be done . . . The only thing left was to attach it [Title IX] to the education bill." The article goes on to note that "In the end, Congress did outlaw sex discrimination in Title VII, but Mink . . . still pushed the change in Title IX."

[2]See "Letters Home: My Life With Title IX," *Women in Sport: Issues and Controversies*, 2nd ed., edited by Greta Cohen, NAGWS (2001), for a description of the swiftly changing structure of the sport experience for females in the 1950s, 1960s, and 1970s.

[3]AAPE changed its name to the American Association for the Advancement of Physical Education (AAAPE) in 1885, later to the American Physical Education Association (APEA), still later to the American Association for Health, Physical Education and Recreation, and ultimately to the American Alliance for Health, Physical Education, Recreation and Dance.

[4]"Sport" has come to refer to a more broad-based activity when compared with the term "athletics," which focuses more on competition. The terms have over the last century swapped meanings several times, but when the NAGWS changed to DGWS and thereby traded "athletics" for "sport," it was trying to emphasize its application to a broad range of physical activity, including instructional, recreational, and competitive.

[5]Three-court basketball involved two forwards, two centers, and two guards. No player could dribble the ball more than three times, and all had to remain within their one-third of the court. The game progressed to a two-court format, then to rovers, and finally to a five-person full-court game. Iowa's high schools resisted

the move from six-person basketball teams for its girls significantly longer than any other state did. Finally, Iowa's high schools, with judicial urging, moved to the five-person game, thus permitting its female high school students to compete more effectively for scholarship dollars.

[6]1984 was the first Olympic Marathon for women, and the world waited with held breath to see whether females could live through the event.

[7]Laura Lyon invented the sports bra in 1904. Aren't you glad you learned this tidbit of trivia?

[8]For a good overview of the early days of college football and the development of sport governance on a national basis, see *Sport and Play in American Life* by Stephen Figler, Saunders College Publishing, 1981. The book is old, but its coverage of the topic is broad.

[9]The 19th Amendment, ratified in 1920, gave women the right to vote.

[10]From 1958 to 1974 the precursor's name was the Division of Girls and Women in Sport, and it was still located under the umbrella of AAHPER.

[11]Before going to the convention, concerns had developed among the leadership of the DGWS as well as the United States Olympic Committee about the apparent increase of females seeking to participate on men's teams to garner access to coaching and elite-level competition.

[12]Larkins was also involved with the USOC and had become aware of the need to provide more fully for the athletic needs of female athletes.

[13]The introduction and more information about the meeting are found in the *1963-64 NCAA Yearbook* .

[14]For an excellent and cogent presentation of the events surrounding the dialogue between the DGWS and the NCAA, see the affidavit of Donna Lopiano filed in the United States District Court for the District of Columbia in the lawsuit *Association for Intercollegiate Athletics for Women v NCAA*, 735 F. 2d 577 (1984).

[15]Neinas' response on behalf of the NCAA was included in a letter to Richard Larkins, who had made the inquiry on behalf of the women in DGWS.

[16]The balance of the text is found in Walter Byers' letter to Katherine Ley of August 21, 1967. A transcript of the letter is found in the *Affidavit of Donna Lopiano*, in the lawsuit of the *AIAW v NCAA*, filed in the United States District Court for the District of Columbia.

[17]This statement by Byers reflects the inaccurate perception that intercollegiate athletics did not exist at the time for women. Although seasons were short, in part because of the failure of colleges to provide funding for coaches or team expenses, regional (and national championships in some sports) were taking place. The denial by Byers of the existence of women's intercollegiate athletics reflected the profession's devaluation of the activities of women and their coaches. This devaluation of female coaches' records extended through much of the following decade as they stood as candidates for coaching positions in the post–Title IX era. "If it didn't say NCAA, it didn't exist" was the evaluative tool often used to judge prior coaching experience.

[18]See *AAHPER Update*, May 1973, page 11 for a full report of the process of changing DGWS and AIAW viewpoints on financial aid.

[19]Reality tells us that only 1 in 25,000 scholarship athletes is ever offered a professional contract of any sort.

[20]As the developing AIAW began obtaining television contracts for the national championships that it was sponsoring for women, the NCAA took greater notice. The NCAA, as it signed contracts for the broadcast rights to its male championships, required the broadcasting company to commit to broadcast any women's championship only if sponsored by the NCAA and not by the AIAW. The television contracts between the AIAW and its broadcasters were then renounced by the broadcasters, leaving the AIAW in a difficult financial position. Also, the NCAA offered to pay the expenses for its member schools (most had dual membership with the AIAW and the NCAA) if they would attend the NCAA women's championships and not the AIAW championships. The AIAW filed an antitrust lawsuit but was ultimately not successful in overcoming the stranglehold of the NCAA.

[21]For a complete review of Blaufarb's comments, see *AAHPER Update*, February 1975, page 1.

[22]See "Retrospect on a Year of Title IX Discussions," *Update*, AAHPER, February 1975, page 3.

[23]Mergers took place within college physical education departments as well as in athletics departments.

[24]See appendix F for contact information for NACWAA and its programs.

6

Title IX in the Courts, 1972 to 1992

How did we get to where we are today? Besides the law, regulations, policy interpretations, and corollary materials such as the *Investigator's Manual* and the 1996, 1998, and 2003 clarification letters, a long line of lawsuits has helped refine our understanding of Title IX. This chapter and the next track the major steps of understanding that have been contributed by decisions and settlements in lawsuits, and, in one instance, corrective legislation.

We can identify two major eras in the growth of legal understanding about Title IX—the period before 1992 and the period after 1992. The pivotal 1992 event around which everything else seems to fall in two sections was the U.S. Supreme Court's unanimous decision in *Franklin v Gwinnett*, from which we learned that compensatory and punitive damages are possible under Title IX. We discuss *Franklin* toward the end of this chapter, but before initiating that discussion, we offer the vital prologue found in several other significant cases.

To understand Title IX, we need to understand the cases that illuminate the reach of its power. Without such cases as *Cannon v University of Chicago* (1979), we would not know that an individual has enforcement options beyond simply filing an in-house or OCR complaint. Without *North Haven Board of Education v Bell* (1982), we would not know that the protections of Title IX include employees as well as students. Without *Grove City College v Bell* (1984), we would not know that indirect federal funding triggers Title IX jurisdiction. Today we take for granted many of these understandings, but sometimes others of us are ignorant of them to the detriment of our programs and our students. Let's jump in and see what the decisions and settlements from the birth of Title IX through its 20th birthday tell us.

CASE LAW

Decisions in lawsuits provide insight into how the courts view issues of contention concerning specific legal issues. Such decisions add to a body of literature known as case law. Although the term "case law" has a meaning different from "precedent," the insights that case law provides are of value even if they don't automatically carry with them the weight of a precedent. The cases discussed here, however, except for *Blair*, provide both the insight of case law and the weight of precedent; the U.S. Supreme Court decided each case and thus each carries precedent value across the breadth of the United States.

In the early years of Title IX, most cases finding their way to the U.S. Supreme Court dealt mainly with issues of procedure, jurisdiction, and remedies. Let's look at the following cases and see what we've learned about these issues.

Cannon v University of Chicago (1979)

The main question asked and answered by the *Cannon v University of Chicago* case is this: May an individual sue an institution without first exhausting all administrative remedies, such as an in-house complaint or OCR complaint? The answer is yes.

But we might first ask, may individuals sue on their own behalf under Title IX? The "term of art" (indicating that the term has a special legal meaning beyond its mere words) known as "private right of action" is the legalese way of asking the same question. "Private right of action" refers to a person's ability to take a case to court rather than only to an administrative body such as the OCR. The presence or absence of a private right of action makes a great deal of difference in the sharpness of the enforcement teeth surrounding any law. When a private right of action exists, the plaintiff has an expanded range of possible remedies. When a private right of action exists, a plaintiff can similarly seek redress in an expanded range of forums.

The significance of a private right of action is found in the autonomy afforded to the complainant or plaintiff. Complainants or plaintiffs have the right to decide what forum, administrative agency, or courthouse is the best for their particular cases. They may bypass administrative complaints and the time consumed by them, if desired. Without a private right of action, plaintiffs would not be able to seek either compensatory or punitive damages under Title IX because neither is available through the administrative complaint procedure; damages are only available through a lawsuit. The availability of damages (determined by the pivotal 1992 *Franklin* decision) carries with it a threat of significant financial consequence, which has encouraged many institutions to comply with Title IX rather than go to court to defend noncompliance.

OCR administrative complaints do not allow damages, although they do carry the *threat* of loss of federal funding to the institution. As we have discussed in previous chapters, the loss of federal funding has never been implemented in the more than three decades of the life of Title IX. The idle threat is thus an ineffective motivation for compliance. Therefore, the existence of a private right of action is significant.

Cannon is the case by which the existence of a private right of action under Title IX was determined.[1] Cannon believed that she had been denied admission to medical school because of her gender. The medical school was a recipient of federal financial assistance, and thus the school was under the jurisdiction of Title IX. Could Cannon exercise her rights under Title IX only by filing a complaint with OCR, or did her options include a private right of action to file a lawsuit in court? The answer is not found within Title IX or its regulations; both are silent on the issue.

In *Cannon* the United States Supreme Court decided that a private right of action is indeed available under Title IX when

(1) someone who is discriminated against on the basis of sex is a member of the class for whose special benefit Title IX was enacted,

(2) the legislative history of Title IX indicates Congress' intent to create a private cause of action for a person excluded, on the basis of sex, from participation in a federally funded program,

(3) implication of a private remedy under Title IX is fully consistent with the orderly enforcement of Title IX, and

(4) the subject matter of a private action under Title IX (invidious sex discrimination) does not involve an area basically of concern to the states.

When these four requirements are met, a private right of action also exists. Few Title IX issues would fail to meet the four requirements; *Cannon* demonstrated that lawsuits join OCR complaints as enforcement avenues for Title IX.

North Haven Board of Education v Bell (1982)

The *North Haven Board of Education v Bell* case asks and answers two main questions:

- Title IX covers students; does it also cover employees?
- Did Congress provide at least a tacit approval of the regulations for Title IX?

The answer to both questions is yes.

North Haven provides a good historical review of the early days of Title IX. The case also provides a basis from which to understand much later cases such as *Lowrey v Texas A&M University* (1997) and *Lakoski v James* (1996),[2] which narrow the application of Title IX when employees are the plaintiffs.

Elaine Dove was a tenured public school teacher. After taking a one-year maternity leave, she tried to return to her job, but the school district barred her from doing so. Dove filed a Title IX complaint with HEW.[3] In response to her complaint, HEW began investigating the employment practices of the school district. The school district refused to cooperate with HEW, claiming that Title IX, and thus HEW, had no power to regulate employment practices. The school district sued HEW when it learned that HEW was initiating enforcement proceedings against it. The issue, originally triggered by Dove's being barred from returning to work following a maternity leave, had blossomed into a much broader one. The school district claimed, along with another similarly situated school district that was added to the case, that because the complainant was an employee, not a student, HEW had no jurisdiction to investigate the district's employment practices. The U.S. Supreme Court disagreed.

The divided Supreme Court determined that the reach of Title IX did in fact extend to employees and not just to students. The court reached its determination by reviewing the statutory language of the Title IX regulations, section 106.51 (a)(1), "No *person*, shall, on the basis of sex . . ." [emphasis added], and by reviewing the regulations developed to implement the statute wherein, "No person shall, on the basis of sex . . . be subjected to discrimination in *employment* . . ." [emphasis added]. The court also buttressed its decision by looking at the legislative history leading up to the enactment of Title IX including 1970 hearings in which much of the testimony focused on employment issues. The court also relied on the 1971 offering of education amendments in which Senator Bayh,[4] as their author, provided parallels to the protection of employees provided by Title VI.

> "[Title IX was designed to] provide for the women of America something that is rightfully theirs—an equal chance to attend the schools of their choice, to develop the skills they want."
>
> Senator Birch Bayh, Chronicle of Higher Education, "Title IX at Thirty," June 21, 2002

Besides finding that employees are included under the Title IX umbrella of protection, the court needed to find that HEW did in fact have regulatory power to create, promulgate, and enforce specific regulations for Title IX. To that end, the court found that Congress, even though it did not specifically vote in approval of the regulations, acquiesced when the regulations were presented to it. Similarly, Congress has declined to make use of later opportunities to revisit or revise the regulations, thus adding support to the notion that Congress did indeed approve of them.

Employees have access to antidiscrimination legislation such as Title VII, which protects them in the workplace. *North Haven* adds Title IX protections to those of Title VII, which were already available to employees.[5]

The minority opinion (dissenting) in the *North Haven* case focused on tracking the federal dollars, in contrast to the majority's focus on legislative history and original intent of the statute. The dissenting opinion noted that Dove was not in a federally funded subunit of the school district and therefore was not protected by Title IX. Employees in other areas and subunits of the school district that did receive federal money might have been within the reach of Title IX, but Dove was not. The dissenting opinion in *North Haven,* although of no legal significance, foreshadowed the majority's opinion in an even more significant case two years later known as *Grove City v Bell.*

Grove City College v Bell (1984)

The two important questions asked and answered by the *Grove City College v Bell* case are the following:

- Does the word "program," which is found in the one-sentence law called Title IX, refer to the entire institution or only the subunit or subunits that actually receive federal financial assistance?
- Must the institution receive federal financial assistance directly from the federal government to trigger Title IX jurisdiction?

Although later "overturned" by the Civil Rights Restoration Act in 1988, the *Grove City* decision said in response to the first question that only subunits that actually received federal money were included in the term "program." The decision regarding the second question continues to stand; the court determined that institutions need not receive federal assistance directly from the federal government to trigger Title IX jurisdiction.

All postsecondary institutions within the jurisdiction of Title IX were required to be in compliance with Title IX by 1978. Every institution was required to file a letter with the federal government stating that it was in compliance. Grove City College refused to file the letter.

Grove City College, a private college in western Pennsylvania that had strenuously avoided any entanglements with the federal government, believed it was not obligated to file the letter because it received no direct federal funding. Its professors held no federal grants, and no federal teaching-improvement dollars had crossed its threshold. Indeed, even its financial aid office saw no federal dollars.

Because of the absence of federal dollars on campus, the college did not think that it needed to file the letter; the Office for Civil Rights thought otherwise. OCR thought that the presence of Better Education Opportunity Grants (BEOG) money traveling from the federal government directly to the college's students, who then used the funds to pay their tuition and fees, was sufficient presence of federal money to trigger jurisdiction. The BEOG money went directly to students; it arrived on campus only indirectly, funneled through the hands of students. Because the BEOG money never passed through the college's financial aid office, the college didn't agree.

After a bit of pushing and shoving resulting in no change in the stance of Grove City College, OCR started the process to remove the BEOG money from the college's students. The college sued to block the loss of its students' BEOG money.

Very little moves quickly with litigation. By the time the *Grove City* case had moved to the U.S. Supreme Court, a new president occupied the White House and the government's position on several issues in the case had changed drastically. The metamorphosis of the government's arguments makes interesting reading, but the effect of the case was profound.

First, the U.S. Supreme Court decided that even indirect federal funding such as the BEOG money was sufficient to trigger jurisdiction. Thus, federal money funneled through students to the college meets the "receiving federal financial assistance" required element of Title IX. This first part of the decision maintained the broad reach of Title IX. The second part of the decision did the opposite as far as intercollegiate athletics programs were concerned.

The second part of the court's decision involved the definition of the word "program" found in the text of Title IX. The court determined that "program" referred only to the actual subunit that received the federal dollars. Therefore, if the only federal money on campus was found in a biology professor's research grant, only the biology department was under the jurisdiction of Title IX. A female student could be discriminated against with impunity while taking a class in the art department or serving as an intern in the classics department because neither department was the recipient of federal funding. On the other hand, if the biology department discriminated against her, she could file either a Title IX complaint with OCR or a Title IX lawsuit. To many people, the patchwork quilt pattern of protection from discrimination resulting from the *Grove City* decision didn't make sense. Why would Congress have enacted antidiscrimination legislation only to limit its jurisdiction in such irrational ways?

The *Grove City* decision had a greater, more far-reaching effect on intercollegiate athletics than it did on other subunits of the institution. Many departments on campus might have federal money flowing to them, but athletics departments characteristically don't. The federal money found in the financial aid department and used to fund athletes' tuition triggered Title IX jurisdiction over the financial aid department but not over the athletics department. After *Grove City*, institutional goodwill would have to be relied on for fair, nondiscriminatory treatment; Title IX no longer applied within subunits not receiving federal financial assistance.

The effect of *Grove City* was swift and massive. Faith in institutional goodwill would soon prove to be misplaced. Within weeks of the decision, scholarships for female athletes were canceled at several colleges across the nation, women's teams were slated for termination at others, OCR complaints were closed, and lawsuits were dismissed. In general, the removal of Title IX jurisdiction revealed the ephemeral nature of the goodwill required for continued equitable treatment for female athletes.

The effect of *Grove City* on interscholastic athletics programs was not the same as its effect on intercollegiate programs because federal financial assistance to school districts generally comes to the school district rather than to a specific subunit. Once in the school district, federal dollars are mixed with other funding and dollars from all sources are "contaminated," thus conferring Title IX jurisdiction on all corners of the school district, including its athletics programs.

The devastating effect of the program-specific portion of the *Grove City* decision was to survive for four years; an entire collegiate generation of potential female athletes was powerless to find assistance through Title IX for sex-based discrimination.[6]

Blair v Washington State University (1987)

The main question asked and answered by the *Blair v Washington State University* case is this: Should football and so-called revenue sports and all other subsets of teams be treated equally by Title IX? In short, the answer is yes.

Some believe that football and other so-called revenue-producing sports should be excluded from Title IX jurisdiction, but such exclusion would undermine the purpose of Title IX and, more to the point, would be contrary to the well settled law.

Young children who crave an ice cream just before dinner or simply must have a new toy, right now, today, this minute, have perfected the technique of asking and reasking the question or posing the question to different people until they finally receive a yes. Some Title IX questions, once forcefully answered, are not asked again. Others seem to be resurrected periodically with the hope that the answer will be different. The football-exclusion question seems to be one with resurrection powers.

The question of whether football or any sport labeled as revenue producing (whether labeled correctly or not) should be excluded from Title IX jurisdiction was addressed and forcefully answered early in the life of Title IX by the failure of the Tower amendment. On May 20, 1974, less than two years after the enactment of Title IX, Senator John Tower of Texas proposed that Title IX should be amended to remove so-called revenue-producing sports from its calculations. Labeling was important to the Tower amendment. It did not matter whether the designated revenue sport ever produced any revenue, either net or gross. All that mattered was that the sport was labeled as potentially revenue producing. According to the proposed Tower amendment, a school that decided to protect its men's basketball, baseball, or football teams from the reach of Title IX could do so simply by labeling those sports as potentially revenue producing. The school would never need to show that the designated sports had ever or would ever earn even one penny. The motivation for designating a sport as potentially revenue producing was, theoretically, that the sport would be removed from all Title IX calculations. When it came time to determine whether equity existed, equity would need to exist only between women's sports and men's minor sports, both of which were historically underfunded.

Senator Tower's proposal was unsuccessful.[7] When the Tower amendment failed to make it out of committee in 1974 the issue was determined; Title IX is to treat football and so-called revenue sports equally with all other subsets of teams. The reach and calculations of Title IX include all sports.

Thirteen years later, in 1987, the *Blair* case highlighted the issue again but within a different forum. The *Blair* case did not apply federal law but instead used a state law drafted similarly to Title IX. Many states have "state Title IX" legislation; Washington is one of them. Although the *Blair* decision carries no weight in the case law of Title IX, its decision expresses judicial support for the failure of the Tower amendment and supports the well-accepted proposition that Title IX does not discriminate among specific sports but applies to all equally. Language from the *Blair* appellate decision, which reversed in part the lower court, serves as a strong reiteration of a long-term standard of Title IX: "The football program may not be excluded from the calculations of participation opportunities, scholarships, or distribution of nonrevenue funds" (*Blair* at 1385).

> States Step up to Push for Equity in Absence of Federal Enforcement
>
> *Comment on state of Title IX legislation, Education Week, June 18, 1997*

In its fourth decade, the inclusion of football and other so-called revenue sports within the jurisdiction of Title IX remains settled, but the question still arises periodically. The stakes are large; if such sports were removed from Title IX jurisdiction, Title IX would lose its ability to auger for any semblance of equity in athletics programs. Like the young child's question about ice cream, the question about so-called revenue sports again came forward during the Department of Education's 2002-2003 commission hearings, even in the face of irrefutable data showing that the production of net revenue is not a realistic dream in most athletics programs. The result of the 2002-2003 commission process was the continued inclusion of the proportionality prong as an appropriate member of the three-prong test for participation. All sports continue to remain within the jurisdiction of Title IX. See chapter 9 for a discussion of issues considered by the commission.

No matter how many times the question is asked, the answer remains the same: Football and "potentially revenue-producing" sports are not excluded from the reach of Title IX.

Franklin v Gwinnett County Public Schools (1992)

The important question asked and answered by *Franklin v Gwinnett County Public Schools* is this: Are monetary damages available to the successful Title IX plaintiff? The answer is yes.

In the autumn of 1991 the United States Supreme Court heard arguments in a sexual harassment case. A female student claimed that an employee of the school had sexually harassed her. The student had originally filed an OCR complaint, but the results did not satisfy her; the employee had left the district, and the complaint was ended. The student wanted stronger notice to be taken of her victimization, so she exercised her private right of action as she filed a Title IX lawsuit in federal court. Onlookers for the case held mixed expectations for the outcome, but none anticipated the actual result.

The one sentence of Title IX and the regulations were both silent on the availability of monetary damages. Clarence Thomas had just joined the court following a well-publicized confirmation hearing involving allegations against him of sexual harassment. The composition of the Court did not bode well for a verdict in favor of adding sharper teeth to antidiscrimination legislation such as Title IX. According to pundits

> Decision Sends Clear Message to Violators: Money Increases Incentive.
>
> *Comment on the unanimous U.S. Supreme Court decision in* Franklin v Gwinnett, USA Today, *February 27, 1992*

who offer prior comment on what the Court will do, a favorable decision in *Franklin* was unlikely and a unanimous favorable decision was next to impossible. On February 28, 1992, the Court surprised everyone by handing down its unanimous decision affirming the availability of monetary damages in Title IX lawsuits.[8] The surprise of the decision was quickly followed by the realization that the enforcement power of Title IX had been dramatically changed. The decision put every institution on notice that it now faced a realistic threat of losing substantial and unpredictable amounts of money for noncompliance. In response, many institutions decided that compliance was more fiscally sound than noncompliance.

No longer would victims of sex discrimination have in their favor only an empty threat that an institution would lose its federal funding. No longer would doors be closed as victims sought the aid of attorneys in Title IX cases. No longer would delay be the strategy of choice for institutions unwilling to change. Title IX enforcement took a major step forward with the *Franklin* decision.

LEGISLATION: CIVIL RIGHTS RESTORATION ACT OF 1987 (1988)

You'll remember that the U.S. Supreme Court's 1984 *Grove City* decision interpreted the word "program" to mean a subunit of an institution, thereby gutting Title IX jurisdiction over programs such as college physical education and athletics, which typically receive no direct federal funding. The judiciary has the task of interpreting law; Congress

The Civil Rights Restoration Act clarified that the word "program" applies to an entire institution receiving federal funding, so a track and field program that does not receive federal funds still falls under Title IX jurisdiction.

has the task of enacting it. Following the *Grove City* decision, Congress needed four years to enact legislation that, in effect, told the Supreme Court that its interpretation of the word "program" was incorrect. This legislation was the Civil Rights Restoration Act (CRRA).

The Civil Rights Restoration Act of 1987 was passed, over presidential veto, in 1988. Among other things, the CRRA made clear previously unclear or misinterpreted language in several antidiscrimination statutes, including Title IX and its predecessor-in-language, Title VI. Following the CRRA, the term "program" as used by Title IX correctly applies to the entire institution, not merely the subunit that actually receives federal funding. Thus, if any federal dollar finds its way on campus, the entire campus falls under the jurisdiction of Title IX.

Although athletics departments and departments of physical education rarely receive any federal financial support themselves, their institutions do. Following the CRRA, it matters not if a particular department receives the federal funds. It matters only that somewhere on campus federal dollars are present.

So, the CRRA firmly established Title IX jurisdiction, again, over collegiate athletics and physical education departments and, in effect, reversed the part of the *Grove City* decision that had previously defined "program" as subunit.

SETTLEMENTS AND CONSENT ORDERS

Some lawsuits are concluded by settlement or consent between the parties and approved by the court but with the outcome not determined by the court. The results of such lawsuits carry no value as legal precedents because the court rendered no decision. But the lawsuits do provide insight into the negotiation of Title IX issues among the parties and often reflect the parties' understanding of the state of the law that they would have faced had the case proceeded to a judicial determination. For that reason, we discuss here one of the more prominent settlements.

The *Haffer v Temple University* (1988) case asks and answers two main questions:

- Can a student effectively exercise her private right of action in a Title IX lawsuit alleging rampant discrimination in the athletics program?
- Is there a realistic and legally accepted method of comparing benefits received by men and women and thereby evaluating compliance with Title IX?

The answer to both questions is yes.

The extremely long-lived *Haffer* case took eight years from its filing date to the entry of a consent order in 1988. The case spanned both the 1984 *Grove City* decision and the Civil Rights Restoration Act of 1987 (passed over presidential veto in 1988), which in effect reversed the program-specific effect of *Grove City*. The *Haffer* case overcame a multitude of hurdles and changing legal landscapes.

The facts of the *Haffer* case were not unique; female athletes made up 42 percent of the athlete population and received 13 percent of the budget, and discrimination against the female athletes occurred in all of the 13 program areas. Rollin Haffer decided that she was willing to stand up, at great cost to her college experience and beyond, and try to cause Temple University, which received over $19 million in federal financial aid, to change its ways. Haffer elected to use a lawsuit rather than an OCR complaint as her vehicle.

Haffer was the first collegiate athletics case to enter the court system rather than wend its way through the OCR administrative complaint process.[9] *Haffer* initially began life as a Title IX case, but once the Supreme Court handed down its *Grove City* decision, all claims but the financial aid claim were dismissed. The *Grove City* decision, which held sway from 1984 to 1988, put intercollegiate athletics programs beyond the reach of Title IX because they were subunits of the institution and did not directly receive federal assistance. Financial aid, however, was administered by the financial aid office on campus, which did receive federal dollars and thus remained under the eye of Title IX. After *Grove City*, *Haffer* altered its focus to equal protection claims under the 14th Amendment.

The *Haffer* case is significant for several reasons. The case illustrates the fortitude required to pursue a Title IX claim in the courts during the years when Title IX was young. It set the stage for techniques of evaluating discrimination in intercollegiate sport settings. The format used in *Haffer* of comparing the benefits received by the men's program with the benefits received by the women's program became the model. The *Haffer* case also painfully illustrates the effect of the *Grove City* decision on cases that were pending at the time, and it stands as a witness to the lack of institutional goodwill for the cause of equity, which was to survive *Grove City*.

In many ways, the *Haffer* case was a crucible that tested an ordinary but strong-willed young student-athlete and her committed legal counsel, none of whom had taken a Title IX case to court before, against a well-financed and determined university. The *Haffer* case noted that there is indeed a connection between institutional support and revenue, and that funding restraints are not a viable excuse for continued discrimination. Because of the time span of *Haffer*, the case also proved that evidence from before *Grove City* could be used if circumstances continued to be similar to support a claim on continuing discrimination after the Civil Rights Restoration Act. The case laid solid groundwork for methods of determining the comparability of treatment of athletes generally.

IN BRIEF

The first 20 years of Title IX are marked by an increase in understanding of its jurisdiction and structural personality. *Cannon* tells us that Title IX includes a private right of action. *North Haven* tells us that Title IX applies to employees as well as to students. *Grove City* tells us that even indirect federal funding triggers its jurisdiction. *Blair* reminds us that all sports are included equally in Title IX. The Civil Rights Restoration Act defines "program" to mean institution-wide, thus assuring that physical education and athletics programs lie within the perimeters of Title IX. The *Haffer* settlement gives us a hint of things to come concerning measuring compliance. *Franklin*, perhaps the most important case in the first 20 years, affirms the availability of monetary damages and thereby opens the door for more aggressive enforcement of Title IX.

Four Questions and Four Answers

1. **Has it ever been definitively decided that all sports, even football, are included in the reach and calculations of Title IX?**

    Yes. In 1974 the Tower amendment was proposed. Its effect would have been to remove sports designated as potentially revenue producing from the reach of Title IX.

    The Tower amendment failed. Other attempts to remove football, such as seen in the *Blair* case, or to remove sports declared to be revenue producing have also failed. The well-settled law is that Title IX treats all sports equally, regardless of their designation as potentially revenue producing.

2. **Why is the 1992 *Franklin* decision of great significance in the enforcement of Title IX?**

    Before *Franklin*, the only punishment believed to be available if a school was found to be in violation of Title IX was the loss of the school's federal financial aid. Because no school found in violation of Title IX had ever lost one penny of its federal financial aid, the threat was hollow and without effect. Delay, delay, delay became the three most effective strategies for a school that did not want to move toward compliance—delay until the complainant wearied of the fight, delay until the complainant graduated and moved on with life, delay until the law might change.

Following *Franklin,* the threat of financial loss was suddenly real. An institution faced the threat of unlimited damages being assessed against it. No longer was delay an effective strategy. The availability of monetary damages caused lawyers to step into the fray, motivated by contingency fees. Plaintiffs were no longer fighting the struggle by themselves. Many schools elected to spend their money on upgrading their women's program rather than on defending a losing battle in court with its concomitant risk of even greater financial loss in the form of damages.

3. **How would you characterize the focus of the lawsuits during the first 20 years of Title IX?**

Most of the lawsuits in the early years dealt with Title IX nuts and bolts, such as what sports were included, who Title IX protected, and what damages were allowed. Were all issues and questions of the early years focused on issues found in, or absent from, the law and the regulations?

The settlement in *Haffer* started to provide compliance details, but it was not until post-1992 cases were completed that we began to see court decisions illuminate the contents of the policy interpretations. Only after *Franklin* did we gain significant knowledge through the courts about how to measure compliance and how to apply the policy interpretations.

4. **What was the effect of *Grove City* and how long did it last?**

The big splash in the press resulting from *Grove City* came from only one part of its decision: the definition of "program" as restricted to a particular subunit of the institution. That portion received the press coverage because it effectively did what the NCAA, the Tower amendment, and others could not. *Grove City* removed college athletics from the reach of Title IX.

The institution-wide portion of the *Grove City* decision remained in force for four years until Congress enacted, over presidential veto, the Civil Rights Restoration Act of 1987.

The second portion of the *Grove City* decision remains today. The second portion notes that even indirect federal funding such as BEOG grants is sufficient to trigger Title IX jurisdiction.

NOTES

[1]Other cases, including *Guardians Association v Civil Service Commission of the City of New York*, 463 U.S. 582 (1983), discussed private rights of action in discrimination cases. The *Guardians* case dealt with Title VI, but because the language of Title IX tracks that of Title VI, corollary implications of support for a private right of action exist. Today, there is no doubt about private right of action under Title IX even though the private right of action has eroded somewhat for employees. See chapter 7 for details concerning the erosion of private rights of action for employees under Title IX. Other cases relating to the existence of private rights of action for employees using antidiscrimination laws, but not directly to Title IX, include *Alexander v Sandoval*, 523 U.S. 275 (2001).

[2] Chapter 7 discusses the *Lowrey* and *Lakoski* cases. Both limit the usefulness of Title IX when employees are the plaintiffs.

[3]HEW, following reorganization, passed its Title IX enforcement responsibilities on to the Department of Education. The change in agency name and organizational structure did not have any effect on Title IX enforcement, jurisdiction, or requirements.

[4]Senator Birch Bayh of Indiana (his son, Evan Bayh is currently serving as a senator from Indiana) was the primary Senate force behind the passage of Title IX in 1972. On the 30th anniversary of the law, Senator Birch Bayh noted that "basically, we said if you accept federal funds, it comes from women and men who are taxpayers, so you should treat women students and faculty equally." Concerning the progress of Title IX, Bayh went on to comment, "There was a soccer field I used to jog around. One day, all of a sudden I realized, that half of the players were little girls and half of them were little boys. I realized then that that was, in part, because of Title IX" (Michael Marot, "A WNBA Executive Pays Tribute to Title IX," Associated Press, May 8, 2002). Senator Bayh, besides being a prime mover and author of Title IX, was also the author of two proposed constitutional amendments relating to women's rights.

[5]See the discussion of the *Lowrey* case in chapter 7 for material about limitations on an employee's protections under Title IX.

[6]Interestingly, females were not the only group to suffer significant declines in progress during the four years of *Grove City* influence. In 2002 the decrease in the number of men's wrestling teams triggered Title IX hearings and threats of gutting Title IX protections within the athletic community because, the argument went, the advance of women's programs had been carried out at the expense of men's wrestling teams. But the greatest loss of men's wrestling programs took place during years when Title IX did not apply to women's intercollegiate athletics. See chapter 9 for a full discussion of the argument and the broader issues of current Title IX debates.

[7]The Javits amendment, which followed the unsuccessful Tower amendment, was enacted. The Javits amendment recognized that some sports cost more to equip and field than others did. Inequity should not be assumed based solely on the difference in dollar expenditures between sports but on benefit provided. See chapter 9 for a discussion of the Javits amendment.

[8]Monetary damages are available in Title IX lawsuits that allege intentional discrimination. The issue of intent, however, is not a major barrier in athletics cases. The Court's *Franklin* opinion referred to the length of time that Title IX had been present (20 years at the time of the *Franklin* decision) and noted that continuing discrimination within athletics after so many years and so much material concerning Title IX requirements within athletics programs was most likely intentional rather than accidental.

[9]*Haffer* benefited from the *Cannon* decision concerning private right of action. Rollin Haffer was not limited to filing an OCR complaint but, because of the existence of a private right of action under Title IX, could and did file a Title IX lawsuit.

7

Title IX in the Courts
After *Franklin v Gwinnett,*
1992 to 2004

After the 1992 *Franklin* case, lawsuits rather than OCR complaints became the enforcement avenue of choice in most circumstances. The range of issues litigated since 1992 covers everything from how to evaluate compliance in the area of participation opportunities to the implications of cutting teams to whether the NCAA is within Title IX jurisdiction. The legal logic is sometimes straightforward and sometimes convoluted, but the knowledge to be gained is integral to an understanding of Title IX.

CASES CONCERNING ENFORCEMENT
AND "SUITABLE PLAINTIFFS"

Many of the post-*Franklin* cases have focused on questions of the validity of various compliance measures, particularly the proportionality prong of the three-prong test for participation. In this section we'll talk about those cases, but we'll also talk about cases that focus their attention on the usefulness of Title IX to various groups of plaintiffs such as athletes who will graduate before a final decision in a case (*Cook v Colgate*, 1993), male athletes (*Gonyo v Drake*, 1993), and employees (*Lowrey v Texas A&M University*, 1997).

Cook v Colgate University (1993)

The main question asked and answered by *Cook v Colgate University* is whether class-action lawsuits provide greater protection against being found moot[1] (and thus not decided on their merits) than do cases with individual plaintiffs. The answer is yes.

A women's ice hockey club existed at Colgate, but several members wanted to have a varsity team. Colgate's policies included a provision for making such a request no more frequently than every two years. Various club members had requested the creation of a varsity team in 1979, 1983, 1986, and again in 1988 without success. Finally, in 1990 several frustrated ice hockey club members filed a Title IX lawsuit to force the university to create a varsity team. The plaintiffs were elated when the district court ordered Colgate to grant their request for a team even if they, who by then were about to graduate, would not be on the team. Colgate appealed, arguing that because all the plaintiffs would have graduated by the time the next hockey season began the district court's order was no remedy for the plaintiffs.

If by the time the court prescribes a remedy, the remedy has no real application to the harmed plaintiffs, the decision is moot (a question whose answer is pointless). Because the plaintiffs had sued Colgate as individuals rather than as representatives of a class made up of future potential ice hockey team members, the court of appeals agreed with Colgate and vacated the district court's order as moot. No women's varsity ice hockey team would be formed.

If the plaintiffs had brought their case as a class action, Colgate University would likely have fielded a varsity women's ice hockey team as originally ordered by the district court.[2] In the law, procedural issues rather than conceptual ones occasionally carry the day. Following the *Cook v Colgate* decision, most Title IX cases involving claims of participation violations have been filed as class actions to avoid being ruled moot when the named plaintiffs graduate.[3]

Favia v Indiana University of Pennsylvania (1993)

The *Favia v Indiana University of Pennsylvania* case answered several important questions:

- Are fiscal difficulties an excuse for discrimination?
- Is a promise to expand participation opportunities in the future sufficient to avoid current compliance problems?
- May participation be measured by counting the number of teams for each sex?
- Is the presence of intent to discriminate required for Title IX to be violated?

The answer to these four questions turned out to be no.
The *Favia* case also answered two other questions of significance:

An increasing number of women are playing rugby, but most schools offer it as a club rather than varsity sport. Ice hockey, previously offered mainly as a club, is now a fast growing varsity sport for women.

- When an equal number of male and female teams are cut but the remaining representation is unequal, do Title IX issues arise?
- Should the courts give deference to OCR's policy interpretation (the location of the three-prong accommodation test for participation opportunities)?

The answer to both of these questions turned out to be yes.

Much like other colleges and universities in the late 1980s and early 1990s, Indiana University of Pennsylvania (IUP) faced massive, institution-wide budget cuts. The athletic department was asked to trim $350,000 from its budget to help bridge the gap. The department planned to do so by, among other actions, cutting two men's teams (soccer and tennis) and two women's teams (gymnastics and field hockey). Members of the two women's teams joined other female athletes in a class-action suit seeking a permanent injunction barring IUP from cutting the two women's teams.

Before the proposed cutback of teams, 503 IUP students participated in athletics, 37 percent of whom were females. After the cutback there were to be only 397 athletes, 30.5 percent of whom would be females. Sixty-five of the athletes who were slated to lose their teams were females, and only 41 were males.

According to IUP's testimony, the women's teams slated for termination involved sports decreasing in national interest. IUP was partially correct. Women's gymnastics had indeed seen a decline in popularity in the five years before IUP's cuts, dropping from 20.6 percent of colleges offering teams to 11.3 percent (Acosta and Carpenter, 2004). Field hockey, however, had not experienced as significant a drop in popularity. Field hockey was offered by 34.8 percent of colleges five years before the IUP cuts and by 28.9 percent five years later in 1991 (Acosta and Carpenter, 2004).[4] On a local basis at the time of IUP's cuts, nine schools in IUP's conference had field hockey teams.

To help temper the blow of cutting teams, IUP promised to add women's soccer when the financial status of the athletics department improved. IUP might have selected soccer because it is the fastest growing sport for women and was so even in the years surrounding the *Favia* case. Twenty-nine percent of schools offered soccer for women in 1986, and 45.8 percent did so in 1991. The massive growth continued even through 2004, when 88.6 percent of the nation's intercollegiate athletics programs had soccer for women (Acosta and Carpenter, 2004).

Before the cuts, IUP had nine teams for men and nine for women. After the cuts, there were to be seven for men and seven for women. The athletic director believed that making equal cuts of teams was an acceptable method of meeting equity even if the result of such cuts landed unequally on the historically underrepresented sex. Although his belief was apparently one of goodwill, his belief was incorrect.

The Title IX requirement to provide equitable participation opportunities to the historically underrepresented sex was the focus of the *Favia* case, but the evidence presented in *Favia* was not limited to participation. The situation at IUP mirrored the situation experienced by most female college athletes of the same era. For instance, the coach of the field hockey team wore two hats. She was a full-time physical education teacher as well as a coach. She received no monetary compensation for her coaching duties but was "paid" by being released from teaching a two-credit course that otherwise would have been part of her physical education workload. The coach kept the team's uniforms in the trunk of her car along with other equipment because no on-campus storage was available. For every $8 spent on male athletes, IUP spent only $2.75 on its female athletes. Several male coaches of men's teams received complimentary cars and golf club memberships. No coach of a women's team enjoyed such perks. Male athletes garnered 79 percent of the scholarship dollars. IUP encouraged spectator support for men's teams by offering raffles for a full semester of tuition at each men's basketball and football home game. IUP did not offer similar enticements to spectators at women's competitions. Although IUP was in Division II, the vice president said that football needed to be safeguarded because it brought prestige to the campus. In short, female athletes did not share the supportive campus climate of privilege that male athletes enjoyed.

The court found in favor of the women athletes, restored their teams, and issued a permanent injunction against terminating the two women's teams. The succinct language found in the decision answered many questions of the day:

- "A cash crunch is no excuse."
- "You can't replace programs with promises."
- "Men's athletics have reaped the benefits of favoritism" (*Favia*, 1992).

Budget constraints rather than ill will were the driving force behind IUP's plan to terminate teams. Does the presence of gender-neutral motivations such as budget constraints matter? No. The outcome is what matters. In *Favia* the outcome of the proposed, apparently gender-neutral, cuts was to maintain and indeed exacerbate the inequality already present at IUP. Discrimination, even in the absence of ill intent, is sufficient to trigger a violation of Title IX.

The focus of the *Favia* decision was the three-prong test for measuring compliance with the Title IX requirement for equitable participation opportunities. IUP could not meet any of the three possible measures of equitable participation opportunities for women. Females made up 56 percent of the student body, but only 37 percent of the athletes were females (prong 1, proportionality, fails to be met). Female athletes at IUP were obviously both able and interested in participation (prong 2, meeting interest and ability, fails to be met), and IUP had no continuing history of upgrading

> "... there can never be an economic justification for discrimination. No one should ever be permitted to say that I can't comply with the law because I can't afford it. It is the same as saying, 'I should be allowed to practice racism (or sexism) if I can't afford to initiate a change in the way I live or do business.'"
>
> Women's Sports Foundation, Internet Resource Center, *March 8, 2000*.

their women's program (prong 3, history of upgrading, fails to be met). The *Favia* court, in finding for the plaintiffs, reaffirmed that "OCR's Policy Interpretation [the location of the three-prong test] deserves our great deference"(*Favia*, 1992), a holding articulated six years earlier in the U.S. Supreme Court decision in *Chevron USA v Natural Resources Defense Council, Inc.* (467 U.S. 837 [1984]).

IUP appealed the case, but the U.S. Supreme Court denied certiorari (refused to hear it). The Supreme Court's refusal to hear the case set a pattern for a long line of similar cases relating to the proportionality prong. The Supreme Court is presented with a great many more cases than it can hear. The Court may hear a case when it disagrees with the lower court decision, when courts of appeal from various circuits have created a confusing pattern of decisions on similar topics, or for any number of other motivations. But when it has been presented with clear fact patterns relating to the same issue (in this case proportionality) and consistently refuses to hear such cases, it is safe to assume that the Court agrees with the decisions of the lower courts. Such has been the situation with every case relating to proportionality seeking review by the Supreme Court. *Favia*, in its role as a pioneering case, provided many answers to Title IX questions. A decade later, those answers continue to hold sway.

Gonyo v Drake University (1993)

The main question asked and answered by the *Gonyo v Drake University* case is this: If cutting a men's team reduces the proportion of men participating in athletics, may the men use Title IX to reinstate their team? The answer is no.

Drake University found it necessary to reduce its athletics budget. The termination of the wrestling team was one of the actions the institution took in response. Members of the discontinued men's wrestling team sued Drake University in a class-action lawsuit seeking reinstatement. The plaintiffs claimed breach of contract (relating to their recruitment followed swiftly by the cancellation of the team to which they had been recruited) as well as invoking both Title IX and the equal protection clause of the 14th Amendment to claim discrimination.

The disappointed wrestlers argued that the proportionality prong of the Title IX participation test should protect them against losing their opportunity to participate. The court disagreed. The court noted that the goal of Title IX was to provide equal opportunity to participate rather than to maintain the status quo of current participatory distributions. At the time of the case, over 75 percent of Drake's athletes were males, whereas only 42 percent of the student body were males. Even after the termination of the wrestling team, the proportion of Drake's male athletes far exceeded the representation of males in the student body. The court dismissed the wrestlers' case. From *Gonyo* we learn that the termination of a men's team signals no discrimination when posttermination participation ratios continue to favor males.

Roberts v Colorado State University (1993)

The *Roberts v Colorado State University* case asked and answered two important questions:

- May the court order an institution to reinstate a specific sport?
- Is expansion of women's program in the 1970s sufficient evidence of growth to demonstrate accommodation of interest?

The answer to the first question is yes; the answer to the second is no.

The year 1993 was a busy one for Title IX. *Roberts v Colorado State University* joins *Cook v Colgate*, *Favia v IUP*, and *Gonyo v Drake* in providing valuable information about the functioning of Title IX in a post-*Franklin* world.

Colorado State University faced a $600,000 deficit in its athletic department. To help meet the shortfall, the department dropped its baseball and softball teams. Members of the women's softball team filed a Title IX lawsuit arguing that their team should be reinstated. The court of appeals agreed.

The central question of the *Roberts* case is whether the court can order a college to reinstate a specific team in order to meet a systemic failure to accommodate the interests of its students. The case also involves the broader issue of how to evaluate whether an institution has indeed accommodated the interests and abilities of its students. The first question, answered in the affirmative by the court, is clear: A court may order the reinstatement of a specific team.

The second issue, how to measure accommodation, continues to be debated even in the fourth decade of Title IX.[5] Title IX requires that an institution effectively accommodate the interests and abilities of the historically underrepresented sex. In brief, the institution may show that it is accommodating those interests in one of three ways.[6] The institution can

1. show that its athletes are participating in the same proportion as their representation in the student body, or
2. show that the institution has a historic and continuing pattern and practice of upgrading its historically underrepresented sex (women's) program, or

3. show that the interests are in fact being accommodated, including the selection of sports offered and the competitive level at which they are offered (club versus varsity).

Which if any of the three ways of demonstrating compliance did Colorado State University (CSU) meet? The fact that CSU was terminating a viable women's team was clear evidence that it was not fully meeting the interests and abilities of at least the members of the softball team. Second, CSU had expanded its women's program in the 1970s when Title IX was first on the scene but could not show a continuation of upgrading. The only prong remaining for CSU's use was the proportionality prong, and CSU failed to meet that test as well because, as with many institutions, the gender proportionality of CSU's athletes

The *Roberts v Colorado State University* case determined that a court can order a school to reinstate a specific sport such as softball.

did not match the proportionality of males and females in the student body at large.[7]

So, when the court ordered CSU to reinstate women's softball, we learned that a specific sport could be designated for reinstatement instead of requiring the school to enlarge participation opportunities for women generally. We also learned that the somewhat subjectively measured second prong, a history of upgrading the women's program, meant a continuing and consistent pattern of upgrading, not just an early start with no follow-up, as had been the case at CSU.

Seven years after the *Roberts* decision, the Office for Civil Rights declared that Colorado State University was in compliance and ceased monitoring its program.

Lowrey v Texas A&M University System dba Tarleton State University (1997)

The *Lowrey* case asked and answered two important questions:

- Does an employee have a private right of action?[8]
- Can a person sue under Title IX for discrimination suffered by a third party?

The answer to the second question is a simple no. The answer to the first question is a little more complex. For retaliation based on Title IX nonemployment issues, an employee does have a private right of action. For employment-related claims, the employee does not.

The 1979 *Cannon* case (chapter 6) demonstrated that Title IX included a private right of action (which means that a Title IX plaintiff may sue an institution without having first exhausted all administrative remedies). Lowrey asserted that right when she sued her employer, Tarleton State University, for sex discrimination against both her and student-athletes.

Lowrey was employed by Tarleton State University. She wore many hats: physical education instructor, head women's basketball coach, and, for a time, women's athletic coordinator. The *Lowrey* case involves a complicated interrelationship of Title VII and Title IX. Although complicated, the results of the *Lowrey* case are important to understand. To do so, we first need to look at an earlier case, *Lakoski*, decided by the same court.

In *Lakoski v University of Texas Medical Branch* (1996), the court found that when an employee pursued sex discrimination claims in the workplace, Title VII, not Title IX, was the appropriate forum. *Lakoski* concluded, in effect, that no private right of action exists for workplace-related claims of sex discrimination under Title IX. Title VII, not Title IX, was the appropriate legislation for workplace claims. To allow claims to proceed under both Title VII and Title IX (having very different procedures and potential remedies) would not be legislatively prudent.

The *Lakoski* decision would seem to have destroyed the portion of Lowrey's Title IX case that related to employment. But did Lowrey have a right to proceed in her Title IX case on behalf of her students? The *Lakoski*[9] decision by the U.S. Court of Appeals for the Fifth Circuit did not bar Title IX usage in sex discrimination cases when the victim of the discrimination is a student; it barred Title IX usage only when the plaintiff is an employee. But Lowrey lacked legal standing to pursue a Title IX case for discrimination by the school against her students.[10] So Lowrey could not use Title IX to pursue her own claims of discrimination by the school against her because the *Lakoski* decision found that Title VII, not Title IX, was the correct mode; and Lowrey couldn't use Title IX to sue on behalf of her students[11] because that right belonged only to her students, not to her as a third party.

Lowrey, it seemed, was being blocked at every turn concerning Title IX. For a variety of reasons, most having to do with procedure, Lowrey needed to find some way to proceed under the auspices of Title IX. To do so, the court would need to find some type of discrimination actionable under Title IX that did not arise out of Lowrey's employment but for which Lowrey had legal standing to sue. It did. The *Lowrey* court found that because Lowrey had been involved in pressing the school to redress its discrimination against students (a Title IX issue not arising our of her employment), any retaliation against her by the school could be found to be based on her support of the students' Title IX problems rather than on her own victimization in the workplace. Therefore, her Title IX claim of retaliation, but not her other Title IX claims, all of which were employment based, provided her with a private right of action under Title IX for retaliation and only retaliation.

So, although the legal logic in *Lowrey* is cloudy, what we learn from it is clear:

1. An employee cannot sue for workplace discrimination using Title IX, at least not in the Fifth Circuit. Sex discrimination in employment is remediable by Title VII, not Title IX.

2. An employee can sue, however, for retaliation using Title IX if the retaliation arises out of a non-employment-based Title IX issue. Even if the plaintiff is an employee and the discriminator is the employer, Title IX can be used for retaliation claims.

Cohen v Brown University (1997)

Cohen v Brown University asks and answers two important questions:

- When counting participation opportunities, should the number of slots on a team be counted or should actual participants be counted?

- May an institution survey the interest among its male and female students and then, based on the ratio of interest reported, use a similar ratio for determining compliance ("relative interests theory")?

The court determined that actual participants should be counted, thus avoiding fake or illusory reports of participation. And no, an institution may not use surveys and ratios to determine compliance. To do so would freeze opportunities for women at a level engendered by past discriminatory practices.

Brown University offered its female students a large array of teams, but the situation was by no means perfect. The ratio of male to female students in the student body was 48 percent to 52 percent, but its athlete ratio was 63.3 percent male and 36.7 percent female in 1990-91, when it faced budget constraints. In response to the budget woes, two women's teams (volleyball and gymnastics) and two men's teams (golf and water polo) were demoted to club status. Terminating the same number of men's and women's teams is not a safe passage to compliance, as we learned in *Favia*. The number of participants, not the number of teams, is the appropriate basis for evaluation.

The demoted female team members sued Brown under Title IX for reinstatement. The word "quota" found its way into the rhetoric of the argument, and the spotlight again fell on the policy interpretations and the three-prong accommodations test found therein.

Brown proffered several arguments on its behalf. Brown proposed surveying student interest and then using the "relative interest" expressed by its male and female students to serve as the proportionality cum "relative interest" method by which to evaluate compliance. The court rejected this argument and added, "Interest and ability rarely develop in a vacuum; they evolve as a function of opportunity and experience. The policy interpretation recognizes that women's lower rate of participation in athletics reflects women's historical lack of opportunities to participate in sports."[12]

The *Cohen* case was lengthy, complicated, and expensive. But the questions involved were simple. The policy interpretations were clear and were justifiable as a method of determining compliance, including its three-prong test for participation. The notion of "relative interest" advanced by Brown University was not an appropriate alternative.

Brown University expended millions of dollars to defend its position rather than follow the law. The court explicitly rebuked Brown University's attempt to paint the inflammatory words "quota" and "affirmative action" on the side of Title IX. Title IX does not require a school to drag female students into its athletics program, nor does it require that an institution always provide a team in the presence of females interested in participating.

One oft-heard argument used to support the denial of opportunities to female athletes is that women are simply not interested to the same degree that men are. The *Cohen* court made it clear that it viewed such an argument with great suspicion. In sum, the various written decisions in the *Cohen* case addressed not only the law and its requirements but also the rhetoric surrounding Title IX. The case makes interesting and useful reading.

Boucher v Syracuse University (1999)

Boucher v Syracuse University answered this question: Can the "history of upgrading" prong for determining compliance with the access to participation opportunities requirement be used successfully? The answer is yes.

Women from two club teams at Syracuse University filed a lawsuit based on the level of their participation opportunities. They wanted varsity status. The plaintiffs also sued for the loss of scholarships that, they alleged, would have come their way if they were varsity team members rather than club team members. The court said that because the plaintiffs were not varsity members, their claim for scholarship dollars lost was not appropriate because of the students' lack of legal standing on that particular issue. The plaintiffs, however, could continue to sue based on the denial of varsity status.

At the time of the *Boucher* case, Syracuse's student body was 50 percent female, yet only 32.4 percent of its athletes were female. Thus, the university could not counter the plaintiffs' request for advancement to varsity status by showing that it had met the proportionality prong. Syracuse would need to use one of the other two prongs. Syracuse chose "history of upgrading." The court accepted the "history of upgrading" argument, although Syracuse had not added any women's teams from 1982 to 1995 (remember, Title IX did not apply to college athletics from 1984 to 1988). In 1995, however, Syracuse had added two teams for women. Although the university had not consistently added women's sports, it had, the court determined, consistently upgraded its support

Javelin throwers with interest and ability in the 1920s and the 1990s.

© Smith College archives

for its female athletes. The university had continuously increased the number of women's scholarships and had improved facilities, coaches, and other support services. At the time of the lawsuit, the number of female athletes had increased by 47 percent in the years since 1982, whereas the number of male athletes had increased by only 3 percent. Syracuse had no Title IX policy in place, but it had been expanding its women's program and had promised the court that it would add softball. The court believed the promise and therefore dismissed the case. Recall that the *Cohen v Brown University* case makes it clear that schools need to add teams, not just increase support for existing teams. The difference between the two cases involves the additional teams added at Syracuse, two in 1995, and softball at the conclusion of the case.

Pederson v Louisiana State University (2000)

The two main questions answered by *Pederson v Louisiana State University* are the following:

- Is ignorance, even if fueled by chauvinism rather than enmity, an excuse for violating Title IX?
- Is intent to treat the sexes differently sufficient to trigger monetary damages, or must intent to violate Title IX be shown?

The answer to the first question is no. Ignorance is not an excuse. Regarding the second question, the intent to treat the sexes differently is sufficient to trigger monetary damages.

Soccer and softball teams were the desire of able female athletes at Louisiana State University (LSU). Unfortunately, no varsity teams existed. Indeed, LSU had added no new women's team for 14 years. Not surprisingly, LSU found it difficult to claim a historical pattern and practice of upgrading its women's programs (prong 2 of the three-prong test). Nor could LSU meet the prong that it fully accommodated the interests and abilities of its students because team loads of soccer and softball players were standing at the ready, waiting for the opportunity to play. Thus, LSU had only one chance left: proportionality. LSU was unable to meet any of the three prongs, so it was in violation of Title IX. The court mused concerning the validity of the proportionality prong, but because LSU couldn't meet any of the three prongs, the validity of the proportionality prong in the eyes of the court was of no consequence one way or the other.

Initially "arrogant ignorance" rather than intent was labeled as the root cause. Because no intent was found, the plaintiffs were deprived of the potential for monetary damages. However, the court of appeals reversed the district court and found that LSU did in fact intentionally discriminate. The court of appeals noted, "LSU's hubris in advancing . . . the argument that women were not interested in participating" is remarkable, because, of course, fewer women participate in sports, given the voluminous evidence that LSU has discriminated against women in refusing to offer them comparable athletic opportunities to those it offers its male students.[13] Intent to treat females differently from males is sufficient to show the intent required for the imposition of monetary damages. Intent to violate Title IX is not necessary.[14]

The court in *Pederson* also supported the strength and validity of the policy interpretations and the three-prong test found therein by saying, "The proper analytical framework for assessing a Title IX claim can be found in the policy interpretations to Title IX, which require an analysis of the disproportionality between the university's male and female participation, the university's history of expanding opportunities for women, and whether the university effectively accommodates the interests of its female students."[15]

CASES CONCERNING TERMINATION OF MEN'S TEAMS

Men's "minor" sports teams have been cut, sometimes because of changing interest and demographics and sometimes because of disingenuous decision making by administrators who are attempting to meet the proportionality prong of the three-part test for participation (a form of roster management) without touching football or men's basketball. In any case, the loss of participation opportunities for either males or females is lamentable. But is the termination of a men's team actionable under Title IX? Let's look at a couple of cases.

Neal v Board of Trustees of California State Universities (1999)

The *Neal* case asked and answered a key question: Can roster management (capping the number of participants on men's teams) be legally used as a method of manipulating the ratio between men and women for purposes of showing compliance with the proportionality prong of the accommodations test? The answer turned out to be yes.

The National Organization for Women (NOW) filed a lawsuit against the California State University[16] system, of which California State University of Bakersfield (CSUB) is a part. A portion of the consent decree in the case involved increasing female participation toward the ratio of females in the student body on each campus. Cal State Bakersfield reduced the number of male participants rather than increase the number of female participants. The school did so to make the ratio of males to females look better even if it meant that fewer participants, both male and female, would benefit from the athletic experience. What CSUB was doing when it reduced the number of male participants would become known as roster management.

Roster management is a euphemism for limiting male participation to meet the proportionality prong of the three-part accommodation test. The men's wrestling team, of which Neal was a member, bore the brunt of the roster management scheme at CSUB. Roster management is legal under Title IX even though it is contrary to the educational mission of the nation's colleges and universities.

The *NOW* case and the *Neal* case are not related except that the institution's response to the first set the stage for the second. Because CSUB decided to practice roster management to meet the requirements of the *NOW* case, Neal's wrestling team was canceled. Because Neal's wrestling team was canceled, Neal sued the institution. The court, in denying the wrestlers' claim in *Neal* that Title IX prohibited such behavior (roster management), also reaffirmed the strength of the policy interpretations from which the three-prong test emanates. "[W]here Congress has expressly delegated to an agency the power to 'elucidate a specific provision of a statute by regulation' that agency's regulations should be accorded 'controlling weight unless they are arbitrary, capricious, or manifestly contrary to the statute.'"[17] The court noted, "Every court, in construing the policy interpretation and the text of Title IX, has held that a university may bring itself into Title IX compliance by increasing athletic opportunities for the underrepresented gender (women in this case) or by decreasing athletic opportunities for the overrepresented gender (men in this case)."[18]

Chalenor et al. v University of North Dakota (2002)

The *Chalenor* case answered a related and equally important question: May an institution that is attempting to meet the proportionality prong of the three-part test cut a men's team rather than increase female participation? Again, the answer is yes.

Budget constraints as well as concerns over finding a way to meet the proportionality prong of the accommodations test (because the university could not meet either of the other two prongs) were the justifications the University of North Dakota used for cutting the men's wrestling team. The team members sued the university for violating their rights under Title IX. The university refused to reinstate the team even after private donors came forward to fund the team. As with a long line of cases, both before and after the pivotal 1992 *Franklin* decision, the *Chalenor* court found that terminating a men's team does not violate Title IX when the men are not the protected class (historically underrepresented sex).

Playing the numbers game by cutting men's participation rather than increasing women's participation to meet the proportionality prong of the three-prong accommodations test certainly violates the spirit of Title IX and tortures the mission of athletics on any campus, but it is not illegal.

CASES SPECIFICALLY CONCERNING SEXUAL HARASSMENT

Title IX does not define sexual harassment, but it does protect against it. The absence of a reference to sexual harassment in the one-sentence law of Title IX, its regulations, or the policy interpretations doesn't lessen the inclusion of sexual harassment prohibitions within the purview of Title IX. Sexual harassment includes treating someone differently based on sex or sex-based matters. Well-established law indicates that sexual harassment is a form of sex discrimination. The inclusion of sexual harassment in sex discrimination is not the question; what is meant by the term "sexual harassment" is.

Before we look at what the cases tell us, we need to set a few ground rules. Title VII has more fully addressed sexual harassment,[19] but Title IX has energetically borrowed much of the Title VII jurisprudence concerning sexual harassment issues. As we look at the cases, some of which involve Title VII, be aware that the principles addressed also apply to Title IX.

What is sexual harassment? Title IX is silent on the issue. Sexual harassment is of two types: quid pro quo and hostile environment. Title VII defines both types, which are used by extension as the definitions of sexual harassment for Title IX.

The first type, quid pro quo, is easy to recognize. Quid pro quo sexual harassment involves trading something such as a better grade, team captaincy, or a role as a first-string player for a sexual favor.

The second, hostile environment, is more difficult to define. Oafs, cads, and bounders have always existed and perhaps always will. But not every crude, inappropriate, or rude remark with a sexual connotation that makes someone uncomfortable constitutes hostile environment sexual harassment. Only those remarks and behaviors that are sufficiently pervasive and rise to an unreasonable level are actionable as sexual harassment. The threshold is high. Determining what meets the threshold in a specific instance is up to the courts, but a series of cases have told us in a general way several things about pursuing sexual harassment lawsuits.

Does it matter who is who in a relationship of harassment? The courts have had to face that question in a variety of harassment combinations. Where sexual harassment is concerned, there is no shortage of harasser-to-harassee combinations. In educational settings, we think most frequently of the teacher or coach harassing the student. In addition, harassment between employees, between students, and even within the same gender has provided the courts with fodder for enlightening decisions.

Gender of the Harasser and Harassee: *Oncale v Sundowner Offshore Services* (1998)

The *Oncale* case asked this question: Can sexual harassment exist if both the harasser and the harassee are the same sex? The answer is yes.

Oncale is a Title VII case, but because Title IX borrows heavily from Title VII whenever sexual harassment issues arise, the *Oncale* decision is important to our discussion.

Oncale worked on an offshore oil rig, and his coworkers apparently didn't like him. Whether the male coworkers thought that he was gay or simply used gay terminology during their harassment of him is irrelevant. The issue revolved around whether the gender of the harasser and the person being harassed had to be different for harassment to be actionable. According to the unanimous U.S. Supreme Court decision in the *Oncale* case, sexual harassment can exist even where the harasser and the harassee are the same gender.

Teacher on Student Sexual Harassment: *Gebser v Lago Vista Independent School District* (1998)

The *Gebser* case asked two important questions:

- Can an employer be held liable for the sexual harassment activities of its employee?
- Must the employer (or other third-party defendant) have notice of the harassment?

The answer to both questions is yes.

An eighth grader and her teacher were engaged in a sexual relationship. The issue of whether the school district could be held liable under Title IX arose when the student filed a lawsuit based on the teacher's misconduct.

In effect, the school district is a third party. Can liability be imposed by using an agency theory, that is, by alleging that the teacher was acting as the agent of the district? No. Can liability be imposed by using a negligence theory, that is, by claiming that the district should have known about the harassment? No.

The U.S. Supreme Court chose neither agency nor negligence as a legal principle upon which to hang liability of a third party, which, in the *Gebser* case, was the school district. The employer, or school district, can be "liable for damages only where the district itself intentionally acted in clear violation of Title IX by remaining deliberately indifferent to acts of teacher-student harassment of which it had actual knowledge" (*Gebser* at 290). In these circumstances, the school district had knowledge of the harassment and had the control to remedy it, so when the school district decided to do nothing about the sexual relationship, it triggered liability for itself. The *Gebser* case stands for the principle that intent, necessary for the imposition of monetary damages, in sexual harassment cases requires both (1) notice of the existence of the harassment[20] and (2) deliberate indifference over a situation or context within its control.[21]

Peer-on-Peer Sexual Harassment: *Davis v Monroe County Board of Education* (1999)

The question that the *Davis* case answered is whether a minimum standard is required in order to impose monetary damages in a Title IX case involving peer-to-peer sexual harassment. The answer was yes.

Lashonda Davis, an elementary school student, was being sexually harassed by a classmate. Besides making vulgar statements such as "I want to get in bed with you" and "I want to feel your boobs," the classmate fondled her. Davis and her mother complained to the teacher, but little happened. The harassment continued and escalated. The principal was notified, also to no avail. After three months Davis' seat was changed to the other side of the room, but the harasser's behavior did not change.

In Davis' physical education class the harasser "purportedly placed a door stop in his pants and proceeded to act in a sexually suggestive manner toward her."[22] Davis' grades as well as her physical and emotional health suffered. Davis contemplated suicide and, in her fifth-grade handwriting, wrote a suicide note. The harasser's other victims joined Davis' voice of complaint, yet the principal still failed to intervene successfully.

In May, at the end of the school year, the harasser pled guilty to sexual battery. When Davis' irate and frustrated mother asked the principal what discipline would follow for the harasser, the principal said, "I guess I'll have to threaten him a little bit harder." Apparently such threats, if ever issued, were unmet by any change in behavior.

Davis brought a Title IX lawsuit that sought monetary damages from the school board, which either refused or was incapable of intervening to stop the harassment. The court determined that such a suit was appropriate; a private right of action exists under Title IX for peer-to-peer harassment.

The U.S. Supreme Court, however, also held that such a private right of action only exists when the defendant (in this case the school board) acts with ". . . deliberate indifference to known acts of harassment in the school board's programs or activities, and (b) the harassment was so severe, pervasive, and objectively offensive that it effectively barred the victim's access to an educational opportunity or benefit." In effect, the Supreme Court answered the question of what type of behavior equates to the intent that we learned in the *Franklin* case is necessary to seek monetary damages in a Title IX case. The presence of intent is more easily demonstrated in the typical athletics case, but in a peer-to-peer sexual harassment case, intent must rise to the level of deliberate indifference to known acts of harassment.[23] To violate Title IX in cases of peer-to-peer sexual harassment, the defendant must both know and not care.

Liability of Employer: *Faragher v City of Boca Raton* (1998)

The *Faragher* case answered this question: Is an employer liable for employee-to-employee sexual harassment? The answer is yes.

Although a Title VII case, *Faragher* tells us a great deal about sexual harassment claims in the workplace. Title IX also covers employees, so the principles gleaned from *Faragher* may generally be applied in Title IX cases as well. Faragher was a city lifeguard, and her supervisor made it clear that certain perquisites of the job were available only if Faragher provided sexual favors to her supervisors. She sued her employer.

The U.S. Supreme Court held that employers were obligated to provide a harassment-free workplace and as long as they "(a) . . . exercised reasonable care to prevent and correct promptly any sexually harassing behavior, and (b) the plaintiff employee unreasonably failed to take advantage of any preventive or corrective opportunities provided by the employer or to avoid harm otherwise they would not be liable, under Title VII for the sexual harassment of one employee to another" (*Faragher* at 775). But Faragher's employer did not take steps to prevent harassment, and Faragher did what she could to take advantage of preventive and corrective opportunities.

Faragher tells us that the employer has an obligation to provide a safe working environment free from sexual harassment. If the employer does not do so and if the employee tries appropriately, even if ineffectively, to prevent or correct the harassment, the employer may be out of compliance with Title IX as well as Title VII even if unaware of the actual harassment. In plain English, if the recourse for preventing harassment that the employer has set up is ineffective, the employer can be held responsible whether they know about a specific harassment or not.

A CASE OF SPECIAL INTEREST: *MERCER v DUKE UNIVERSITY* (2002)

The decision in the *Mercer* case does not have geographically wide legal significance; it applies only in the district in which it was heard. But the issues it raises about punitive damages are worth pondering.

Mercer wanted to play football. She was good. After a shining performance as a placekicker in high school and at a Duke University scrimmage, she became a member of the Duke team. Her team membership was short lived, however, as her coach quickly changed his mind. Besides changing his mind, he allowed intemperate and inflammatory remarks to escape his mouth regarding Mercer and her role at Duke. Mercer sued. Mercer won a multimillion dollar judgment against Duke, all but one dollar of which was in the form of punitive damages. The level of the coach's remarks along with the level of behavior by Duke's administration about the matter eased the way for the jury to award punitive damages.

> "Instead of football, why don't you consider other extracurricular activities, such as beauty pageants?"
> "Consider trying out for the cheerleading squad."
> "Sit in the stands with [your] boyfriend."
>
> *Comments attributed to Duke football coach made to female placekicker Mercer, Mercer v Duke*

The *Mercer* case makes interesting reading and provides a road map for what to avoid in handling a volatile public relations struggle. Initially, it seemed as though the case would be an expensive lesson for Duke in that regard. On appeal, however, in an unpublished opinion that carries no precedent value, the Court of Appeals of the Fourth Circuit found that Title IX did not permit the awarding of punitive damages unsupported by compensatory damages. Ten years before, the U.S. Supreme Court in *Franklin* had unanimously determined that monetary damages were available in cases of intentional discrimination under Title IX and made no exclusion of punitive damages. The conflict between the Supreme Court's *Franklin* opinion and the decision of the Court of Appeals of the Fourth Circuit in *Mercer* (which has no application beyond the *Mercer* case) is interesting. The *Mercer* case has received little press, perhaps because it carries no broader precedent value, but the issue is one to watch.

SETTLEMENTS

Some lawsuits are concluded by settlement between the parties with the approval of the court but without the outcome being determined by the court. The results of such lawsuits carry no value as legal precedents because the court rendered no decision, but they do provide insight into the negotiation of Title IX issues among the parties and often reflect the parties' understanding of the state of the law that they would be facing if the case proceeded to a judicial determination. For that reason, we discuss two of the more prominent settlements here.

Settlements became a more favored option for defendants following the *Franklin* decision. Institutions that had been brought to the brink of having to spend a significant sum to defend a Title IX lawsuit faced a decision: pay lots of money to lawyers for their defense while also risking compensatory and unlimited punitive damages or put the money saved by avoiding continuing litigation into their athletic programs. Many institutions wisely chose the latter.

Kiechel v Auburn University (1993), a post-*Franklin* class-action lawsuit brought by female members of the Auburn University women's soccer club, sought to elevate the club to varsity status. Auburn quickly settled the case by promising, among other things, to create a women's varsity soccer team, to support it on an agreed-to formula, and to create new facilities for the team. The financial cost to Auburn was considerably less than it would pay for a protracted lawsuit, even if it might have eventually won. The quick settlement muted the negative public relations cost, and Auburn gained a forum for more female students to gain the benefits of an athletics experience. In many ways, the *Kiechel* case turned out to be a win-win situation. A bigger win-win would have resulted had Auburn decided before the lawsuit to meet the interests and abilities of its female athletes as required by Title IX.

Sanders v Texas A&M University (1992) is another post-*Franklin* settlement. This class-action lawsuit, settled a year after the start of litigation, resulted in increasing the ratio of females in its athletics program from 23 percent to 44 percent. The pent-up demand for participation opportunities flowed swiftly into the opportunities created. As in *Kiechel*, the decision to settle rather than fight the lawsuit to the end allowed a reallocation of resources otherwise destined for defense attorneys.

IN BRIEF

Proportionality, proportionality, proportionality. After *Franklin,* Title IX lawsuits seem to have a penchant for refining the interpretation of proportionality as one of the three methods for determining the equitable

Complying with Title IX should be a win-win situation, as demonstrated by the decision in the *Kiechel v Auburn University* case, which resulted in club soccer being elevated to varsity soccer.

opportunity to participate. In 1979 the policy interpretations laid out the road map for evaluating compliance. Only five years after the policy interpretations came into effect, the *Grove City* decision removed Title IX from the intercollegiate athletic setting. When Title IX reappeared on the intercollegiate scene in 1988, other issues moved into the spotlight for a few years, but following *Franklin*, participation and its measurement became the focus.

Why has proportionality been the focus during the last decade? An interesting hypothesis is to posit, "If you are not on the team, you don't need a uniform." In other words, if opportunities are denied, the issue of providing equal benefits of uniforms, coaches, equipment, transportation, and the like never matters. Participation measurement is the gatekeeper for all other benefits. No universal Machiavellian plan is in place to keep the gate closed so that men's teams do not have to share scarce resources for uniforms and coaches, but the budgetary ramifications of enlarging the participant base certainly do not go unnoticed on specific campuses. In any case, we have looked at proportionality by analyzing many lawsuits in the last decade, and we know concretely that proportionality is an equal partner with the other two prongs as an appropriate measure for determining compliance with the provision of opportunities. But the length of the line of cases that have brought us to this knowledge does not preclude others from asking the same question repeatedly. One decade is probably insufficient to turn the focus to other yet untested questions.

Besides teaching us that proportionality is a viable member of the tripartite test for participation, the post-*Franklin* courts have also taught us the following:

- Fiscal difficulties are not an excuse for violating Title IX or for postponing compliance.

- The number of participants rather than the number of teams is the key to determining compliance with the Title IX requirement to provide access to participate.

- Proof of the defendant's intent to discriminate is needed to obtain monetary damages.

- Proof of the defendant's intent to violate Title IX is not needed.

- Proof of the defendant's intent to discriminate is not needed to bring forward a Title IX complaint or lawsuit; disparate result is sufficient.

- The court may order specific remedies, including the reinstatement of a particular sport team. The court is not limited to just ordering the defendant to increase opportunities for women.

- The "relative interest theory" is discredited and is not appropriate as a means for determining proportionality.

- Roster management, a euphemism for capping men's teams while not increasing women's opportunities, is technically legal if not educationally sound.

- Generally, terminated men's teams cannot use Title IX to reinstate the team.
- Sexual harassment is within the prohibitions of Title IX.
- The sex of the harasser and harassee need not be different.
- Notice followed by indifference to harassment is needed to obtain monetary damages in sexual harassment cases.

Ten Questions and Ten Answers

1. **If my school doesn't have the money to comply with Title IX, may we postpone compliance?**

   No. The *Favia* case (1993) made it clear that lack of money is not an excuse for failing to provide equal access and equal benefit and to fulfill all other requirements of Title IX. Nor is the lack of money an acceptable reason for postponing compliance. In much the same way as with our mortgage obligations, Title IX does not provide forgiveness just because we've spent all our money on a new TV, lost our job, or decided to worry about the mortgage payment later. The obligation remains and the penalties for failing to meet them accrue in the face of either our poor choices or our inattention.

2. **Can a male whose team is terminated use Title IX to help reinstate it?**

   No. Terminating any participation opportunities is contrary to the mission of school-based athletics programs. Some administrators have chosen to do so, however, when faced with financial exigency. Title IX protects the historically underrepresented sex, which in athletics is typically female. If after the termination the historically overrepresented males still exceed their ratio in the student body, Title IX is of no help to the terminated athletes.

3. **We have to cut teams. We've decided to cut a men's team with 10 members and a women's team with 10 members. We believe that by cutting equal numbers of teams and participants we are within the parameters of Title IX. Are we?**

   No. The number of teams never enters into Title IX calculations. Instead, compliance with the Title IX requirement to provide access to participation is measured by the number of participants. *Gonyo* (1993) makes it clear that the number of teams is of no import in determining compliance. If female students are underrepresented before an institution cuts an equal number of teams or even an equal number of male and female participants, the inequity will remain after the cuts. Let's look at an example. Assume that before cutting teams, your student-body male-female ratio was 50-50 but your 100-person athletics program was 40 percent female and 60 percent male. After you execute the plan proposed in this question, you'll have 30 females (37.5 percent) and 50 males (62.5 percent). Although the cut involves an equal number of athletes between the sexes and appears gender neutral, the effect is not gender neutral.

4. **We see our dilemma spelled out in question 3, but programmatically the cut is what we have to do. We don't intend to discriminate against our female students, but the unequal result is an unavoidable consequence. If we lack the intent to discriminate, will Title IX forgive us?**

   No. *Pederson* tells us that the intent to treat the sexes differently (not the intent to violate Title IX) is sufficient not only to trigger Title IX jurisdiction but also to trigger the availability of monetary damages. The absence of intent to treat the sexes differently may still trigger Title IX jurisdiction, if not monetary damages, if the result is one of disparate impact, as noted in *Favia*.

5. **Title IX applies to employees as well as students. Is it as useful in employment cases as it is in student-related cases?**

   No. Title VII and Title IX overlap in many of the protections provided to an employee. To avoid legislative inefficiency, much of the protections for employees are actionable by a private right of action through Title VII to the exclusion of Title IX. But a few areas still exist in which an employee has a Title IX private right of action. Among those areas is retaliation. The *Lowrey* and *Lakoski* cases provide good insight into the issue.

6. **Brown University proposed using a "relative interest" format rather than the male-female ratio of students in the student body for determining proportionality. Is "relative interest" an acceptable method?**

   No. The answer is no because the court in *Cohen v Brown* said so and because to use the "relative interest" test would arbitrarily freeze participation opportunities for women at a level reflective of past discrimination, thereby aiding those who would continue to discriminate rather than aiding the alleviation of discriminatory practices.

7. **If we increase the maximum number of students permitted on women's teams, will that help us to comply with Title IX even if the slots are not filled?**

No. The calculation involves actual participants, not slots. If you offer slots where there is no interest and deny access where there is interest, you are not meeting the interests and abilities of the underrepresented sex.

8. **Is it legal to put a cap on the number of men allowed on a team rather than increase the opportunities for women? If we put a cap on the men's team rosters, our ratio of male to female athletes looks better.**

Capping team roster size is legal, but doing so is not within the spirit of Title IX because it does not provide fuller access to opportunities long denied to females. The action is a sham and a shell game, but it is legal. It is a substitute for reevaluating bloated or expansive budgets for some favored men's teams, but it is legal.

9. **Title IX is confusing. That's why I've bought this excellent book. Would I be better off if I stopped reading and stayed confused? Can I use ignorance of the law as an excuse for not complying with it?**

No. Ignorance is no excuse. The "arrogant ignorance" found at LSU in the *Pederson* case did not provide safety from the reach of Title IX. So, thanks for buying the book and keep reading.

10. **Does Title IX protect against sexual harassment?**

Yes. Title IX covers both quid pro quo and hostile environment types of sexual harassment.

The sex of the victim and the victim's harasser need not be different. The employer of an employee who is harassing a student may be liable under Title IX for the employee's harassing behavior if the employer had actual notice (knowledge) and remained deliberately indifferent to the harassment. Thus, students need to be made aware of the identity of the person to whom complaints of sexual harassment must be made. Coaches and teachers to whom students may complain about the harassment should be counseled to refer the student to the person officially, not just logically, designated to receive the complaint. Failure to complain to the correct person bars the victim from the potential availability of monetary damages. The *Gebser* case provides good insight into this issue.

NOTES

[1]When a decision in a case becomes irrelevant because the plaintiff's situation will no longer be affected by the outcome, the court often declines to render a decision on the merits or issues of the case and instead simply decides that the issues are now moot and in effect throws out the case. For example, by the time the *Colgate* case reached the court of appeals, all the plaintiffs had graduated or were about to do so, and a decision by the court ordering the establishment of a team for them to play on during their undergraduate years would be moot, meaningless.

[2]The creation of the ice hockey team had to wait until the court approved a settlement in yet another Title IX case against Colgate: *Bryant v Colgate*, New York District Court, No. 93-CV-1029, 1997. The *Bryant* settlement included a provision for starting an ice hockey team for women. The intervening four years from the ruling of mootness in the *Cook* case to the settlement in the *Bryant* case represent a collegiate generation of female students deprived of an opportunity to benefit from experiences offered to their male counterparts.

[3]Several years are required for Title IX lawsuits to reach conclusion. The time is usually longer than the college life span of a particular student and thus class-action cases are preferable.

[4]The Acosta and Carpenter study currently covers 27 years of data, 1977 to 2004. The study is available online at webpages.charter.net/womeninsport as well as at www.nagws.org, the Web site of the National Association for Girls and Women in Sport.

[5]See chapter 9 for a fuller discussion of the status of the current proportionality argument.

[6]For a fuller discussion of the three-prong test, see chapters 4 and 9.

[7]In 2000 the Office for Civil Rights discontinued monitoring Colorado State University, eight years after it began, finding that CSU was in compliance with Title IX. Among other things, in 1998-99, 51.6 percent of the student body was made up of women and 48.6 percent of its athletes were women. This ratio is much more in line than the ratio was during the *Roberts v Colorado* lawsuit of the early 1990s. CSU has made progress in many areas but still has more to do; the salaries of the coaches of women's teams at CSU averaged only 80 percent of those of the nonfootball coaches of men's teams at CSU in 2000.

[8]The right to sue an institution using Title IX without first exhausting all administrative remedies, such as an in-house or OCR complaint, is referred to as a private right of action.

[9]The *Lakoski* decision was appealed to the U.S. Supreme Court. The Court denied certiorari (refused to hear the case).

[10]"For purposes of this decision, it is important to distinguish between a cause of action for *discrimination* under title IX [sic] and a cause of action for *retaliation* under that title. It is axiomatic that Lowrey cannot state a claim for discrimination on behalf of her students. Therefore, were we asked to afford Lowrey a remedy for the rights of her students, we would hold that she does not have standing to assert the rights of a third person under [t]itle IX" (*Lowrey* at 251).

[11]Although Lowrey lacked the legal standing required to file a Title IX lawsuit on behalf of her students, she could have filed an OCR complaint on their behalf. This is true because no legal standing is required for filing administrative Title IX complaints.

[12]The *Cohen* court recognized the possibility that years of experience in discriminatory athletic settings on the high school level may reduce a woman's eagerness to engage in what she perceives to be merely a continuation of a discriminatory setting on the college level.

[13]The testimony of LSU's director of athletics indicated his categorization of females as uninterested in athletics. The testimony in the case makes interesting reading and illuminates the thought processes of those who saw females as cheerleaders, not participants, of the athletics program at LSU.

[14]See *Alexander v Sandoval*, 121 S. Ct. 1511 (2001). *Sandoval* is a Title VI case but is applicable to Title IX. *Sandoval* requires the showing of intent to discriminate for a private right of action claiming monetary damages to succeed. A showing of disparate effect is not enough. But in athletics cases, as distinct from sexual harassment cases, intent is relatively easy to demonstrate, and thus *Sandoval* is unlikely to have a significant chilling effect on Title IX cases seeking damages.

[15]See the policy interpretations in appendix B for the specific language of the three-prong test.

[16]The *NOW* lawsuit served to force the entire California State University system to adopt, by settlement, a plan to increase participation availability so that it more clearly mirrored the representation of females in the student body. The ratios improved, but sadly, at some institutions, the ratios improved not by the addition of opportunities for females but by the removal of opportunities for males.

[17]The ability of federal agencies to issue guidance is well established, and although such power in relation to Title IX has been the subject of several lawsuits, the power remains unaltered.

[18]Although every court that has heard such cases has determined that decreasing men's opportunities is an acceptable method, none has recommended such an action.

[19]Title VII, enacted in 1964, protects the employee and job applicant from discrimination in the workplace. Title VII protects against many types of discrimination, including discrimination based on religion, color, race, and sex, but it does not protect students.

[20]Concerning the need for notice, see also *P.H. v School District of Kansas City*, 265 F. 3d 653 (8th Cir. 2001), finding that no liability exists where there was no notice of a male teacher having a sexual relationship with a male student; see also *Warren v Reading School District*, 278 F. 3d 163 (2002), finding that a principal and guidance counselor had notice that a male teacher was sexually abusing a fourth-grade boy. The principal was certainly an "appropriate person" as the highest ranking employee, but the guidance counselor, to whom the principal referred the complaint, was not.

[21]The Office for Civil Rights issued extremely helpful guidance on sexual harassment and Title IX, available for downloading at http://www.ed.gov/about/offices/

list/ocr/docs/sexhar00.html. Note, however, that the guidance was prepared before the decision concerning notice found in the *Davis* case. Therefore, the information in the guidance about the topic of notice is not accurate, but all other parts of the guidance are both accurate and useful.

[22]The *Davis* case illustrates the seriousness of peer harassment within the early grades of school and the potential danger when parents and school children are not made aware of the "person in authority" to whom complaints must be made in order to preserve a plaintiff's right to sue for monetary damages.

[23]The standard to trigger the availability of monetary damages in Title IX sexual harassment cases was set initially in the *Gebser* case a year before the *Davis* decision. Unlike the *Davis* decision, which involved student-on-student harassment, the *Gebser* case involved faculty-on-student harassment.

PART III

Title IX in the 21st Century

Title IX has had enormous consequences. In part III we'll look at the depth and breadth of that effect in today's world and review current issues concerning its application.

8

Numbers: Effects of Title IX

Understanding the past allows us to recognize change wrought in the present. By understanding both the past and the present, we can design programs that will auger well for a positive future. This chapter employs existing databases, some small and rudimentary, others massive and complex, to illuminate progress, the pace of progress, possibilities for progress and, in some areas, lack of progress.

Let's first look at some of the social, emotional, behavioral, and physical benefits that are available to females who participate in sport.

BENEFITS OF SPORT PARTICIPATION FOR FEMALES

In 1995 Nike's television commercial relating to girls and women who participate in sport drew a great deal of attention. The commercial included photos of young women playing various sports. The action was fast; the camera scanned the young women quickly and then zoomed in on each participant. In turn, the female athletes looked into the camera and said, "If you let me play sports . . ." and then each completed her sentence with a reason why she played. All were positive statements and represented benefits that girls and women gained from sport participation. The airing of the commercial demonstrates not only Nike's awareness of an expanding market for its wares but also society's growing acceptance of females who sweat on the nation's playing fields and in the nation's gyms.

The following statements from a variety of sources use the Nike formula to express the benefits to female participants.

If you let me play sports . . .

- I will like myself more (White and Sheets, 2001).
- I will be more popular at school (White and Sheets, 2001).
- I will be less likely to get breast cancer (*British Journal of Cancer,* 2000).

- I will be more likely to graduate from high school and go on to college (Women's Sports Foundation, 1989).
- I will feel more confident, have more self-esteem, and take pride in what I do on and off the playing field (Women's Sports Foundation, 1985).
- I will like my body and know I look better because of the physical exercise sport provides for me (President's Council on Physical Fitness and Sport, 1997).
- I will not smoke or will smoke less than do my nonathletic classmates (*Medicine and Science in Sports and Exercise*, 1996).
- I will be less likely to develop osteoporosis later in life (Teegarden, Proulx, et al., 1996).
- I will be happier when I play sports and will suffer less depression in my life (Colton and Gore, 1991).
- I will learn what it means to be strong (White and Sheets, 2001).
- I will learn how to work with others toward a mutual goal (White and Sheets, 2001).
- I will be able to discipline myself; I will be better able to manage my time (White and Sheets, 2001).
- I will have fun (White and Sheets, 2001).
- I will be less likely to get pregnant before I want to (Women's Sports Foundation, 1998).
- I will be less likely to engage in sexual activities than my female nonathlete friends (Women's Sports Foundation, 1998).
- I will be less likely to stay with a male who beats me (Nike, 1995).
- I will have parents who are more likely to be active in sports and to encourage and support me when I play (*Journal of Sport and Exercise Psychology*, 1997).
- I will know I have a better chance of graduating from college than do my nonathletic female friends (68 percent as opposed to 59 percent) (NCAA, 2000).
- I will do better as a high school athlete in my science classes than will my nonathletic female friends (Hanson and Kraus, 1998).
- I will lower my chances of having a stroke (*Journal of the American Medical Association*, 2000).
- I will not be as likely to use marijuana, cocaine, or other drugs that will harm my body (Women's Sports Foundation, 2000).
- I will enhance my position in society (Justus, 1995).

Research suggests that young girls and young women who participate in the competition, teamwork, and skill development of athletics realize immediate and long-term benefits.

Because the benefits of sports participation are of value to both males and females but have special value to females, in the words of the Feminist Majority, "We need to create a climate in which sports and fitness are for everyone, not just a few, and in which everyone's abilities are tested and respected."

PARTICIPATION

The often heard phrase "If you build it, they will come" is true of females and sport opportunities. Indeed, they have come. Each year the participation of females in sport breaks new records.

High Schools

In concert with changing societal acceptance, the shadow cast by Title IX, even before its mandatory compliance date of 1978, had a great effect on participation. In 1971 over a quarter of a million (294,015) girls participated in organized high school sports, but that figure represented only about 5 percent of all athletes in high schools.[1]

Only seven years later, in 1978, over two million participated (2,083,040). By 1978 females represented about 32 percent of all high school athletes. So, in the seven years preceding the mandatory compliance date of Title IX, participation of high school females increased by 600 percent (Policy, 1979).

In the academic year 2002-2003 over 12 million students sat in the nation's high school classrooms. Almost 56 percent of them participated in high school sports. In 2002-2003 the highest number of girls in history (2.8 million) (National Federation of State High School Associations, 2003) were participating in sports and gaining the health, social, and behavioral benefits available.

Some people erroneously think that opening the gym doors for females means a closing of the doors for boys. In fact, 2002-2003 represents not only a record year for the numbers of girls participating in high school athletics but also a record year for boys; 2,856,358 girls and 3,988,783 boys participated. Just as a parent's heart can expand to find room for a new son or daughter, high school athletic programs found a way to expand opportunities for girls while also expanding opportunities for boys. Although in 2002-2003 females represented only 41 percent of the high school athlete population, their numerical growth was greater than the growth that occurred among their male counterparts; girls gained 858,869 participants and boys gained 572,349 participants in the period between 1993 and 2003, with both setting all-time records in the number of participants. Persistent but fading strands of the misapprehension that females are not as interested in sports should not long be able to stand in light of such data. If you build it, they will come.

When females are exposed to or taught sports skills, they will play sports. Opportunities have always been provided for the boys simply because society has always expected and encouraged boys to play sports. Playing sports is part of the male image. For many years, females were not allowed the same opportunities or provided the same encouragement. Society was sending a message to females that knowledge of and participation in sport were not an acceptable form of activity.

Times have changed, and girls and women are participating not just in schools but in all manner of sport-related clubs and community-based facilities.

> Wrestling with Reality: Women Wrestlers Try to Pioneer Their Way to a Sanctioned Sport
>
> NCAA News, *November 22, 1999*

Colleges and Universities

The Association for Intercollegiate Athletics for Women (AIAW),[2] born only a few months before the enactment of Title IX, governed women's intercollegiate athletics for about a decade before the NCAA developed a consistent, official interest in women's programs. People needing the NCAA's imprimatur on data concerning the status of women in intercollegiate athletics would have to wait more than a decade from the NCAA's takeover of women's athletics to receive it.

The NCAA's 1992 *Gender Equity Study* arrived with great fanfare in the press, but it was neither the first nor the most comprehensive source for data that tracked the changing face of athletics for women in the United States. The arrival of the NCAA study was, however, both symbolic and useful well beyond the actual data found within.

The NCAA study was released within weeks of the *Franklin v Gwinnett* decision (which noted the availability of compensatory and punitive damages in Title IX cases), and both occurred within months of the 20th anniversary of Title IX. The existence of NCAA-sanctioned data documenting the presence of a great disparity between males' and females' athletics programs surprised some and reinforced the knowledge of many others. The NCAA data caused those who had not realized it before to acknowledge that discrimination or at least great disparity ran rampant through the athletics programs at NCAA member schools, in all three divisions. The confluence of the release of the study with the unexpected, unanimous decision of the Supreme Court in the *Franklin* case and the focus on the 20th anniversary of Title IX served well the cause of increasing the awareness of the promise of Title IX and the continuing noncompliance with its requirements by many schools.

The 1999-2000 *NCAA Gender Equity Report*[3] is available for downloading online[4] and is consistent with more long-term studies in demonstrating an enduring increase in participation by female athletes at no cost to the status of male participation levels.

Study Results Echo Inequity Women Know All Too Well

Comment on the release of the first NCAA Gender Equity Study in USA Today, March 12, 1992

The Acosta and Carpenter study *Women in Intercollegiate Sport*[5] with data beginning in 1978, 14 years before the first NCAA *Gender Equity Study* (1992), provides a broad view of the massive growth in participation at the college level, including the final few years of AIAW competition. Its breadth also provides a view of the changing palette of popularity of various sports. Among the information found in the Acosta and Carpenter study is the following:

- In 2004 the average number of teams offered for females per school was near an all-time high of 8.32. In 1972 the number was 2.50 per school, and in 1978, the mandatory compliance date for Title IX, the number was 5.61.

- In the two-year period of 2002 to 2004, 270 new women's teams were added. In the six years from 1998 to 2004, 1,155 new teams were added for a total of 8402 in 2004.

- All three divisions continued to show an increase in the number of sports offered over the years to their female student-athletes. In 2004, Division I schools averaged 9.26 teams per school, Division II averaged 6.90, and Division III averaged 8.51.

- Soccer, offered at only 2.8 percent of the nation's intercollegiate women's athletics programs in 1977, was found in 88.6 percent of the schools in 2004, an increase of more than 4,000 percent.

- Crew or rowing, an often favored sport in part because of the large number of participants a team can carry (thus helping to meet the proportionality prong of the three-prong participation test), was offered in only 6.9 percent of colleges in 1977. By 2004 the sport was found at 14 percent of colleges.

- Golf, found in almost half of colleges (48.7 percent) in 2004, more than doubled its popularity in the last quarter century (from 19.9 percent in 1977).

- Gymnastics, one of the sports that has seen teams cut on the men's side of the equation, has similarly diminished in popularity on the women's side. In 1977 gymnastics was the 9th most frequently offered sport for women found on college campuses; in 2004 it ranked 13th with only 11 percent of colleges having it among their women's program.

- Lacrosse, found in 28.5 percent of colleges in 2004, has doubled its representation since 1977 (13 percent).

At the enactment of Title IX in 1972, 170,000 men participated in intercollegiate sports compared with 30,000 women participants (Bock, 2002). On the 30th anniversary of Title IX, there were 209,000 college men and 151,000 women playing on NCAA teams, with thousands more at NAIA and junior colleges. Within NCAA schools, females represented about 42 percent of the athlete population. Thirty years earlier their mothers made up only 15 percent of the college athlete population. If you build it, they will come.

Today, a larger pool of females exists from which to draw female athletes than existed at the birth of Title IX. From 1971 to 1976 collegiate enrollment figures for women grew from 3.4 million to over 5.2 million. In that five-year time period intramural participation by women increased 108 percent from 276,167 to 576,167, and club sports saw an increase of 102 percent from 31,852 to 64,375 (King, 2002). If you build it, they will come. They will come even when they are not provided with their share of the budget (see figure 8.1).

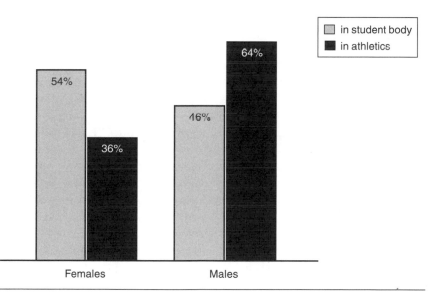

Figure 8.1 Comparison of percentage of males and females in the student body to the percentage of athletic budgets designated for each sex.

NCAA, 2002

Just a few years later in the 1977-1978 academic year, 48 percent (5,408,000) of the 11,267,000 national undergraduate collegiate enrollment was female, but only 30 percent of the students in the gyms and on the athletic fields were females.

Minorities

The generic access to sport participation opportunities occasionally carries with it a profound set of results for specific subgroups. Several studies have dealt with the effect of varsity sport participation on a variety of nonsport variables, such as social, educational, and career mobility, among minority students.

A massive but older study, *Minorities in Sports,* issued in 1989 by the Women's Sports Foundation (WSF), provides data on over 14,000 male and female high school students and tracks them for six years. The study includes policy recommendations as well as data about the effect of access to sport participation during and after the school experience.

The WSF's *Minorities in Sports* sought to determine whether the urging by Title IX for access, unfettered by discrimination, for females to the gymnasia and fields of our nation's schools may produce a disparate influence on those gaining access, based in part on their membership in a particular ethnic group. Among the findings of *Minority in Sports* is the somewhat obvious yet often discounted fact that female athletes, particularly Hispanic females, "were more likely than their nonathletic peers to score well on achievement tests, to report high popularity, to stay in high schools, to attend college, to seek a bachelor's degree, and to make progress toward that degree" (Women's Sports Foundation, 1989, 5). Sadly, the study also found that "compared to whites, the upward mobility of minority athletes after high school is limited" (Women's Sports Foundation, 1989, 5). But the study found that when compared with their nonathletic peers of the same ethnic group, "Hispanic athletes from rural schools were almost five times more likely than their nonathletic peers to be attending four-year colleges" two years after high school and "Hispanic female athletes were two to four times more likely than their nonathletic peers to attend and stay in college" (Women's Sports Foundation, 1989, 5). So, in general, athletics participation increases the upward mobility of women, regardless of how ethnicity might limit it, with the effect on Hispanic young women being the greatest.

Are women of color receiving their fair share of opportunities in intercollegiate athletics compared with other women? The Women's Sports Foundation's 2003 *Title IX and Race in Intercollegiate Sport*[6] says yes. The answer is yes in terms of participation and financial aid as compared with other women. Additional questions found within the WSF study are of note, including the finding that Title IX has not resulted in a loss of opportunities for male athletes of color.

Because of their gender, women have been viewed as minorities as they seek to enter the historically male domain of athletics. As a result, females have experienced discrimination based on gender. Being a woman and not being white, however, may mean getting a double dose of discrimination. Women as a group, in spite of discrimination and regardless of ethnicity, have benefited, at least to some degree, because of Title IX and the increasingly open gymnasium doors. The 2003 release of the Women's Sports Foundation's *Title IX and Race in Intercollegiate Sport* found that 15 percent (22,541) of collegiate female athletes were women of color. In 1971 only 7 percent (2,137) had been women of color.

The absolute number of female athletes of color has increased tenfold in 30 years while women as a whole increased only fivefold. Women of color make up 24.9 percent of the female student body, but female athletes of color make up only 14.8 percent. Are they doubly discriminated against?

The apparent double discrimination may result from causes having little to do with racial discrimination at the athletic program level but nonetheless having significant effect on the nonathletic lives of nonwhite female participants. Access to facilities, coaches, or exposure to any kind of sport that requires financial support from the female participant and her family becomes problematic in the absence of sufficient resources. If limited financial resources are available because of broad-based discrimination or other factors, the lack of finances and the resulting decreased access to facilities and coaching may play a role in the underrepresentation of female minority group members, especially in sports such as field hockey, lacrosse, equestrian, golf, and tennis.

LEADERSHIP

Before Title IX, 90 to 95 percent of the coaches and athletic directors in programs for females were themselves female. In most cases males were not sought out for these positions, nor did males want them. Pay for the coaches of girls' and women's teams was seldom more than token and in many instances was in the form of a thank-you rather than in the more useful form of currency. In a few cases, males were affirmatively barred from being considered for positions in programs where female role models were viewed as vital to the program.

Title IX does not require equal numbers of female and male coaches or equal numbers of female and male administrators. It requires only that female athletes have access to the same level of coaching as their brothers do, and the notion of equity requires a gender-neutral hiring process and determination of salary.[7] Title IX and newly blossoming notions of equity produced greater salaries for coaches of female teams, thus making the positions more financially attractive than they had been before.

Coaching opportunities in programs for females increased swiftly at the hands of Title IX because the number of teams for females was expanding markedly. Males filled most of the new coaching positions.[8] By 1985 females coached only half of women's teams (Acosta and Carpenter, 2004),[9] yet males coached all but 2 percent of men's teams. When all of men's and women's teams are combined, women hold only 18.8% of the head coaching jobs in the NCAA (Acosta and Carpenter, 2004).

The early massive expansion of sport offerings for females may have been part of the reason for the increase in males coaching females, but the increase has persisted. In 2004 only 44.1 percent of intercollegiate women's teams had female coaches, yet still only 2 percent of men's teams had female coaches. The influences on the marketplace seem to be complex and may include combinations of continued discrimination, an expansion of nonsport and nonteaching roles for females so that additional employment choices are drawing women to other arenas, the influence of an increasing presence of male athletic directors,[10] and an enduring societal view that it's OK for males to coach females but it's not OK for females to coach males.

As programs for females were increasing, formerly volunteer and part-time coaching positions became full time. Before Title IX, women who were teaching full time in the physical education departments of their institutions held the vast majority of the coaching positions in the then separate women's athletics programs. When the opportunity to coach full time was presented, many of the teacher-coaches had to choose between teaching and coaching. The decision was often difficult because many of the women had strong philosophical tenets concerning both programs. The choice frequently carried with it lifelong consequences. Athletic departments were being merged, and males were becoming the head athletic directors. Organizational charts placed accountability for the newly merged athletics departments outside the physical education department.[11] Choosing to coach full time meant leaving a departmental home, loosening emotional ties, and exchanging a known professional support system for membership in an athletics department that was almost always led by a male athletic director. The future seemed uncertain, and although some women chose to move to coaching on a full-time basis, others decided to teach.

When Title IX was enacted in 1972, women filled more than 90 percent of the coaching positions in women's intercollegiate programs. In 2004, 44.1 percent of the coaches of women's teams were female, close to the lowest representation of females as head coaches of women's teams in history (44%). In 2004 there were 8,402 head coaching jobs of women's NCAA teams, with an increase of 631 jobs since 2000. Males filled the majority of the new jobs, yet no concomitant increase occurred in the number of female coaches for men's teams; females still make up only 2 percent of coaches of men's teams.

Assistant coaches play an important role in athletics. As women's teams became more visible and competitive, the need for assistant coaches increased. Before Title IX, paid assistant coaches were few, although many women and some men volunteered to serve in those positions. Because volunteers served as assistant coaches, there was little consistency in the personnel holding assistant coaching positions. Slowly, the role of the paid assistant and volunteer assistant became critical. In 2004 there were 9,215 paid assistant coaching jobs within women's NCAA intercollegiate athletics programs. Women held 57.2 percent, or 5,273, of those jobs. Women also held 52.9 percent of the volunteer positions (Acosta and Carpenter, 2004).

Although the gender of an employee is of no concern to Title IX or Title VII as long as no discrimination occurred in the hiring, pay-scale determination, or conditions of employment, the enactment of Title IX was nonetheless the catalyst for unintended consequences in the workplace. Before the enactment of Title IX, women filled more than 90 percent of the head administrative positions in women's intercollegiate programs. In 2004 females directed only 18.5 percent of women's programs, and almost one in five programs had no female anywhere in the athletic administrative structure. Division III programs were the most likely to have a female head administrator (27.5 percent), and Division I programs were the least likely (8.7 percent). In 2004 the athletics programs of NCAA schools having women's athletics programs included 3,350 administrative jobs, an increase of 240 jobs from 2002. Women filled only 41 percent of the 3,350 jobs, and only 187 were as the head athletic director (Acosta and Carpenter, 2004).

The acceptance of females as workforce members and role models has evolved. With acceptance come enhanced opportunities for women to expand their professional horizons. Today's female university student has more options for pursuing diverse fields of study, and she does. Thirty years ago women did not have such opportunities because they were expected to be homemakers or, if they wanted to work outside the home, to pursue workplace options among secretarial, nursing, or education-based professions. Today, young women seek careers in such diverse fields as medicine, law, science, engineering, computer science, and the corporate world, where the financial rewards, mobility, and growth are substantially greater than what was available in the limited fields of education, nursing, and office worker in 1972. Today, women make up nearly 50 percent of the paid workforce for the first time in history, with two-thirds of mothers with young children joining the workforce (AAUW, 2003). The realm of athletics, in which there are few female role models, may not be a choice that young women often contemplate.

MONEY, MONEY, MONEY

The only place where Title IX counts dollars is in the area of financial aid; all other areas are evaluated based on benefit received. But when you go grocery shopping and the benefit that you bring home is food, entering the store with more money in your pocket allows you to buy more benefit. Women's budgets allow for buying much less benefit (see figure 8.2).

Data from the NCAA's periodic *Gender Equity Report*, a variety of General Accounting Office studies, and data gathered by the annual Equity in Athletics Disclosure Act of 1994 (EADA) provide this perspective about funding comparisons between men's and women's programs:

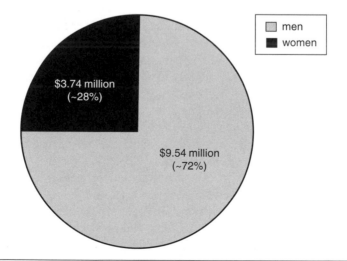

Figure 8.2 Division 1A spending on athletics.
NCAA, 2002

- Although 54 percent of college students were female, in 2002 females received only 36 percent of the sports operating budget dollars.
- Since 1972, for every new dollar spent on women, two new dollars have been spent on men (Justus, 1995).
- Division IA schools spent almost three times as much on their men's programs ($9.54 million) as they did on their women's program ($3.74 million).
- In the 2002-2003 academic year women received 42 percent of athletic scholarships, which in actual dollars amounted to $133 million less than men received. Although that discrepancy may be appalling, it was an improvement from 1997, when male athletes received $179 million more than female athletes did.
- In 2001-02 $369,200 was expended for recruiting in the average Division IA men's program, whereas $159,300 was spent on the female counterparts (NCAA, 2002).
- In 1999 Division I men's programs enjoyed operating budgets averaging $882,100. Women's programs had $486,200 to spend (NCAA, 2002).
- In 1999 Division III men's programs had operating budgets averaging $137,000 compared with $94,700 for women.
- Although the Equal Pay Act and Title VII pertain more closely to salary disparities than does Title IX, a look at the differences might be useful. Both men and women are experiencing salary increases, but the increases for women are less than a third of the increases provided to men.
- Coaches of women's teams in 2000 made about $3,000 more than they did in 1999, but coaches of men's teams made $9,200 more.

Recruiting budgets make a big difference in how many athletes, male and female, come to campuses. When the money spent on recruiting is restricted from one sex, it is not difficult to understand why there might be fewer athletes of that sex (see figure 8.3).

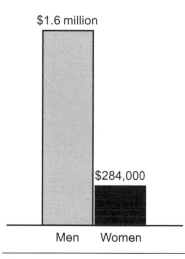

Figure 8.3 Average money spent per school on recruiting (Division 1A). NCAA, 2002

THEN AND NOW: AN OVERVIEW

Participation for both males and females has increased greatly since the enactment of Title IX. The percentage growth of females has outstripped the percentage growth of males, but participation of females is only now approaching men's pre–Title IX levels (see figures 8.4, 8.5, and 8.6). The same applies to high school athletics programs.

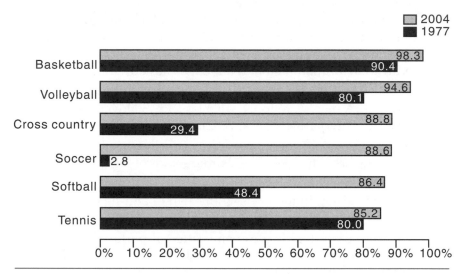

Figure 8.4 Most offered intercollegiate sports for women by percentage of schools with teams, 1977 and 2004.

Acosta and Carpenter, 2004

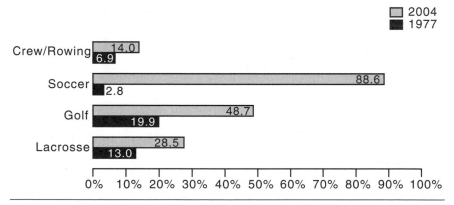

Figure 8.5 Fastest growing women's sports (schools offering varsity teams).

Acosta and Carpenter, 2004

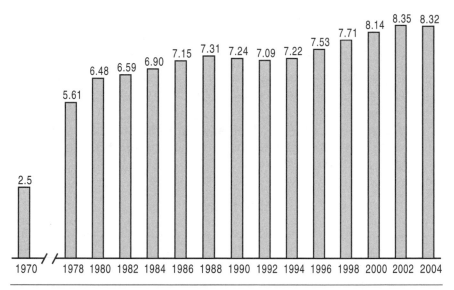

Figure 8.6 Average number of intercollegiate women's varsity teams per NCAA campus.

Acosta and Carpenter, 2004

- In the early 1970s, 30,000 college women and 170,000 college men participated in intercollegiate varsity sports.
- In 2002, 150,000 college women and 209,000 college men participated in NCAA intercollegiate varsity sports.
- In the early 1970s, 294,000 high school girls and 3,700,000 high school boys played varsity sports.
- In 2002, 2,856,358 high school girls and 3,988,783 high school boys played varsity sports.
- Minority participation rates have increased for both male and female student-athletes. Although participation has expanded greatly for females, employment for female coaches and athletic administrators has not paralleled that growth.
- Before Title IX 90 percent of all coaches of women's NCAA women's teams and athletics directors for women's programs were women.
- Since the enactment of Title IX the percentage of women's teams having a female coach has diminished by more than 50 percent and in 2002 stood at 44 percent, the lowest in history and in 2004 stood at 4.1%.
- Females coached 2 percent of men's NCAA teams in 1972 and the percentage remains unchanged today.

- In 2004, females directed 18.5% of women's programs.
- In 2004, 17.8% of women's athletics programs had no female anywhere in the athletic administrative structure.
- In 2004, 12.2% of the full-time sports information directors were female. In 1972 few programs had a sports information director of either gender.
- In 2004, 30% of the full-time athletic trainers in NCAA schools were female. In 1972 few programs had athletic trainers of either gender (Acosta and Carpenter, 2004).

IN BRIEF

Participation rates for females have increased dramatically and continue to do so without ending the continuing concomitant increases for males. Representation of females in the coaching and administrative ranks of athletics programs for girls and women has dropped dramatically since the enactment of Title IX. On the other hand, women's representation in the coaching ranks for boys' and men's teams has not increased in the three decades of Title IX. Budgets have increased for both males and females, but males still have access to funds beyond their representation in the pool of athletes.

Coaching salaries have increased for both males and females, but the increases for males continue to outpace those for females by a significant margin.

Three Questions and Zero Answers

As we did in chapter 5, we're going to ask you to apply your own point of view to the questions below and thus will not be providing you with answers.

1. **Participation rates for females of all age groups have increased since the enactment of Title IX. What positive benefits of the greater access to sport have you seen for your daughter, extended family, and community?**

2. **Budgetary constraints are often posed as the reason for terminating teams or failing to provide teams (even if the real answer is roster management). In instances in high school programs where the impetus truly is budgetary constraints, how might you persuade the local school board or taxpayers to find the necessary funding?**

3. **If you were a college president reading this chapter, would it bother you if your campus was one where the salaries for male coaches were expanding at a much greater pace than the salaries for female coaches? If so, what plan might you develop to provide appropriately for both your male and female coaches?**

NOTES

[1]The National Federation of High Schools maintains a database on the participation of males and females in high school athletics programs. The database also includes information on the changing interest in various sports and is available online at http://www.nfhs.org/scriptcontent/va_custom/va_cm/contentpagedisplay.cfm?content_ID=133.

[2]See chapter 5 for a fuller discussion of the role of the AIAW.

[3]A considerable time lag occurs from when the NCAA collects the data to when the report becomes available.

[4]The entire 1999-2000 NCAA *Gender-Equity Report* is available for downloading without charge at www.ncaa.org/library/research/gender_equity_study/1999-00/1999-00_gender_equity_report.pdf.

[5]The Acosta and Carpenter study's latest update (27 years as of this writing) is available for downloading without charge at webpages.charter.net/womeninsport.

[6]The study is available for downloading without charge at www.womenssportsfoundation.org/cgibin/iowa/search/index.html.

[7]Title VII and the Equal Protection Act cover workplace discrimination against coaches more comprehensively than does Title IX. The *Lowrey* case discussed in chapters 1 and 7 provides an up-to-date review of what Title IX covers and does not cover regarding discrimination against employees, at least in the Fifth Circuit.

[8]Motivation is difficult to quantify, but it seems logical to attribute the influx of males into the coaching ranks for female teams to several factors. Increasing salaries for coaching female teams attracted male candidates. Males could not be barred from obtaining jobs as coaches of female teams because of civil rights legislation such as Title VII and Title IX. The merging of male athletic departments with female athletic departments typically resulted in a male becoming the athletic director rather than the female counterpart. Male athletic directors had a cadre of male friends and associates to whom they looked for new coaches rather than to females unknown to them. Male athletic directors understood NCAA coaching experience when it appeared on an applicant's vita but did not understand similar or greater experience when it was related to the AIAW.

[9]In 1984 and again in 1988 Acosta and Carpenter conducted a study relating to the perceived causes for the declining representation of females in the coaching and administration ranks. Among their findings were that males perceived the causes to be related to such items as the lack of females wanting to coach (a perception unsupported by the marketplace) and females' heavy home and family responsibilities, which would not allow them to coach (a perception refuted by the female

respondents). Females perceived that the strength of the old boys network was functioning and that at least some level of discrimination was in action. A complete summary of this older but interesting data is available at Acosta/Carpenter, Post Office Box 42, West Brookfield, MA 01585.

[10]Acosta and Carpenter's data demonstrate that the gender of the athletic director influences the likelihood of females being hired as coaches of women's teams. For instance, in 2004 44.1 percent of women's intercollegiate teams were coached by women overall, but at Division III colleges where the athletic director was female, 46.3 percent of the head coaching jobs of women's teams were filled by females. In Division I, females filled 53.4 percent of the head coaching jobs of women's teams when the AD was a female.

[11]Women's athletics programs were typically housed in the women's department of physical education under the supervision of the chair of physical education or a woman from the department who was designated as the athletics director. Many other titles were used, but the ultimate role was that of athletics director for women.

9

Issues and Cases in Transit

The life of Title IX has been strewn with attempts to alter it, contain it, maintain it, limit it, gut it, blame it, praise it, laud it, applaud it, repeal it, and appeal it. In chapter 5 we discussed some of the early attempts to divorce athletics from the coverage of Title IX and to exclude so-called revenue sports from its reach. Chapter 6 guided you through the pre-*Franklin* lawsuits that, in the main, sought to define Title IX jurisdiction and coverage. Chapter 7 provided you with a stroll through the post-*Franklin* case law, in which men whose teams had been terminated sought redress, in which employees found that many of the civil rights protections previously sponsored by Title IX were shifting to Title VII, and in which proportionality was repeatedly found to be an appropriate element of the three-prong test for participation.

So what's left for chapter 9? Two things remain. One is legally complex, and the other is emotionally complex. The first concerns the 11th Amendment to the Constitution, and the second concerns attempts to change Title IX through both a lawsuit and a federal commission.

TITLE IX AND THE 11TH AMENDMENT

Let's tackle the legally complex issue first. The 11th Amendment to the United States Constitution says, "The Judicial power of the United States shall not be construed to extend to any suit in law or equity, commenced or prosecuted against one of the United States by Citizens of another State, or by Citizens or Subjects of any Foreign State."

What does the 11th Amendment have to do with Title IX? No one knows at this point. The 11th Amendment, however, has been used as an argument, sometimes successfully and sometimes not, to bar non–Title IX cases based on other forms of federal antidiscrimination legislation from being litigated in federal court. Thus, we need to talk about it.

Although the words of the 11th Amendment don't say so explicitly, it is well-settled law that under some circumstances states have an immunity from being sued in federal court for violation of a federal statute. In the early days of the United States the individual states were concerned that the new federal government would impose federal laws on the states and allow citizens to sue the states when the states violated federal laws. In addition, the states were concerned that when they were sued for violating a federal law, the states would be defendants in what they would perceive to be hostile federal courts. Therefore, the 11th Amendment was passed to give the states immunity from being sued in federal court for violating federal law.

Federal laws would still apply to individuals and to nonstate entities within the states, but the states themselves would have immunity from federal lawsuits. Every now and then the immunity that the 11th Amendment gives to states is abrogated (dispensed with, or thrown out) by the courts. Once immunity is dispensed with, victims of the state's violation of the particular federal law in question are permitted to sue the state in federal court. If you work for a state university and believe that your rights under the Americans with Disabilities Act (ADA) have been violated, you cannot successfully sue the university for lost wages and other monetary damages.[1] You cannot sue because the state that runs the university is immune from the federal lawsuit because of the 11th Amendment. But don't fret; all states have legislation somewhat similar to the federal law known as the ADA, so your rights are protected even if you work for a state university. But you will have to sue the university in state court rather than in federal court, and you will have to use the state statute to do so rather than the ADA.

The 11th Amendment immunity conferred on the states is not an absolute immunity. In some circumstances, the states' immunity from being sued for damages in federal court for violating a federal statute is abrogated (thrown out). Among the requirements that need to exist for Congress (and plaintiffs using Congress' statutes) to get around the states' 11th Amendment immunity are

- an intent expressed by Congress to abrogate 11th Amendment immunity at the time of the enactment of the legislation in question pursuant to its 14th Amendment powers, or
- implication of that intent.

Implication of intent might come from the legislative history or by Congress' demonstration of a level of discrimination by the state against the protected class high enough for the courts to deduce intent.

Does the 11th Amendment provide states with immunity from Title IX? The legislative history of Title IX is sketchy, and express intent is absent. But no 11th Amendment Title IX case has progressed through the courts, possibly because cogent arguments can be made that the state was perpetuating broad-based and pervasive sex discrimination through its education system at the time Title IX was enacted. Furthermore, the remedy selected for Title IX violation is "proportional and congruent to the targeted violation" (*Board of Trustees of the University of Alabama v Patricia Garrett* at 356). If brought to court, 11th Amendment immunity would probably be abrogated in relation to Title IX suits, thus continuing to allow plaintiffs to sue state defendants in federal court.

Many states have enacted legislation similar to Title IX. In the states that have such legislation, the applicability or nonapplicability of the 11th Amendment immunity for state defendants is of little consequence. Victims could sue the state for Title IX violations in state court if, perchance, the 11th Amendment immunity was found to be applicable in Title IX cases.

In states that do not yet have legislation similar to Title IX in place,[2] the effect of potential 11th Amendment immunity makes a more interesting debate topic than it would in states that have legislation of the Title IX type. So, although this is an area to watch, it is unlikely that the authority of Title IX against state institutions would be able to be lessened.

THE "WRESTLERS" LAWSUIT

From mid-2002 to mid-2003, simmering frustration emanating from the termination of a variety of men's "minor" sports teams resulted in the filing of a class-action lawsuit against the U.S. Department of Education. A variety of men's "minor" sports such as wrestling, gymnastics, and swimming, which had seen for years an erosion of their positions in intercollegiate athletics programs, filed the lawsuit, which sought to alter Title IX. (For economy of reference, we'll refer to this group as the wrestlers although we acknowledge that it is not fair to place the entire responsibility on that group.) Institutions that failed to meet any of the three prongs of the participation test all too often decided to manipulate numbers rather than expand opportunities. The only prong that, by its nature, is susceptible to manipulation is the proportionality prong. The manipulation of numbers typically included terminating men's "minor" sports teams rather than, for example, curbing the excesses of football.[3] Interest in any particular sport waxes and wanes over the years. Men's wrestling, gymnastics, and swimming may have been on the wane,[4] but it is difficult to know. If the termination of men's teams had been based on changing interest patterns alone rather than serving as a method of number manipulation, the termination of waning men's wrestling, gymnastics, and swimming teams would have been paired with an expansion of teams representing men's sports waxing in popularity.

Such was not the case. The culprit appears to be manipulation, at least in part, not merely alteration of interest patterns.

For many years, but to no avail, the terminated men's teams (hereafter called the wrestlers) filed lawsuits against their individual schools using a variety of legal premises, including Title IX and the 14th Amendment.[5] Frustrated at losing their teams and then frustrated even more at finding no relief through individual lawsuits, the wrestlers filed a class-action lawsuit against the Department of Education, whose Office for Civil Rights is responsible for enforcing Title IX. The wrestlers may have taken the bold step of filing a class-action suit against the enforcement agency rather than against the allegedly discriminating institution[6] because of a growing sense of frustration as well as awareness that they had friends, such as Speaker of the House Dennis Hastert, a friend of wrestling, in high places.[7] The case against the Department of Education is legally complex,[8] but, in brief, it claimed that the policy interpretations (in which the three-prong test first appeared) and the 1996 letter of clarification (which reiterated the three-prong test) were illegal changes to Title IX made by the Department of Education and should be thrown out. The wrestlers believed or at least hoped that if the able-to-be-manipulated proportionality prong was thrown out, schools would have no incentive to manipulate numbers to the detriment of still existing wrestling teams.

Wrestling Coaches Sue Education Department Over Title IX Enforcement

Chronicle of Higher Education, *February 1, 2002*

Hoping for reinstatement of previously terminated wrestling teams seems likely to have been in vain, but partisanship can sweep away reason. In reality, the best the wrestlers could hope to achieve by their lawsuit was the removal of a motivating factor in the team termination equation. The wrestlers' class-action suit filed in Washington, D.C., had several difficult hurdles to clear before it could even draw breath. The plaintiffs were all membership organizations and as such had to face challenges to their legal standing to bring the case to court.[9] To have the requisite legal standing to bring a lawsuit to court, each association must be able to show that the association itself has been injured or that the association is suing on behalf of its injured members. The United States Constitution permits lawsuits against the federal government or its agencies to enter the federal court system only when its Article III minimal requirements for legal standing are met. Three elements must be satisfied:

- Injury
- Causation
- Redressability

Was the association injured, were its members injured, or were the institutions at which the athletes and coaches worked injured? Was the interpretation of Title IX and its corresponding enforcement by the Department of Education's Office for Civil Rights the cause of the injury, or was the cause of the injury based on the decisions made on each campus? If the court found in favor of the plaintiff organizations, could the injury be remedied?

Even if the court found that the wrestlers had legal standing and granted the wrestlers' requests, the court had no power to force the institutions that had terminated their teams (which were not parties to the lawsuit) to make better decisions or to reinstate previously terminated wrestling teams.[10] Therefore, even if the first two elements for standing could be satisfied, the last, redressability, could not.

Male athletes in less popular sports such as wrestling, swimming, and gymnastics have felt the pain of roster management, a tactic some institutions have used to comply with the letter, but not the spirit, of Title IX.

So, as it turned out, the plaintiff wrestlers were not able to meet the three elements for legal standing relating to two of the three parts of their lawsuit, and on the third they failed to state a claim that the court could resolve. Thus, on June 11, 2003, their lawsuit was dismissed.[11]

High hopes for the outcome of another situation that was unfolding at the same time—the formation of a federally sponsored commission on athletic opportunities—may have tempered the wrestlers' disappointment. This commission, they hoped, could have a more far-reaching effect on Title IX than the lawsuit ever could.[12]

THE COMMISSION

Following the 1992 *Franklin* decision, more Title IX lawsuits entered the courts and more were resolved in favor of the female plaintiffs, by way of either settlement or decision. Title IX had finally found its enforcement momentum. That momentum was intimidating to some people and became an even greater irritant as the years of enforcement went onward. The proportionality debate continued.

"Denny [Rep. Dennis Hastert] will stand up for wrestling."

Dale Anderson, former wrestler at Michigan State University, commenting on Rep. Hastert's appointment as Speaker of the House. NCAA News, February 1, 1999

In May 1995 Representative Dennis Hastert, who was later to become Speaker of the House, urged hearings on the validity of the three-prong test for proportionality. The House Subcommittee on Postsecondary Education held the hearings. Mr. Hastert, a former wrestling coach, former president of the Wrestling Coaches Association, and inductee to the Wrestling Hall of Fame, testified at the hearings. The proportionality prong of the three-prong test for participation was his target. Mr. Hastert's testimony made his position clear: He believed that there was a direct and destructive connection between the proportionality prong and colleges' decisions to terminate men's "minor" sports teams. The proportionality debate continued.

The 1995 hearings produced no changes. The proportionality prong remained one of three options for showing equitable participation. College administrators continued to make disingenuous and unconscionable decisions to terminate men's "minor" sports teams rather than increase opportunities for women. The proportionality debate heated up.

The 1995 Congressional hearings produced no change, and neither would the review of the proportionality option by the enforcement agency, OCR. The year 1996 saw the promulgation of the clarification letter by the Office for Civil Rights; the 1996 clarification letter[13] supported the three-prong test for participation found in the policy interpretations. The judiciary similarly found no reason to reinterpret the issue. Eight of the 12 United States Courts of Appeal had ruled on Title IX cases involving proportionality, and all 8 supported it as an appropriate legal measure for assessing equitable participation. The loudness of the proportionality debate was unabated even though Congress, OCR, and the courts had all tried to close the discussion.

Half a dozen years later, Mr. Hastert, by then the Speaker of the House, supported the creation of a Department of Education–Office for Civil Rights' commission to review Title IX in general and the proportionality prong in particular. So, on June 27, 2002, the federal Commission on Opportunities in Athletics was announced under the direction of the new Secretary for the Department of Education, Roderick Paige. The commission's charge was to "strengthen enforcement" and "expand . . . opportunities to ensure fairness for all athletes."[14]

Many people saw the commission as just "another chapter in an old debate,"[15] but this turned out to be the last chapter in the proportionality debate. If the commission were to lead to a change in Title IX, it was likely to be a massive change away from significant enforcement. On the other hand, if the commission's activities were to lead to a reaffirmation of Title IX, only those who refused to listen would fail to realize that further debate about Title IX and attacks on it would be futile. Because of the breadth of the potential swing of the pendulum, supporters and foes alike watched the commission's process with held breaths and strenuous political activation. Foes and supporters alike viewed the outcome of the commission as vital; it was like sudden death overtime.

Both foes and supporters of Title IX found something to dislike in the backgrounds, experiences or lack thereof, and perceived biases of various commissioners.[16] The Internet and postal service carried heavy loads of letters urging commissioners and members of Congress to support particular points of view. The local and national press prepared Title IX articles and programs that shared one element: They were guaranteed to irritate someone. Amicus "briefs" and position papers[17] were sent to the commission, yet some surmised that the commissioners did not read them. Ineptitude and ignorance on the parts of commissioners, commission staff, and Department of Education administrators were apparent to many observers.

> "From charter to final vote, the commission was more concerned with what men had lost than with what women never had."
>
> Newsday, *February 3, 2003, Michael Dobie*

Both sides criticized the selection of invited speakers, and all were dissatisfied with the lack of opportunity for public input. The commission may have been a paradigm of all federal review processes when the topic touches nerves central to the lives of so many. Eight questions were posed for commission response:

1. Are Title IX standards for assessing equal opportunity in athletics working to promote opportunities for male and female athletes?

2. Is there adequate Title IX guidance that enables colleges and school districts to know what is expected of them and to plan for an athletic program that effectively meets the needs and interests of their students?

3. Is further guidance or other steps needed at the junior and senior high school levels, where the availability or absence of opportunities will critically affect the prospective interests and abilities of student-athletes when they reach college age?

4. How should activities such as cheerleading or bowling factor into the analysis of equitable opportunities?

5. The [Education] Department has heard from some parties that whereas some men athletes will "walk on" to intercollegiate teams—without athletic financial aid and without having been recruited—women rarely do this. Is this accurate and, if so, what are its implications for Title IX analysis?

6. How do revenue-producing and large-roster teams affect the provision of equal athletic opportunities?

7. In what ways do opportunities in other sports venues, such as the Olympics, professional leagues, and community recreation programs, interact with the obligations of colleges and school districts to provide equal athletic opportunity? What are the implications for Title IX?

8. Apart from Title IX enforcement, are there other efforts to promote athletic opportunities for male and female students that the department might support, such as public-private partnerships to support the efforts of schools and colleges in this area?

Can you find which of the eight questions touch areas beyond Title IX jurisdiction? Can you put yourself in the place of either a supporter of Title IX or someone seeking substantive changes and then judge any of the questions as slanted? If you were creating questions for a federal commission to consider, would you have added or subtracted from the list of eight? Most people who were closely watching the commission and its progress would have had heartfelt and vehement answers to those questions, even if those answers might have been diametrically opposed to those of other observers.

The 12-month period covering the life span of the commission was one of tumult and turmoil for anyone who was watching. Hearings occurred at several venues across the nation. Invited speakers testified, and a few members of the public testified, sometimes on the topic and sometimes not.[18] Commissioners displayed their ignorance of the law and their failure to do their homework, biases surfaced, and votes occurred with illogical lack of consistency. Tempers flared, and emotions ran high. Overall, the 12 months were intense for all concerned. Trepidation continued to rise.

By itself, the commission's report, whatever it was to contain, would not determine any change or reaffirm Title IX. Even so, the commission's report remained the focus and fear of people on both sides. By itself, the report had no power, but how it would be used created great anxiety. Its potential contents took on an importance beyond their actual power. The report could either be ignored in toto or used as support to accomplish whatever predetermined decisions the Department of Education might have had in mind through enforcement emphases or, through executive order, whatever the president of the United States might have wanted all along. Nonetheless, the commission occupied a central place in the field of attention from June 2002 to February 2003, when the final report was issued.

The final report titled "Open to All: Title IX at Thirty" was issued on February 26, 2003, 11 years after the *Franklin v Gwinnett* decision was handed down. The final report included 23 recommendations, 15 of which received a unanimous vote by commission members. Perhaps in an attempt to allay fears, Roderick Paige, secretary of education, announced that the Department of Education would "move forward" only on the 15 unanimous proposals. Fears were not allayed.[19]

A careful reading of the contents of the unanimously approved proposals raised even greater concern. In some cases, the wording was so vague that it allowed anything to be done. Some proposals involved areas beyond the reach of Title IX, and others were so innocuous as to be meaningless. When read as a group, the proposals display viewpoints so disparate that one wonders how the package could receive a unanimous vote. Look at the 15 unanimous proposals and see whether you see a mix of boilerplate and revolution. (Because they ultimately had no bearing on the result, they are not presented on these pages but are available for your reading pleasure at www.ed.gov/about/BDSCOMM/LIST/athletics/report.html.)[20]

Reactions to the final report[21] included the widest possible divergence of opinion and emotion by those whose attention the commission had held for the eight months of the creation of the report and the four months of waiting for a response to its contents.[22] Following the issuance of the final report, a minority report[23] was presented by two members of the commission who felt that the process and the final report were both flawed. Indeed, a reading of the transcripts[24] of the commission's hearings and public deliberations and a review of the final report would certainly raise doubt about the process as well as the preparation of the commission's members, regardless of what point of view one holds on Title IX issues. Contrary to the wishes of its drafters, the minority report was not part of the official package sent forth from the commission.

The months after the issuance of the report were quiet, not from lack of interest but because all were waiting for the other shoe to drop: What would the Department of Education do about the report? Finally, on July 11, 2003, Gerald Reynolds, assistant secretary for civil rights, issued the *2003 Further Clarification of Intercollegiate Athletics Policy Guidance Regarding Title IX Compliance.* The 2003 further clarification joins the policy interpretations, the 1996 clarification letter, and a host of lawsuits, all of which have upheld the validity of the proportionality prong of the three-prong test for access to participation opportunities (a copy of the 2003 clarification letter appears in appendix E).

Let's look at the highlights of the further clarification letter of 2003. By way of the letter, OCR and the U.S. Department of Education reaffirmed the three-prong test for participation opportunities and reminded schools that satisfaction of any of the three prongs would be acceptable. No member of the three-prong test is favored. The letter also reminded schools that nothing in any part of Title IX or its clarifying documents requires or even recommends cutting or limiting male participation. Indeed, the letter noted, to do so is a disfavored practice. The letter also noted that booster funding and other private funding of teams, although allowed, does not relieve the school from finding ways of meeting the unchanged requirements of Title IX. Further, OCR promised to coordinate information better among its various regional offices.

The clarification letter of 2003 solidified the tremendous changes that women's sport has seen since this 1922 crew team suited up and climbed into their shell.

The long and belabored debate was finally over. Title IX, including the proportionality prong, is clear, enforceable, applicable, and unchanged. The *NCAA News* ran its story on the issuance of the 2003 further clarification under the headline "Department of Education Closes the Book on Title IX."[25] NCAA President Myles Brand noted in the article that "All young women and men engaged in athletics have reason to cheer today . . . [a]nd all of us who support their athletics endeavors, myself proudly included, should join in their celebration." President Brand is correct. Finally, 31 years after the enactment of Title IX, only those who choose to be blind and deaf or those of unabated ill will would continue to debate Title IX requirements rather than find ways to move expeditiously toward compliance. The "same old debate" was finally over.

IN BRIEF

This chapter brings the process of really knowing Title IX full circle and up to date. A timeline might serve as the best review:

- June 23, 1972—Title IX is enacted into law (20 U.S.C. Section 1681 et seq.).
- 1974—The Tower amendment proposes to delete "revenue-producing" sports from Title IX jurisdiction and calculations. The amendment died in committee.
- 1974—The Javits amendment is added to Title IX. The amendment directed that regulations, when issued, must include language that would provide "reasonable provisions considering the nature of particular sports." In other words, the regulations would need to recognize that some sports require greater cost to outfit partici-pants, some sports involve more officials, and so forth, and that such differences do not, by themselves, constitute a variance of support that would trigger a Title IX problem.
- 1975—H.R. 8394 is introduced. The bill proposed that any revenue generated by a sport could be used first to offset any expenses of the generating sport before being shared with any other part of the athletic program's budget or other sport. Thus, the bill proposed that a sport that generated money could generate all it could spend before it would face any Title IX compliance issues. The bill died in committee.

  1975—Regulations are signed into law by President Ford (34 C.F.R. 106). The regulations included provisions relating to athletics as well as general areas of education. Colleges did not need to comply with Title IX before 1978.
- 1975—Senate bill 2146, proposed by Senator Helms, attempts to remove jurisdiction of Title IX regulations from all of the nation's athletic programs unless an institution required all of its students, as part of their curriculum requirements, to participate in athlet-ics. The bill was also reintroduced six months later, but the Senate refused to act on either version.
- 1978—HEW asks for comments about its proposed method of assessing compliance, which includes a proposal that compli-ance would be presumed if substantially equal expenditures per capita went to its male and female athletes and future expansion of opportunities for women. This was known as the presumption of compliance standard. The final policy interpretations issued at the conclusion of debate about various HEW proposals did not include the presumption of compliance standard.
- 1978—All postsecondary schools are supposed to be in compliance with Title IX regulations.

- 1979—HEW issues a policy interpretation focusing mainly on athletics. This marks the birth of the three-prong test for determining whether a school is in compliance with the requirement to provide appropriate participation opportunities.
- 1984—The U.S. Supreme Court decides *Grove City v Bell*, which tells us that (1) even indirect federal funding can trigger Title IX jurisdiction and (2) Title IX jurisdiction applies only to the subunit within the institution that actually receives federal funding. Thus, although the first is good news for broad application of Title IX as a tool to counter sex discrimination, the second effectively removes all collegiate-level athletics programs from Title IX jurisdiction. High schools were less affected by *Grove City* because federal money generally comes into the institution's general operating budget rather than to a specific department within the institution.
- 1988—The Civil Rights Restoration Act of 1987 is enacted over the veto of President Reagan. The CRRA, in effect, redefines the Title IX word "program" to mean institution-wide rather than subunit. Thus, the act removed the negative effect of the second part of the *Grove City* decision, and college athletics were again under the jurisdiction of Title IX.
- 1990—The Office for Civil Rights issues Title IX *Investigator's Manual* to aid OCR employees in evaluating an institution's compliance.
- 1992—The *Franklin v Gwinnett County Public Schools* decision by the U.S. Supreme Court unanimously supports the notion that compensatory and punitive damages may be available in Title IX cases of intentional sex discrimination. The Court makes it clear that 20 years after enactment of Title IX, violations by an athletic program are probably intentional.
- 1992—The NCAA, 20 years after enactment of Title IX, completes its first comprehensive study on the status of female athletes within its member institutions. The NCAA acknowledges the widespread discrimination that professionals and participants had recognized for years.
- 1992 onward—A long line of Title IX cases alleging discrimination in access to participation continues, with decisions typically in favor of the plaintiff female athletes. The three-prong test for participation first found in the policy interpretations issued in 1979 is a focus of many of these cases and is upheld as a valid measure. The issuance of the policy interpretations, by extension, is validated as

a legal exercise of HEW's powers. Additionally, a long line of cases brought by representatives of men's teams facing retrenchment makes it clear that although administrators abdicate educational principles when they retrench men's teams to alter participation ratios rather than honor the mission of athletics participation on campuses, they do not violate Title IX.

- 1994—The Equity in Athletics Disclosure Act (EADA) is enacted. EADA causes more information to be available concerning a variety of campus decisions and their results regarding gender equity.
- 1995—The House Subcommittee on Postsecondary Education holds hearings at the behest of Representative Hastert. A major focus of the hearings is the three-prong test for participation found in the policy interpretations, which were issued 16 years previously. The hearings produced no change.
- 1996—OCR issues a clarification letter not to rework the three-prong test but to reassert and remind institutions of the content of the three-prong test as found in the policy interpretations. OCR has a legal right to issue a clarification where there appears to be a need to explain a valid regulation or policy interpretation.
- 2001-2002—Several high-profile cases claim, by various means, that the cancellation of a men's team by an institution desiring to play the "numbers game" instead of expanding athletics opportunities for its students, is, besides being a poor administrative decision, a violation of Title IX. The cases were not successful.
- February 2002—The National Wrestling Coaches Association (NWCA) files a lawsuit against the Department of Education in the U.S. District Court in Washington, D.C., claiming that the now 23-year-old policy interpretation (source of the three-prong test) was invalid.
- February 2002—Confirmation hearings are held on Gerald Reynolds, proposed by President Bush to be assistant secretary for OCR.
- March 2002—Before the Senate makes a decision on the confirmation of Reynolds, President Bush uses a recess appointment as a vehicle to circumvent the confirmation process and thereby appoints Reynolds.
- May 2002—The Department of Justice, answering for the Department of Education, files its response to the NWCA lawsuit, basing its response not on the validity of the three-prong test but on procedural issues.

- June 2002—The National Wrestling Coaches Association (NWCA) files a cross-motion asking that the Department of Education be ordered to withdraw the 1979 policy interpretations and the 1996 clarification letter.
- June 2002—Reynolds announces the formation of the Commission on Opportunities in Athletics.
- September 2002—Representative Patsy Mink, Hawaii, one of the creators of Title IX, dies.
- November 2002—The Commission on Opportunities in Athletics ends its public comment forums. It expends $700,000 for its work.
- February 2003—The commission issues its report. Secretary of Education Paige says that he will only move forward with the unanimous 15 recommendations (out of 23 recommendations) by the commission.
- June 11, 2003—The National Wrestling Coaches Association (NWCA) lawsuit against the Department of Education is dismissed.
- July 11, 2003—Gerald Reynolds issues the *2003 Further Clarification of Intercollegiate Athletics Policy Guidance Regarding Title IX Compliance*, which reaffirms Title IX and the three-prong test for measuring participation opportunities, thereby finally ending the debate about Title IX enforcement generally and the three-prong test for participation opportunities particularly.
- August 15, 2003—The College Sports Council, a group including the National Wrestling Coaches Association (NWCA), announces that they will file an appeal of the June 11, 2003, dismissal of the "wrestlers" case, despite lack of apparent substantive grounds.[26]
- May 2004—The "wrestlers" appeal is denied.

Three Questions and Three Answers

1. **Is it illegal to terminate a men's team and blame it on gender equity?**

    The action is legal, but the blame is usually misplaced, and the original decision is usually misguided. If the policy interpretations, the long line of "wrestlers" lawsuits against individual institutions, the 1996 clarification letter, and the class-action "wrestlers" lawsuit against the Department of Education left questions among administrators or team members about whether terminating men's teams was legal, the 2003 further clarification letter should surely settle the matter. Terminating men's teams to manipulate the ratio of male to female athletes so that it more closely matches the ratio of the general student body is legal even if it is not a good idea.

2. **Why wasn't the "wrestlers" class-action lawsuit against the Department of Education successful?**

The plaintiffs were associations and as such lacked legal standing in this particular case. Also, although the Department of Education is capable of being sued successfully, the "wrestlers" case failed largely because it did not identify how the Department of Education could do anything to either stop or remedy the injury allegedly perpetrated on the individual wrestlers, swimmers, and gymnasts or their teams.

3. **State universities that violate the Americans with Disabilities Act (ADA) cannot be sued in federal court for those violations because of the immunity found in the United States Constitution's 11th Amendment. Does the 11th Amendment also mean that Title IX cannot be enforced by a lawsuit in federal court?**

No. The courts have not dealt with the question of the 11th Amendment in relation to Title IX. Abrogation of the 11th Amendment immunity enjoyed by states requires specific elements such as a showing that Congress intended to have states liable for violations of a particular statute. Congress can show its intent expressly in the statutory language or impliedly by including in the legislative history created contemporaneously with the passage of a particular statute pursuant to its powers under the 14th Amendment information that can be successfully interpreted by the courts to carry with it that intent. Among the items that provide evidence of implied intent to dispense with 11th Amendment immunity are a showing of a pattern of discrimination on the part of the state and a showing that the remedy imposed by Congress for violation of the particular statute is "congruent and proportional to the targeted violation."[27] The Family and Medical Leave Act has been found to abrogate 11th Amendment immunity, but the ADA and the Age Discrimination in Employment Act of 1967 have been found not to abrogate it, thus leaving states immune from suit in federal court for violating either of those last two statutes. Title IX was enacted with little legislative history. Evidence of state discrimination, however, existed contemporaneously to its passage. Furthermore, it might be easily argued that the remedies imposed for violations of Title IX are "congruent and proportional to the targeted violation." So, at the moment, the issue of 11th Amendment immunity and Title IX has not been litigated. If it were to be litigated, we are willing to look into our crystal ball and prophesy that Title IX would be found to carry with it an abrogation of 11th Amendment immunity, thereby retaining for plaintiffs the right to sue state entities in federal court such as state universities for violations of Title IX.

NOTES

[1]See *Board of Trustees of the University of Alabama v Patricia Garrett*, 531 U.S. 356, 121 S. Ct. 955 (2001), which is the landmark case on the issue of relating to the 11th Amendment and the ADA.

[2]Some states that have some sort of legislation similar to Title IX (some are rudimentary) are Alaska, California, Florida, Georgia, Hawaii, Illinois, Iowa, Maine, Minnesota, Nebraska, New Jersey, New York, Rhode Island, South Dakota, Washington, and Wisconsin.

[3]Average roster size for college football teams used to exceed 120 players plus support staff. Recently, the number of scholarships given in Division I per school has declined by about one-third. Professional football teams typically field a squad of only 48 players.

[4]During the period from 1984 to 1988, Title IX did not have jurisdiction over intercollegiate athletics, yet men's minor sports teams were still being canceled. Were they being canceled because of waning interest or to transfer their minimal resources to the ever voracious football programs?

[5]For cases about the issue of whether Title IX prohibits institutions from capping or terminating men's teams see, among others, *Cohen v Brown University*, 101 F. 3d 155 (1st Cir. 1996), 520 U.S. 1186 (1997) cert. denied; *Williams v School Dist. of Bethlehem*, 998 F. 2d 168 (3d Cir. 1993); *Boulahanis v Board of Regents*, 198 F. 3d 633 (7th Cir. 1999), 530 U.S. 1284 (2000) cert. denied; *Neal v Board of Trustees of California State Universities*, 198 F. 3d 763 (9th Cir. 1999); *Miami Univ. Wrestling Club v Miami University*, 302 F. 3d at 609-10; *Chalenor et al. v Univ. of N.D.*, 291 F. 3d at 1042 (8th Cir. 2002); *Kelley v Board of Trustees, University of Illinois*, 35 F. 3d 265 (7th Cir. 1994), 531 U.S. 1128 (1995) cert. denied.

[6]No "similarly situated plaintiffs have directly challenged the validity of the 1975 Regulations, the 1979 Policy Interpretations, or 1996 Clarification by way of an action brought against the Department of Education, or its predecessor HEW" (*National Wrestling Coaches Association v United States Department of Education*, 263 F. Supp. 2d 882 [D.C. Cir. 2003]).

[7]Representative Dennis Hastert had been inducted into the Wrestling Hall of Fame and among other wrestling connections had been a president of the National Wrestling Coaches Association.

[8]Both the defendant (the enforcement agency) and the plaintiffs in the case were unusual. The plaintiffs, instead of being a specific team or a group of individuals, were associations. The associational nature of the plaintiffs added what was to become an insurmountable barrier to successful progress of the lawsuit.

[9]See *Steel Co. v Citizens for a Better Environment*, 523 U.S. 83 (1998) and *Lujan v Defenders of Wildlife*, 504 U.S. 555 (1992) for good discussions of the application of Article III's standing requirements to associations and organizations.

[10]The "wrestlers" case involved the actions and decisions of third parties—those on each campus who make decisions about which teams to maintain and which to terminate. The court in the "wrestlers" case in quoting *Lujan*, 504 U.S. 555 (1992) said, "[w]hen . . . a plaintiff's injury arises from the government's allegedly unlawful regulation . . . of someone else . . . causation and redressability ordinarily hinge on the response of the regulated . . . third party to the government action. . . . The existence of . . . standing depends on the unfettered choices made by independent actors not before the courts . . . whose exercise of broad and legitimate discretion the courts cannot presume to control or predict, and it becomes the burden of the plaintiff to adduce facts showing that those choices have been or will be made in such a manner as to produce causation and permit redressability of injury."

[11]The "wrestlers" case makes interesting and informative reading, regardless of the simplicity of the outcome. The court discussed not only the issue of standing but, in large measure, put to rest the substantive questions the case would have raised if it had been allowed to proceed. For instance, the "wrestlers" had contended that all parts of the three-part test discriminate against males because, they claimed, males have a greater interest in athletics than do females. The court makes clear that the "greater interest" argument is on shaky ground and that in any case, Title IX and its regulations were drafted in such a way as to allow the historically underrepresented sex to be protected with greater vigor than the historically overrepresented sex. The "wrestlers" court quotes another "wrestlers" case lost earlier in the year, *Miami University Wrestling Club v Miami University*, 302 F. 3d at 615 when it noted that Title IX "focuses on opportunities for the underrepresented gender, and does not bestow rights on the historically overrepresented gender." The *Cohen v Brown University* case discussed in chapter 7 also addresses the issue by saying, "It would require blinders to ignore that the motivation for the promulgation of the regulation on athletics was the historic emphasis on boys' athletic programs to the exclusion of girls' athletic programs in high schools as well as colleges" (*Cohen* II, 101 F. 3d at 175, which was also quoting *Williams v Sch. Dist. of Bethlehem*, 998 F. 2d at 175).

[12]The "wrestlers" announced on August 15, 2003, that they would appeal the dismissal. A careful reading of the court's published opinion in the June 11, 2003, dismissal leaves no or little room for appeal, and thus it seems likely that any continued effort on the part of the "wrestlers" in this regard is futile and ill advised.

[13]The 1996 clarification letter appears in appendix C.

[14]A debate of the various factors contributing to the formation of the commission might use as fodder the following issues:

*Lack of Title IX enforcement by OCR over the decades

*Poor administrative decisions by athletic directors and top administrators, such as terminating men's teams rather than increasing women's opportunities

*Failure to tackle football and its favored position in the hierarchy of athletics

*Failure to reform administrative decision-making processes relating to athletics on campus

*Discovery that inviting women to the table might mean that men eat a bit less

*Delay in dealing with equity issues for years

*A cadre of misinformed and gullible people large enough to be manipulated

*Fan base encouraged by athletic directors to remain sport specific in loyalty instead of developing programwide loyalty

*Lip service by college presidents to the misguided belief that football will produce future revenue and thereby support the mission of the institution

*Power base in federal government who believed themselves to be unrestrainable

*Power base in government emboldened by sense of the "macho"

*Power base in government who believed that life is about the score, not the cost and not the right

Perhaps some or all of the preceding were part of the recipe for the creation of the commission. Certainly, the commission was born in times of turmoil and frustration.

[15]See the syllabus, *Title IX Briefing Book*, Good Sports Inc., November 2002, for a strong point of view regarding whether the commission and its charge would cover new or old ground.

[16]See Ellen Staurowsky's article "The Title IX Commission's Flawed Lineup," *Chronicle of Higher Education*, February 14, 2003, for one person's point of view about the commission's membership. For a list of commission members and their overall points of view about how Title IX might be changed (following the hearing process), see "Federal Panelists' Ideas for Changing Title IX," *Chronicle of Higher Education*, January 3, 2003, A43.

[17]The Web site www.aahperd.org/nagws/template.cfm?template=title9/ main.html provides a full range of resources relating to the commission, its proceedings, and the position papers submitted to it. For a review of two of the major position papers, look also at the following Web sites:

www.aahperd.org/nagws/template.cfm?template=titleix_papers.html

www.womenssportsfoundation.org/cgibin/iowa/issues/rights/ article.html?record=914

[18]Transcripts of the commission's hearings can be found at www.ed.gov/about/ BOSCOMM/LIST/athletics/transcripts.html as well as at www.aahperd.org/ nagws/template.cfm?template=title9/bush.html.

[19]For a collection of views see Suggs, Welch, "Cheers and Condemnation Greet Report on Gender Equity," *Chronicle of Higher Education*, March 7, 2003.

[20]See also Suggs, Welch, "Cheers and Condemnation Greet Report on Gender Equity," *Chronicle of Higher Education*, March 7, 2003.

[21]A full copy of the final report is available on the Internet at www.ed.gov/about/ BOSCOMM/LIST/athletics/report.html.

[22]The headlines demonstrate the breadth of opinions: "Title IX Panel Debates Major Changes, but Endorses Few," *Chronicle of Higher Education,* January 31, 2003; "A Good Law Whose Time Has Passed," *New York Times,* January 31, 2003; "Advocates for Men's and Women's Sports Trade Charges as Title IX Panel Gets Ready to Vote," *Chronicle of Higher Education,* January 29, 2003; "Title IX Plans Assailed as Broad and Harmful," *New York Times,* February 1, 2003; "Advisory Panel Backs Easing Rules for Title IX," *New York Times,* January 31, 2003; "Women's Groups Castigate Education Department for Actions of Title IX Commission," *Chronicle of Higher Education,* December 20, 2002.

[23]"The Minority Views on the Report of the Commission on Opportunity in Athletics" was submitted in February 2003 by two commission members, Donna de Varona and Julie Foudy. The minority report reflected a "disagreement with the tenor, structure and significant portions of the content of the Commission's report, which fails to present a full and fair consideration of the issues or a clear statement of the discrimination women and girls still face in obtaining equal opportunity in athletics . . . [and] our belief that many of the recommendations made by the majority would seriously weaken Title IX's protections and substantially reduce the opportunities to which women and girls are entitled under current law; . . . [and] that only one of the proposals would address the budgetary causes underlying the discontinuation of some men's teams, and that others would not restore opportunities that have been lost" (p. 1). The report provides a review of participation data to bolster its point of view and one by one tracks the recommendations of the full report of the commission.

[24]The transcripts as well as all related commission documents are available at http://ed.gov/search results.jhtml?oq=commission+on+athletics+opportunities& rq=1&tx=transcripts.

[25]See the July 21, 2003, issue of the *NCAA News* for a full review, through the eyes of NCAA President Brand, of the further clarification. The issue is available online at www.ncaa.org.

[26]See Suggs, Welch, "Men's Sports Coaches Announce New Challenge to Title IX Guidelines," *Chronicle of Higher Education,* August 18, 2003.

[27]*Board of Trustees of University of Alabama v Patricia Garrett,* 531 U.S. 356, 121 S. Ct. 148 (2001) involves the ADA and the 11th Amendment. See 356. See also *Nevada Department of Human Resources v Hibbs,* 123 S. Ct. 1972 (2003), which involved the Family and Medical Leave Act. One of the earlier cases relating to the 11th Amendment was *Seminole Tribe of Florida v Florida,* 517 U.S. 44, 116 S. Ct. 1114 (1996). The dissent in the close 5-4 *Seminole* decision makes a strong appeal for the abrogation of the 11th Amendment immunity in many instances.

APPENDIX A

Title IX Regulations

Note: *The following regulations have been abridged for purposes of brevity.*

Federal Register on November 13, 2000, 65 *Fed. Reg.* 68050

Part 106—Nondiscrimination on the Basis of Sex in Education Programs or Activities Receiving Federal Financial Assistance

Subpart A—Introduction

106.1 Purpose and effective date.

106.2 Definitions.

106.3 Remedial and affirmative action and self-evaluation.

106.4 Assurance required.

106.5 Transfers of property.

106.6 Effect of other requirements.

106.7 Effect of employment opportunities.

106.8 Designation of responsible employee and adoption of grievance procedures.

106.9 Dissemination of policy.

Subpart B—Coverage

106.11 Application.

106.12 Educational institutions controlled by religious organizations.

106.13 Military and merchant marine educational institutions.

106.14 Membership practices of certain organizations.

106.15 Admissions.

106.16 Educational institutions eligible to submit transition plans.

106.17 Transition plans.

Subpart C—Discrimination on the Basis of Sex in Admission and Recruitment Prohibited

106.21 Admission.

106.22 Preference in admission.

106.23 Recruitment.

Subpart D—Discrimination on the Basis of Sex in Education Programs or Activities Prohibited

106.31 Education programs or activities.

106.32 Housing.

106.33 Comparable facilities.

106.34 Access to course offerings.

106.35 Access to schools operated by LEAs.

106.36 Counseling and use of appraisal and counseling materials.

106.37 Financial assistance.

106.38 Employment assistance to students.

106.39 Health and insurance benefits and services.

106.40 Marital or parental status.

106.41 Athletics.

106.42 Textbooks and curricular material.

Subpart E—Discrimination on the Basis of Sex in Employment in Education Programs or Activities Prohibited

106.51 Employment.

106.52 Employment criteria.

106.53 Recruitment.

106.54 Compensation.

106.55 Job classification and structure.

106.56 Fringe benefits.

106.57 Marital or parental status.

106.58 Effect of State or local law or other requirements.

106.59 Advertising.

106.60 Pre-employment inquiries.

106.61 Sex as a bona-fide occupational qualification.

Subpart F—Procedures [Interim]

106.71 Procedures

Subpart A—Introduction

[Items not of significance to the scope of this book are deleted.]

106.2 Definitions.

As used in this part, the term:

(a) *Title IX* means title IX of the Education Amendments of 1972, Pub. L. 92-318, as amended by section 3 of Pub. L. 93-568, 88 Stat. 1855, except sections 904 and 906 thereof; 20 U.S.C. 1681, 1682, 1683, 1685, 1686.

(g) *Federal financial assistance* means any of the following, when authorized or extended under a law administered by the Department:

(1) A grant or loan of Federal financial assistance, including funds made available for:

(i) The acquisition, construction, renovation, restoration, or repair of a building or facility or any portion thereof; and

(ii) Scholarships, loans, grants, wages or other funds extended to any entity for payment to or on behalf of students admitted to that entity, or extended directly to such students for payment to that entity.

(2) A grant of Federal real or personal property . . .

(3) Provision of the services of Federal personnel.

(5) Any other contract, agreement, or arrangement which has as one of its purposes the provision of assistance to any education program or activity, except a contract of insurance or guaranty.

(h) *Program or activity* and *program* means all of the operations of

(1) (i) A department, agency, special purpose district, or other instrumentality of a State or local government; or . . .

(2) (i) A college, university, or other postsecondary institution, or a public system of higher education; or . . .

(ii) A local educational agency (as defined in 20 U.S.C. 8801), system of vocational education, or other school system;

(3) (i) An entire corporation, partnership, other private organization, or an entire sole proprietorship—

(A) If assistance is extended to such corporation, partnership, private organization, or sole proprietorship as a whole; or

(B) Which is principally engaged in the business of providing education, health care, housing, social services, or parks and recreation; or . . .

(i) *Recipient* means any State or political subdivision thereof, or any instrumentality of a State or political subdivision thereof, any public or private agency, institution, or organization, or other entity, or any person, to whom Federal financial assistance is extended directly or through another recipient and which operates an education program or activity which receives such assistance, including any subunit, successor, assignee, or transferee thereof.

106.3 Remedial and affirmative action and self-evaluation.

106.4 Assurance required.

106.5 Transfers of property.

106.6 Effect of other requirements.

(c) *Effect of rules or regulations of private organizations.* The obligation to comply with this part is not obviated or alleviated by any rule or regulation of any organization, club, athletic or other league, or association which would render any applicant or student ineligible to participate or limit the eligibility or participation of any applicant or student, on the basis of sex, in any education program or activity operated by a recipient and which receives Federal financial assistance.

106.7 Effect of employment opportunities.

The obligation to comply with this part is not obviated or alleviated because employment opportunities in any occupation or profession are or may be more limited for members of one sex than for members of the other sex.

106.8 Designation of responsible employee and adoption of grievance procedures.

(a) *Designation of responsible employee.* Each recipient shall designate at least one employee to coordinate its efforts to comply with and carry out its responsibilities under this part, including any investigation of any complaint communicated to such recipient alleging its noncompliance with this part or alleging any actions which would be prohibited by this part. The recipient shall notify all its students and employees of the name, office address and telephone number of the employee or employees appointed pursuant to this paragraph.

106.9 Dissemination of policy.

Subpart B—Coverage

[Items not of significance to the scope of this book are deleted.]

106.14 Membership practices of certain organizations.

(a) *Social fraternities and sororities.* This part does not apply to the membership practices of social fraternities and sororities which are exempt from taxation under section 501(a) of the Internal Revenue Code of 1954, the active membership of which consists primarily of students in attendance at institutions of higher education.

(b) *YMCA, YWCA, Girl Scouts, Boy Scouts and Camp Fire Girls.* This part does not apply to the membership practices . . .

(c) *Voluntary youth service organizations.* This part does not apply to the membership practices of voluntary youth service organizations which are exempt from taxation . . . and the membership of which has been traditionally limited to members of one sex and principally to persons of less than nineteen years of age.

Subpart C—Discrimination on the Basis of Sex in Admission and Recruitment Prohibited

[Items not of significance to the scope of this book are deleted.]

106.21 Admission.

(a) *General.* No person shall, on the basis of sex, be denied admission, or be subjected to discrimination in admission, by any recipient to which this subpart applies, except as provided in . . .

(b) *Specific prohibitions* . . .

(i) Give preference to one person over another on the basis of sex, by ranking applicants separately on such basis, or otherwise;

(ii) Apply numerical limitations upon the number or proportion of persons of either sex who may be admitted; or

(iii) Otherwise treat one individual differently from another on the basis of sex.

(2) A recipient shall not administer or operate any test or other criterion for admission which has a disproportionately adverse effect on persons on the basis of sex unless the use of such test or criterion is shown to predict validly success in the education program or activity in question and alternative tests or criteria which do not have such a disproportionately adverse effect are shown to be unavailable.

(c) *Prohibitions relating to marital or parental status.* In determining whether a person satisfies any policy or criterion for admission, or in making any offer of admission, a recipient to which this subpart applies:

(1) Shall not apply any rule concerning the actual or potential parental, family, or marital status of a student or applicant which treats persons differently on the basis of sex;

(2) Shall not discriminate against or exclude any person on the basis of pregnancy, childbirth, termination of pregnancy, or recovery therefrom, or establish or follow any rule or practice which so discriminates or excludes;

(3) Shall treat disabilities related to pregnancy, childbirth, termination of pregnancy, or recovery therefrom in the same manner and under the same policies as any other temporary disability or physical condition; and

(4) Shall not make pre-admission inquiry as to the marital status of an applicant for admission, including whether such applicant is "Miss" or "Mrs." A recipient may make pre-admission inquiry as to the sex of an applicant for admission, but only if such inquiry is made equally of such applicants of both sexes and if the results of such inquiry are not used in connection with discrimination prohibited by this part.

106.23 Recruitment.

(a) *Nondiscriminatory recruitment.* A recipient to which this subpart applies shall not discriminate on the basis of sex in the recruitment and admission of students. . . .

Subpart D—Discrimination on the Basis of Sex in Education Programs or Activities Prohibited

[Items not of significance to the scope of this book are deleted.]

106.31 Education programs or activities.

(a) *General.* Except as provided elsewhere in this part, no person shall, on the basis of sex, be excluded from participation in, be denied the benefits of, or be subjected to discrimination under any academic, extracurricular, research, occupational training, or other education program or activity operated by a recipient which receives Federal financial assistance.

(b) *Specific prohibitions.* Except as provided in this subpart, in providing any aid, benefit, or service to a student, a recipient shall not, on the basis of sex:

(1) Treat one person differently from another in determining whether such person satisfies any requirement or condition for the provision of such aid, benefit, or service;

(2) Provide different aid, benefits, or services or provide aid, benefits, or services in a different manner;

(3) Deny any person any such aid, benefit, or service;

(4) Subject any person to separate or different rules of behavior, sanctions, or other treatment;

(5) Apply any rule concerning the domicile or residence of a student or applicant, including eligibility for in-state fees and tuition;

(6) Aid or perpetuate discrimination against any person by providing significant assistance to any agency, organization, or person which discriminates on the basis of sex in providing any aid, benefit or service to students or employees;

106.33 Comparable facilities.

A recipient may provide separate toilet, locker room, and shower facilities on the basis of sex, but such facilities provided for students of one sex shall be comparable to such facilities provided for students of the other sex.

106.34 Access to course offerings.

A recipient shall not provide any course or otherwise carry out any of its education program or activity separately on the basis of sex, or require or refuse participation therein by any of its students on such basis, including health, physical education, industrial, business, vocational, technical, home economics, music, and adult education courses.

(b) This section does not prohibit grouping of students in physical education classes and activities by ability as assessed by objective standards of individual performance developed and applied without regard to sex.

(c) This section does not prohibit separation of students by sex within physical education classes or activities during participation in wrestling, boxing, rugby, ice hockey, football, basketball and other sports the purpose or major activity of which involves bodily contact.

(d) Where use of a single standard of measuring skill or progress in a physical education class has an adverse effect on members of one sex, the recipient shall use appropriate standards which do not have such effect.

(e) Portions of classes in elementary and secondary schools which deal exclusively with human sexuality may be conducted in separate sessions for boys and girls.

106.37 Financial assistance.

(a) *General.* Except as provided in paragraphs (b) and (c) of this section, in providing financial assistance to any of its students, a recipient shall not:

(1) On the basis of sex, provide different amount or types of such assistance, limit eligibility for such assistance which is of any particular type or source, apply different criteria, or otherwise discriminate;

(2) Through solicitation, listing, approval, provision of facilities or other services, assist any foundation, trust, agency, organization, or person which provides assistance to any of such recipient's students in a manner which discriminates on the basis of sex; or

(3) Apply any rule or assist in application of any rule concerning eligibility for such assistance which treats persons of one sex differently from persons of the other sex with regard to marital or parental status.

(b) *Financial aid established by certain legal instruments.*

(c) *Athletic scholarships.* (1) To the extent that a recipient awards athletic scholarships or grants-in-aid, it must provide reasonable opportunities for such awards for members of each sex in proportion to the number of students of each sex participating in interscholastic or intercollegiate athletics.

(2) Separate athletic scholarships or grants-in-aid for members of each sex may be provided as part of separate athletic teams for members of each sex to the extent consistent with this paragraph and 106.41.

106.41 Athletics.

(a) *General.* No person shall, on the basis of sex, be excluded from participation in, be denied the benefits of, be treated differently from another person or otherwise be discriminated against in any interscholastic, intercollegiate, club or intramural athletics offered by a recipient, and no recipient shall provide any such athletics separately on such basis.

(b) *Separate teams.* Notwithstanding the requirements of paragraph (a) of this section, a recipient may operate or sponsor separate teams for members of each sex where selection for such teams is based upon competitive skill or the activity involved is a contact sport. However, where a recipient operates or sponsors a team in a particular sport for members of one sex but operates or sponsors no such team for members of the other sex, and athletic opportunities for members of that sex have previously been limited, members of the excluded sex must be allowed to try-out for the team offered unless the sport involved is a contact sport. For the purposes of this part, contact sports include boxing, wrestling, rugby, ice hockey, football, basketball and other sports the purpose or major activity of which involves bodily contact.

(c) *Equal opportunity.* A recipient which operates or sponsors inter-scholastic, intercollegiate, club or intramural athletics shall provide equal athletic opportunity for members of both sexes. In determining whether equal opportunities are available the Director will consider, among other factors:

(1) Whether the selection of sports and levels of competition effectively accommodate the interests and abilities of members of both sexes;

(2) The provision of equipment and supplies;

(3) Scheduling of games and practice time;

(4) Travel and per diem allowance;

(5) Opportunity to receive coaching and academic tutoring;

(6) Assignment and compensation of coaches and tutors;

(7) Provision of locker rooms, practice and competitive facilities;

(8) Provision of medical and training facilities and services;

(9) Provision of housing and dining facilities and services;

(10) Publicity.

Unequal aggregate expenditures for members of each sex or unequal expenditures for male and female teams if a recipient operates or sponsors separate teams will not constitute noncompliance with this section, but the Assistant Secretary may consider the failure to provide necessary funds for teams for one sex in assessing equality of opportunity for members of each sex.

Subpart E—Discrimination on the Basis of Sex in Employment in Education Programs or Activities Prohibited

[Items not of significance to the scope of this book are deleted.]

106.51 Employment.

(a) *General.* (1) No person shall, on the basis of sex, be excluded from participation in, be denied the benefits of, or be subjected to discrimination in employment, or recruitment, consideration, or selection therefore, whether full-time or part-time, under any education program or activity operated by a recipient which receives Federal financial assistance.

106.61 Sex as a bona-fide occupational qualification.

A recipient may take action otherwise prohibited by this subpart provided it is shown that sex is a bona-fide occupational qualification for that action, such that consideration of sex with regard to such action is essential to successful operation of the employment function concerned. A recipient shall not take action pursuant to this section which is based upon alleged comparative employment characteristics or stereotyped characterizations of one or the other sex, or upon preference based on sex of the recipient, employees, students, or other persons, but nothing contained in this section shall prevent a recipient from considering an employee's sex in relation to employment in a locker room or toilet facility used only by members of one sex.

APPENDIX B

Policy Interpretation: Title IX and Intercollegiate Athletics

Note: *The policy interpretations that follow have been abridged for purposes of brevity.*

Federal Register, vol. 44, no. 239, Tuesday, Dec. 11, 1979

III. Scope of Application

This Policy Interpretation is designed specifically for intercollegiate athletics. However, its general principles will often apply to club, intramural, and interscholastic athletic programs, which are also covered by regulation. Accordingly, the Policy Interpretation may be used for guidance by the administrators of such programs when appropriate.

IV. Summary of Final Policy Interpretation

The Policy Interpretation is divided into three sections:

- Compliance in Financial Assistance (Scholarships) Based on Athletic Ability: Pursuant to the regulation, the governing principle in this area is that all such assistance should be available on a substantially proportional basis to the number of male and female participants in the institution's athletic program.

- Compliance in Other Program Areas (Equipment and supplies; games and practice times; travel and per diem, coaching and academic tutoring; assignment and compensation of coaches and tutors; locker rooms, and practice and competitive facilities; medical and training facilities; housing and dining facilities; publicity; recruitment; and support services): Pursuant to the regulation, the governing principle is that male and female athletes should receive equivalent treatment, benefits, and opportunities.

- Compliance in Meeting the Interests and Abilities of Male and Female Students: Pursuant to the regulation, the governing principle in this area is that the athletic interests and abilities of male and female students must be equally effectively accommodated.

VII. The Policy Interpretation

This Policy Interpretation clarifies the obligations which recipients of Federal aid have under Title IX to provide equal opportunities in athletic programs. In particular, this Policy Interpretation provides a means to assess an institution's compliance with the equal opportunity requirements of the regulation which are set forth at 45 CFR 88.37(c) and 88.4a(c).

A. Athletic Financial Assistance (Scholarships)

1. The Regulation. Section 86.37(c) of the regulation provides:

[Institutions] must provide reasonable opportunities for such award (of financial assistance) for member[s] of each sex in proportion to the number of students of each sex participating in inter-collegiate athletics.

2. The Policy: The Department will examine compliance with this provision of the regulation primarily by means of a financial comparison to determine whether proportionately equal amounts of financial assistance (scholarship aid) are available to men's and women's athletic programs. The Department will measure compliance with this standard by dividing the amounts of aid available for the members of each sex by the numbers of male or female participants in the athletic program and comparing the results. Institutions may be found in compliance if this comparison results in substantially equal amounts or if a resulting disparity can be explained by adjustments to take into account legitimate, nondiscriminatory factors. Two such factors are:

a. At public institutions, the higher costs of tuition for students from out of state may in some years be unevenly distributed between men's and women's programs. These differences will be considered nondiscriminatory if they are not the result of policies or practices which disproportionately limit the availability of out-of-state scholarships to either men or women.

b. An institution may make reasonable professional decisions concerning the awards most appropriate for program development. For example, team development initially may require spreading scholarships over as much as a full generation (four years) of student athletes. This may result in the award of fewer scholarships in the first few years than would be necessary to create proportionality between male and female athletes.

3. Application of the Policy

a. This section does not require a proportionate number of scholarships for men and women or individual scholarships of equal dollar value. It does mean that the total amount of scholarship aid made available to men and women must be substantially proportionate to their participation rates.

b. When financial assistance is provided in forms other than grants, the distribution of non-grant assistance will also be compared to determine whether equivalent benefits are proportionately available to male and female athletes. A disproportionate amount of work-related aid or loans in the assistance made available to the members of one sex, for example, could constitute a violation of Title IX.

4. Definition: For purposes of examining compliance with this Section, the participants will be defined as those athletes:

a. Who are receiving the institutionally-sponsored support normally provided to athletes competing at the institution involved, e.g., coaching, equipment, medical and training room services, on a regular basis during a sport's season; and

b. Who are participating in organized practice sessions and other team meetings and activities on a regular basis during a sport's season; and

c. Who are listed on the eligibility or squad lists maintained for each sport; or

d. Who, because of injury, cannot meet a, b, or c above but continue to receive financial aid on the basis of athletic ability.

B. Equivalence in Other Athletic Benefits and Opportunities

1. The Regulation: The Regulation requires that recipients that operate or sponsor interscholastic, intercollegiate, club or intramural athletics "provide equal athletic opportunities for members of both sexes." In determining whether an institution is providing equal opportunity in intercollegiate athletics the regulation requires the Department to consider, among others, the following factors:

(1) Whether the selection of sports and levels of competition effectively accommodate the interests and abilities of member of both sexes;

(2) Provision and maintenance of equipment and supplies;

(3) Scheduling of games and practice times;

(4) Travel and per diem expenses;

(5) Opportunity to receive coaching and academic tutoring;

(6) Assignment and compensation of coaches and tutors;

(7) Provision of locker rooms, practice and competitive facilities;

(8) Provision of medical and training services and facilities;

(9) Provision of housing and dining services and facilities; and

(10) Publicity.

Section 86.41(c) also permits the Director of the Office for Civil Rights to consider other factors in the determination of equal opportunity. Accordingly, this Section also addresses recruitment of student athletes and provision of support services.

This list is not exhaustive. Under the regulation, it may be expanded as necessary at the discretion of the Director of the Office for Civil Rights.

2. The Policy: The Department will assess compliance with both the recruitment and the general athletic program requirements of the regulation by comparing the availability, quality and kinds of benefits, opportunities, and treatment afforded members of both sexes. Institutions will be in compliance if the compared program components are equivalent, that is, equal or equal in effect. Under this standard, identical benefits, opportunities, or treatment are not required, provided the overall effects of any differences is negligible.

If comparisons of program components reveal that treatment, benefits, or opportunities are not equivalent in kind, quality or availability, a finding of compliance may still be justified if the differences are the result of nondiscriminatory factors. Some of the factors that may justify these differences are as follows:

a. Some aspects of athletic programs may not be equivalent for men and women because of unique aspects of particular sports or athletic activities. This type of distinction was called for by the "Javits' Amendment" to Title IX which instructed HEW to make "reasonable (regulatory) provisions considering the nature of particular sports" in intercollegiate athletics.

Generally, these differences will be the result of factors that are inherent to the basic operation of specific sports. Such factors may include rules of play, nature/replacement of equipment, rates of injury resulting from participation, nature of facilities required for competition, and the maintenance/upkeep requirements of those facilities. For the most part, differences involving such factors will occur in programs offering football, and consequently these differences will favor men. If sport-specific needs are met equivalently in both men's and women's programs, however, differences in particular program components will be found to be justifiable.

b. Some aspects of athletic programs may not be equivalent for men and women because of legitimately sex-neutral factors related to special circumstances of a temporary nature. For example, large disparities in recruitment activity for any particular year may be the result of annual fluctuations in team needs for first-year athletes. Such differences are justifiable to the extent that they do not reduce overall equality of opportunity.

c. The activities directly associated with the operation of a competitive event in a single-sex sport may, under some circumstances, create unique demands or imbalances in particular program components. Provided any special demands associated with the activities of sports involving participants of the other sex are met to an equivalent degree, the resulting differences may be found nondiscriminatory. At many schools, for example, certain sports notably football and men's basketball traditionally draw large crowds. Since the costs of managing an athletic event increase with crowd size, the overall support made available for event management to men's and women's programs may differ in degree and kind. These differences would not violate Title IX if the recipient does not limit the potential for women's athletic events to rise in spectator appeal and if the levels of event management support available to both programs are based on sex-neutral criteria (e.g., facilities used, projected attendance, and staffing needs).

d. Some aspects of athletic programs may not be equivalent for men and women because institutions are undertaking voluntary affirmative actions to overcome effects of historical conditions that have limited participation in athletics by the members of one sex. This is authorized at 86.3(b) of the regulation.

3. Application of the Policy, General Athletic Program Components

a. Equipment and Supplies (86.41(c)(2)). Equipment and supplies include but are not limited to uniforms, other apparel, sport-specific equipment and supplies, general equipment and supplies, instructional devices, and conditioning and weight training equipment.

Compliance will be assessed by examining, among other factors, the equivalence for men and women of:

(1) The quality of equipment and supplies;

(2) The amount of equipment and supplies;

(3) The suitability of equipment and supplies;

(4) The maintenance and replacement of the equipment and supplies; and

(5) The availability of equipment and supplies.

b. Scheduling of Games and Practice Times (86.41(c)(3)). Compliance will be assessed by examining, among other factors, the equivalence for men and women of:

(1) The number of competitive events per sport;

(2) The number and length of practice opportunities;

(3) The time of day competitive events are scheduled;

(4) The time of day practice opportunities are scheduled; and

(5) The opportunities to engage in available pre-season and post-season competition.

c. Travel and Per Diem Allowances (86.41(c)(4)). Compliance will be assessed by examining, among other factors, the equivalence for men and women of:

(1) Modes of transportation;

(2) Housing furnished during travel;

(3) Length of stay before and after competitive events;

(4) Per diem allowances; and

(5) Dining arrangements.

d. Opportunity to Receive Coaching and Academic Tutoring (86.41(c)(5)).

(1) Coaching—Compliance will be assessed by examining, among other factors:

(a) Relative availability of full-time coaches;

(b) Relative availability of part-time and assistant coaches; and

(c) Relative availability of graduate assistants.

(2) Academic tutoring—Compliance will be assessed by examining, among other factors, the equivalence for men and women of:

(a) The availability of tutoring; and

(b) Procedures and criteria for obtaining tutorial assistance.

e. Assignment and Compensation of Coaches and Tutors (86.41(c)(6)). In general, a violation of Section 86.41(c)(6) will be found only where compensation or assignment policies or practices deny male and female athletes coaching of equivalent quality, nature, or availability.

Nondiscriminatory factors can affect the compensation of coaches. In determining whether differences are caused by permissible factors, the range and nature of duties, the experience of individual coaches, the number of participants for particular sports, the number of assistant coaches supervised, and the level of competition will be considered.

Where these or similar factors represent valid differences in skill, effort, responsibility or working conditions they may, in specific circumstances, justify differences in compensation. Similarly, there may be unique situations in which a particular person may possess such an outstanding record of achievement as to justify an abnormally high salary.

(1) Assignment of Coaches—Compliance will be assessed by examining, among other factors, the equivalence for men's and women's coaches of:

(a) Training, experience, and other professional qualifications;

(b) Professional standing.

(2) Assignment of Tutors—Compliance will be assessed by examining, among other factors, the equivalence for men's and women's tutors of:

(a) Tutor qualifications;

(b) Training, experience, and other qualifications.

(3) Compensation of Coaches—Compliance will be assessed by examining, among other factors, the equivalence for men's and women's coaches of:

(a) Rate of compensation (per sport, per season);

(b) Duration of contracts;

(c) Conditions relating to contract renewal;

(d) Experience;

(e) Nature of coaching duties performed;

(f) Working conditions; and

(g) Other terms and conditions of employment.

(4) Compensation of Tutors—Compliance will be assessed by examining, among other factors, the equivalence for men's and women's tutors of:

(a) Hourly rate of payment by nature of subjects tutored;

(b) Pupil loads per tutoring season;

(c) Tutor qualifications;

(d) Experience;

(e) Other terms and conditions of employment.

f. Provision of Locker Rooms, Practice and Competitive Facilities (86.41(c)(7)). Compliance will be assessed by examining, among other factors, the equivalence for men and women of:

(1) Quality and availability of the facilities provided for practice and competitive events;

(2) Exclusivity of use of facilities provided for practice and competitive events;

(3) Availability of locker rooms;

(4) Quality of locker rooms;

(5) Maintenance of practice and competitive facilities; and

(6) Preparation of facilities for practice and competitive events.

g. Provision of Medical and Training Facilities and Services (86.41(c)(8)). Compliance will be assessed by examining, among other factors, the equivalence for men and women of:

(1) Availability of medical personnel and assistance;

(2) Health, accident and injury insurance coverage;

(3) Availability and quality of weight and training facilities;

(4) Availability and quality of conditioning facilities; and

(5) Availability and qualifications of athletic trainers.

h. Provision of Housing and Dining Facilities and Services (86.41(c)(9)). Compliance will be assessed by examining, among other factors, the equivalence for men and women of:

(1) Housing provided;

(2) Special services as part of housing arrangements (e.g., laundry facilities, parking space, maid service).

i. Publicity (86.41(c)(10)). Compliance will be assessed by examining, among other factors, the equivalence for men and women of:

(1) Availability and quality of sports information personnel;

(2) Access to other publicity resources for men's and women's programs; and

(3) Quantity and quality of publications and other promotional devices featuring men's and women's programs.

4. Application of the Policy—Other Factors (86.41(c)).

a. Recruitment of Student Athletes. The athletic recruitment practices of institutions often affect the overall provision of opportunity to male and female athletes. Accordingly, where equal athletic opportunities are not present for male and female students, compliance will be assessed by examining the recruitment practices of the athletic programs for both sexes to determine whether the provision of equal opportunity will require modification of those practices.

Such examinations will review the following factors:

(1) Whether coaches or other professional athletic personnel in the programs serving male and female athletes are provided with substantially equal opportunities to recruit;

(2) Whether the financial and other resources made available for recruitment in male and female athletic programs are equivalently adequate to meet the needs of each program; and

(3) Whether the differences in benefits, opportunities, and treatment afforded prospective student athletes of each sex have a disproportionately limiting effect upon the recruitment of students of either sex.

b. Provision of Support Services. The administrative and clerical support provided to an athletic program can affect the overall provision of opportunity to male and female athletes, particularly to the extent that the provided services enable coaches to perform better their coaching functions.

In the provision of support services, compliance will be assessed by examining, among other factors, the equivalence of:

(1) The amount of administrative assistance provided to men's and women's programs;

(2) The amount of secretarial and clerical assistance provided to men's and women's programs.

5. Overall Determination of Compliance. The Department will base its compliance determination under 86.41(c) of the regulation upon an examination of the following:

a. Whether the policies of an institution are discriminatory in language or effect; or

b. Whether disparities of a substantial and unjustified nature exist in the benefits, treatment, services, or opportunities afforded male and female athletes in the institution's program as a whole; or

c. Whether disparities in benefits, treatment, services, or opportunities in individual segments of the program are substantial enough in and of themselves to deny equality of athletic opportunity.

C. Effective Accommodation of Student Interests and Abilities.

1. The Regulation. The regulation requires institutions to accommodate effectively the interests and abilities of students to the extent necessary to provide equal opportunity in the selection of sports and levels of competition available to members of both sexes.

Specifically, the regulation, at 86.41(c)(1), requires the Director to consider, when determining whether equal opportunities are available whether the selection of sports and levels of competition effectively accommodate the interests and abilities of members of both sexes.

Section 86.41(c) also permits the Director of the Office for Civil Rights to consider other factors in the determination of equal opportunity. Accordingly, this section also addresses competitive opportunities in terms of the competitive team schedules available to athletes of both sexes.

2. The Policy. The Department will assess compliance with the interests and abilities section of the regulation by examining the following factors:

a. The determination of athletic interests and abilities of students;

b. The selection of sports offered; and

c. The levels of competition available including the opportunity for team competition.

3. Application of the Policy—Determination of Athletic Interests and Abilities.

Institutions may determine the athletic interests and abilities of students by nondiscriminatory methods of their choosing provided:

a. The processes take into account the nationally increasing levels of women's interests and abilities;

b. The methods of determining interest and ability do not disadvantage the members of an underrepresented sex;

c. The methods of determining ability take into account team performance records; and

d. The methods are responsive to the expressed interests of students capable of intercollegiate competition who are members of an underrepresented sex.

4. Application of the Policy—Selection of Sports.

In the selection of sports, the regulation does not require institutions to integrate their teams nor to provide exactly the same choice of sports to men and women. However, where an institution sponsors a team in a particular sport for members of one sex, it may be required either to permit the excluded sex to try out for the team or to sponsor a separate team for the previously excluded sex.

a. Contact Sports—Effective accommodation means that if an institution sponsors a team for members of one sex in a contact sport, it must do so for members of the other sex under the following circumstances:

(1) The opportunities for members of the excluded sex have historically been limited; and

(2) There is sufficient interest and ability among the members of the excluded sex to sustain a viable team and a reasonable expectation of intercollegiate competition for that team.

b. Non-Contact Sports—Effective accommodation means that if an institution sponsors a team for members of one sex in a non-contact sport, it must do so for members of the other sex under the following circumstances:

(1) The opportunities for members of the excluded sex have historically been limited;

(2) There is sufficient interest and ability among the members of the excluded sex to sustain a viable team and a reasonable expectation of intercollegiate competition for that team; and

(3) Members of the excluded sex do not possess sufficient skill to be selected for a single integrated team, or to compete actively on such a team if selected.

5. Application of the Policy—Levels of Competition.

In effectively accommodating the interests and abilities of male and female athletes, institutions must provide both the opportunity for individuals of each sex to participate in intercollegiate competition, and for athletes of each sex to have competitive team schedules which equally reflect their abilities.

a. Compliance will be assessed in any one of the following ways:

(1) Whether intercollegiate level participation opportunities for male and female students are provided in numbers substantially proportionate to their respective enrollments; or

(2) Where the members of one sex have been and are underrepresented among intercollegiate athletes, whether the institution can show a history and continuing practice of program expansion which is demonstrably responsive to the developing interest and abilities of the members of that sex; or

(3) Where the members of one sex are underrepresented among intercollegiate athletes, and the institution cannot show a continuing practice of program expansion such as that cited above, whether it can be demonstrated that the interests and abilities of the members of that sex have been fully and effectively accommodated by the present program.

b. Compliance with this provision of the regulation will also be assessed by examining the following:

(1) Whether the competitive schedules for men's and women's teams, on a program-wide basis, afford proportionally similar numbers of male and female athletes equivalently advanced competitive opportunities; or

(2) Whether the institution can demonstrate a history and continuing practice of upgrading the competitive opportunities available to the historically disadvantaged sex as warranted by developing abilities among the athletes of that sex.

c. Institutions are not required to upgrade teams to intercollegiate status or otherwise develop intercollegiate sports absent a reasonable expectation that intercollegiate competition in that sport will be available within the institution's normal competitive regions. Institutions may be required by the Title IX regulation to actively encourage the development of such competition, however, when overall athletic opportunities within that region have been historically limited for the members of one sex.

6. Overall Determination of Compliance.

The Department will base its compliance determination under 86.41(c) of the regulation upon a determination of the following:

a. Whether the policies of an institution are discriminatory in language or effect; or

b. Whether disparities of a substantial and unjustified nature in the benefits, treatment, services, or opportunities afforded male and female athletes exist in the institution's program as a whole; or

c. Whether disparities in individual segments of the program with respect to benefits, treatment, services, or opportunities are substantial enough in and of themselves to deny equality of athletic opportunity.

APPENDIX C

1996 Clarification Letter (Guidance on Participation and Proportionality)

Note: *The preamble to the following letter has been abridged for purposes of brevity.*
From Norma Cantu—Proportionality Prong
January 16, 1996

Clarification of Intercollegiate Athletics Policy Guidance: The Three-Part Test

The Office for Civil Rights (OCR) enforces Title IX of the Education Amendments of 1972, 20 U.S.C. 1681 et seq. (Title IX), which prohibits discrimination on the basis of sex in education programs and activities by recipients of federal funds. The regulation implementing Title IX, at 34 C.F.R. Part 106, effective July 21, 1975, contains specific provisions governing athletic programs, at 34 C.F.R. 106.41, and the awarding of athletic scholarships, at 34 C.F.R. 106.37(c). Further clarification of the Title IX regulatory requirements is provided by the Intercollegiate Athletics Policy Interpretation, issued December 11, 1979 (44 *Fed. Reg.* 71413 et seq. (1979)).

The Title IX regulation provides that if an institution sponsors an athletic program it must provide equal athletic opportunities for members of both sexes. Among other factors, the regulation requires that an institution must effectively accommodate the athletic interests and abilities of students of both sexes to the extent necessary to provide equal athletic opportunity. The 1979 Policy Interpretation provides that as part of this determination OCR will apply the following three-part test to assess whether an institution is providing nondiscriminatory participation opportunities for individuals of both sexes:

- Whether intercollegiate level participation opportunities for male and female students are provided in numbers substantially proportionate to their respective enrollments; or where the members of one sex have been and are underrepresented among intercollegiate athletes,

- Whether the institution can show a history and continuing practice of program expansion which is demonstrably responsive to the developing interests and abilities of the members of that sex; or where the members of one sex are underrepresented among intercollegiate athletes, and the institution cannot show a history and continuing practice of program expansion, as described above,

- Whether it can be demonstrated that the interests and abilities of the members of that sex have been fully and effectively accommodated by the present program.

Thus, the three-part test furnishes an institution with three individual avenues to choose from when determining how it will provide individuals of each sex with nondiscriminatory opportunities to participate in intercollegiate athletics. If an institution has met any part of the three-part test, OCR will determine that the institution is meeting this requirement. It is important to note that under the Policy Interpretation the requirement to provide nondiscriminatory participation opportunities is only one of many factors that OCR examines to determine if an institution is in compliance with the athletics provision of Title IX. OCR also considers the quality of competition offered to members of both sexes in order to determine whether an institution effectively accommodates the interests and abilities of its students.

In addition, when an "overall determination of compliance" is made by OCR, OCR examines the institution's program as a whole. Thus OCR considers the effective accommodation of interests and abilities in conjunction with equivalence in the availability, quality and kinds of other athletic benefits and opportunities provided male and female athletes to determine whether an institution provides equal athletic opportunity as required by Title IX.

These other benefits include coaching, equipment, practice and competitive facilities, recruitment, scheduling of games, and publicity, among others. An institution's failure to provide nondiscriminatory participation opportunities usually amounts to a denial of equal athletic opportunity because these opportunities provide access to all other athletic benefits, treatment, and services.

This Clarification provides specific factors that guide an analysis of each part of the three-part test. In addition, it provides examples to demonstrate, in concrete terms, how these factors will be considered. These examples are intended to be illustrative, and the conclusions drawn in each example are based solely on the facts included in the example.

Three-Part Test—Part One: Are Participation Opportunities Substantially Proportionate to Enrollment?

Under part one of the three-part test (part one), where an institution provides intercollegiate level athletic participation opportunities for male and female students in numbers substantially proportionate to their respective full-time undergraduate enrollments, OCR will find that the institution is providing nondiscriminatory participation opportunities for individuals of both sexes.

OCR's analysis begins with a determination of the number of participation opportunities afforded to male and female athletes in the intercollegiate athletic program. The Policy Interpretation defines participants as those athletes:

- Who are receiving the institutionally-sponsored support normally provided to athletes competing at the institution involved, e.g., coaching, equipment, medical and training room services, on a regular basis during a sport's season; and

- Who are participating in organized practice sessions and other team meetings and activities on a regular basis during a sport's season; and

- Who are listed on the eligibility or squad lists maintained for each sport, or

- Who, because of injury, cannot meet the three items above but continue to receive financial aid on the basis of athletic ability.

OCR uses this definition of participant to determine the number of participation opportunities provided by an institution for purposes of the three-part test. Under this definition, OCR considers a sport's season to commence on the date of a team's first intercollegiate competitive event and to conclude on the date of the team's final intercollegiate competitive event. As a general rule, all athletes who are listed on a team's squad or eligibility list and are on the team as of the team's first competitive event are counted as participants by OCR.

In determining the number of participation opportunities for the purposes of the interests and abilities analysis, an athlete who participates in more than one sport will be counted as a participant in each sport in which he or she participates. In determining participation opportunities, OCR includes, among others, those athletes who do not receive scholarships (e.g., walk-ons), those athletes who compete on teams sponsored by the institution even though the team may be required to raise some or all of its operating funds, and those athletes who practice but may not compete. OCR's investigations reveal that these athletes receive numerous benefits and services, such as training and practice time, coaching, tutoring services, locker room facilities, and equipment, as well as important non-tangible benefits derived from being a member of an intercollegiate athletic team. Because these are significant benefits, and because receipt of these benefits does not depend on their cost to the institution or whether the athlete competes, it is necessary to count all athletes who receive such benefits when determining the number of athletic opportunities provided to men and women.

OCR's analysis next determines whether athletic opportunities are substantially proportionate. The Title IX regulation allows institutions to operate separate athletic programs for men and women. Accordingly, the regulation allows an institution to control the respective number of participation opportunities offered to men and women. Thus, it could be argued that to satisfy part one there should be no difference between the participation rate in an institution's intercollegiate athletic program and its full-time undergraduate student enrollment.

However, because in some circumstances it may be unreasonable to expect an institution to achieve exact proportionality—for instance, because of natural fluctuations in enrollment and participation rates or because it would be unreasonable to expect an institution to add athletic opportunities in light of the small number of students that would have to be accommodated to achieve exact proportionality—the Policy Interpretation examines whether participation opportunities are "substantially" proportionate to enrollment rates. Because this determination depends on the institution's specific circumstances and the size of its athletic program, OCR makes this determination on a case-by-case basis, rather than through use of a statistical test. As an example of a determination under part one: If an institution's enrollment is 52 percent male and 48 percent female and 52 percent of the participants in the athletic program are male and 48 percent female, then the institution would clearly satisfy part one. However, OCR recognizes that natural fluctuations in an institution's enrollment and/or participation rates may affect the percentages in a subsequent year. For instance, if the institution's admissions the following year resulted in an enrollment rate of 51 percent males and 49 percent females, while the participation rates of males and females in the athletic program remained constant, the institution would continue to satisfy part one because it would be unreasonable to expect the institution to fine tune its program in response to this change in enrollment.

As another example, over the past five years an institution has had a consistent enrollment rate for women of 50 percent. During this time period, it has been expanding its program for women in order to reach proportionality. In the year that the institution reaches its goal—i.e., 50 percent of the participants in its athletic program are female—its enrollment rate for women increases to 52 percent. Under these circumstances, the institution would satisfy part one.

OCR would also consider opportunities to be substantially proportionate when the number of opportunities that would be required to achieve proportionality would not be sufficient to sustain a viable team, i.e., a team for which there is a sufficient number of interested and able students and enough available competition to sustain an intercollegiate team. As a frame of reference in assessing this situation, OCR may consider the average size of teams offered for the underrepresented sex, a number which would vary by institution.

For instance, Institution A is a university with a total of 600 athletes. While women make up 52 percent of the university's enrollment, they only represent 47 percent of its athletes. If the university provided women with 52 percent of athletic opportunities, approximately 62 additional women would be able to participate. Because this is a significant number of unaccommodated women, it is likely that a viable sport could be added. If so, Institution A has not met part one.

As another example, at Institution B women also make up 52 percent of the university's enrollment and represent 47 percent of Institution B's athletes. Institution B's athletic program consists of only 60 participants. If the University provided women with 52 percent of athletic opportunities, approximately 6 additional women would be able to participate. Since 6 participants are unlikely to support a viable team, Institution B would meet part one.

Three-Part Test—Part Two: Is there a History and Continuing Practice of Program Expansion for the Underrepresented Sex?

Under part two of the three-part test (part two), an institution can show that it has a history and continuing practice of program expansion which is demonstrably responsive to the developing interests and abilities of the underrepresented sex. In effect, part two looks at an institution's past and continuing remedial efforts to provide nondiscriminatory participation opportunities through program expansion.

OCR will review the entire history of the athletic program, focusing on the participation opportunities provided for the underrepresented sex. First, OCR will assess whether past actions of the institution have expanded participation opportunities for the underrepresented sex in a manner that was demonstrably responsive to their developing interests and abilities. Developing interests include interests that already exist at the institution. There are no fixed intervals of time within which an institution must have added participation opportunities. Neither is a particular number of sports dispositive. Rather, the focus is on whether the program expansion was responsive to developing interests and abilities of the underrepresented sex. In addition, the institution must demonstrate a continuing (i.e., present) practice of program expansion as warranted by developing interests and abilities.

OCR will consider the following factors, among others, as evidence that may indicate a history of program expansion that is demonstrably responsive to the developing interests and abilities of the underrepresented sex: an institution's record of adding intercollegiate teams, or upgrading teams to intercollegiate status, for the underrepresented sex; an institution's record of increasing the numbers of participants in intercollegiate athletics who are members of the underrepresented sex; and an institution's affirmative responses to requests by students or others for addition or elevation of sports. OCR will consider the following factors, among others, as evidence that may indicate a continuing practice of program expansion that is demonstrably responsive to the developing interests and abilities of the underrepresented sex: an institution's current implementation of a nondiscriminatory policy or procedure for requesting the addition of sports (including the elevation of club or intramural teams) and the effective communication of the policy or procedure to students; and an institution's current implementation of a plan of program expansion that is responsive to developing interests and abilities.

OCR would also find persuasive an institution's efforts to monitor developing interests and abilities of the underrepresented sex, for example, by conducting periodic nondiscriminatory assessments of developing interests and abilities and taking timely actions in response to the results.

In the event that an institution eliminated any team for the underrepresented sex, OCR would evaluate the circumstances surrounding this action in assessing whether the institution could satisfy part two of the test. However, OCR will not find a history and continuing practice of program expansion where an institution increases the proportional participation opportunities for the underrepresented sex by reducing opportunities for the overrepresented sex alone or by reducing participation opportunities for the overrepresented sex to a proportionately greater degree than for the underrepresented sex. This is because part two considers an institution's good faith remedial efforts through actual program expansion. It is only necessary to examine part two if one sex is overrepresented in the athletic program. Cuts in the program for the underrepresented sex, even when coupled with cuts in the program for the overrepresented sex, cannot be considered remedial because they burden members of the sex already disadvantaged by the present program. However, an institution that has eliminated some participation opportunities for the underrepresented sex can still meet part two if, overall, it can show a history and continuing practice of program expansion for that sex.

In addition, OCR will not find that an institution satisfies part two where it established teams for the underrepresented sex only at the initiation of its program for the underrepresented sex or where it merely promises to expand its program for the underrepresented sex at some time in the future.

The following examples are intended to illustrate the principles discussed above. At the inception of its women's program in the mid-1970s, Institution C established seven teams for women. In 1984 it added a women's varsity team at the request of students and coaches. In 1990 it upgraded a women's club sport to varsity team status based on a request by the club members and an NCAA survey that showed a significant increase in girls' high school participation in that sport. Institution C is currently implementing a plan to add a varsity women's team in the spring of 1996 that has been identified by a regional study as an emerging women's sport in the region. The addition of these teams resulted in an increased percentage of women participating in varsity athletics at the institution. Based on these facts, OCR would find Institution C in compliance with part two because it has a history of program expansion and is continuing to expand its program for women to meet their developing interests and abilities.

By 1980, Institution D established seven teams for women. Institution D added a women's varsity team in 1983 based on the requests of students and coaches. In 1991 it added a women's varsity team after an NCAA survey showed a significant increase in girls' high school participation in that sport. In 1993 Institution D eliminated a viable women's team and a viable men's team in an effort to reduce its athletic budget. It has taken no action relating to the underrepresented sex since 1993. Based on these facts, OCR would not find Institution D in compliance with part two. Institution D cannot show a continuing practice of program expansion that is responsive to the developing interests and abilities of the underrepresented sex where its only action since 1991 with regard to the underrepresented sex was to eliminate a team for which there was interest, ability and available competition.

In the mid-1970s, Institution E established five teams for women. In 1979 it added a women's varsity team. In 1984 it upgraded a women's club sport with twenty-five participants to varsity team status. At that time it eliminated a women's varsity team that had eight members. In 1987 and 1989 Institution E added women's varsity teams that were identified by a significant number of its enrolled and incoming female students when surveyed regarding their athletic interests and abilities. During this time it also increased the size of an existing women's team to provide opportunities for women who expressed interest in playing that sport. Within the past year, it added a women's varsity team based on a nationwide survey of the most popular girls high school teams. Based on the addition of these teams, the percentage of women participating in varsity athletics at the institution has increased. Based on these facts, OCR would find Institution E in compliance with part two because it has a history of program expansion and the elimination of the team in 1984 took place within the context of continuing program expansion for the underrepresented sex that is responsive to their developing interests.

Institution F started its women's program in the early 1970s with four teams. It did not add to its women's program until 1987 when, based on requests of students and coaches, it upgraded a women's club sport to varsity team status and expanded the size of several existing women's teams to accommodate significant expressed interest by students. In 1990 it surveyed its enrolled and incoming female students; based on that survey and a survey of the most popular sports played by women in the region, Institution F agreed to add three new women's teams by 1997. It added a women's team in 1991 and 1994. Institution F is implementing a plan to add a women's team by the spring of 1997. Based on these facts, OCR would find Institution F in compliance with part two. Institution F's program history since 1987 shows that it is committed to program expansion for the underrepresented sex and it is continuing to expand its women's program in light of women's developing interests and abilities.

Three-Part Test—Part Three: Is the Institution Fully and Effectively Accommodating the Interests and Abilities of the Underrepresented Sex?

Under part three of the three-part test (part three) OCR determines whether an institution is fully and effectively accommodating the interests and abilities of its students who are members of the underrepresented sex—including students who are admitted to the institution though not yet enrolled. Title IX provides that a recipient must provide equal athletic opportunity to its students. Accordingly, the Policy Interpretation does not require an institution to accommodate the interests and abilities of potential students.

While disproportionately high athletic participation rates by an institution's students of the overrepresented sex (as compared to their enrollment rates) may indicate that an institution is not providing equal athletic opportunities to its students of the underrepresented sex, an institution can satisfy part three where there is evidence that the imbalance does not reflect discrimination, i.e., where it can be demonstrated that, notwithstanding disproportionately low participation rates by the institution's students of the underrepresented sex, the interests and abilities of these students are, in fact, being fully and effectively accommodated.

In making this determination, OCR will consider whether there is (a) unmet interest in a particular sport; (b) sufficient ability to sustain a team in the sport; and (c) a reasonable expectation of competition for the team. If all three conditions are present OCR will find that an institution has not fully and effectively accommodated the interests and abilities of the underrepresented sex.

If an institution has recently eliminated a viable team from the intercollegiate program, OCR will find that there is sufficient interest, ability, and available competition to sustain an intercollegiate team in that sport unless an institution can provide strong evidence that interest, ability, or available competition no longer exists.

a) Is there sufficient unmet interest to support an intercollegiate team?

OCR will determine whether there is sufficient unmet interest among the institution's students who are members of the underrepresented sex to sustain an intercollegiate team. OCR will look for interest by the underrepresented sex as expressed through the following indicators, among others:

- requests by students and admitted students that a particular sport be added;
- requests that an existing club sport be elevated to intercollegiate team status;
- participation in particular club or intramural sports;
- interviews with students, admitted students, coaches, administrators and others regarding interest in particular sports;
- results of questionnaires of students and admitted students regarding interests in particular sports; and
- participation in particular in interscholastic sports by admitted students.

In addition, OCR will look at participation rates in sports in high schools, amateur athletic associations, and community sports leagues that operate in areas from which the institution draws its students in order to ascertain likely interest and ability of its students and admitted students in particular sport(s). For example, where OCR's investigation finds that a substantial number of high schools from the relevant region offer a particular sport which the institution does not offer for the underrepresented sex, OCR will ask the institution to provide a basis for any assertion that its students and admitted students are not interested in playing that sport. OCR may also interview students, admitted students, coaches, and others regarding interest in that sport.

An institution may evaluate its athletic program to assess the athletic interest of its students of the underrepresented sex using nondiscriminatory methods of its choosing. Accordingly, institutions have flexibility in choosing a nondiscriminatory method of determining athletic interests and abilities provided they meet certain requirements. See 44 *Fed. Reg.* at 71417. These assessments may use straightforward and inexpensive techniques, such as a student questionnaire or an open forum, to identify students' interests and abilities. Thus, while OCR expects that an institution's assessment should reach a wide audience of students and should be open-ended regarding the sports students can express interest in, OCR does not require elaborate scientific validation of assessments.

An institution's evaluation of interest should be done periodically so that the institution can identify in a timely and responsive manner any developing interests and abilities of the underrepresented sex. The evaluation should also take into account sports played in the high schools and communities from which the institution draws its students both as an indication of possible interest on campus and to permit the institution to plan to meet the interests of admitted students of the underrepresented sex.

b) Is there sufficient ability to sustain an intercollegiate team?

Second, OCR will determine whether there is sufficient ability among interested students of the underrepresented sex to sustain an intercollegiate team. OCR will examine indications of ability such as:

- the athletic experience and accomplishments—in interscholastic, club or intramural competition—of students and admitted students interested in playing the sport;
- opinions of coaches, administrators, and athletes at the institution regarding whether interested students and admitted students have the potential to sustain a varsity team; and

- if the team has previously competed at the club or intramural level, whether the competitive experience of the team indicates that it has the potential to sustain an intercollegiate team.

Neither a poor competitive record nor the inability of interested students or admitted students to play at the same level of competition engaged in by the institution's other athletes is conclusive evidence of lack of ability. It is sufficient that interested students and admitted students have the potential to sustain an intercollegiate team.

c) Is there a reasonable expectation of competition for the team?

Finally, OCR determines whether there is a reasonable expectation of intercollegiate competition for a particular sport in the institution's normal competitive region. In evaluating available competition, OCR will look at available competitive opportunities in the geographic area in which the institution's athletes primarily compete, including:

- competitive opportunities offered by other schools against which the institution competes; and
- competitive opportunities offered by other schools in the institution's geographic area, including those offered by schools against which the institution does not now compete.

Under the Policy Interpretation, the institution may also be required to actively encourage the development of intercollegiate competition for a sport for members of the underrepresented sex when overall athletic opportunities within its competitive region have been historically limited for members of that sex.

Conclusion

This discussion clarifies that institutions have three distinct ways to provide individuals of each sex with nondiscriminatory participation opportunities. The three-part test gives institutions flexibility and control over their athletics programs. For instance, the test allows institutions to respond to different levels of interest by its male and female students. Moreover, nothing in the three-part test requires an institution to eliminate participation opportunities for men. At the same time, this flexibility must be used by institutions consistent with Title IX's requirement that they not discriminate on the basis of sex. OCR recognizes that institutions face challenges in providing nondiscriminatory participation opportunities for their students and will continue to assist institutions in finding ways to meet these challenges.

The Policy Interpretation is designed for intercollegiate athletics. However, its general principles, and those of this Clarification, often will apply to elementary and secondary interscholastic athletic programs, which are also covered by the regulation. See 44 *Fed. Reg.* 71413. Part two focuses on whether an institution has expanded the number of intercollegiate participation opportunities provided to the underrepresented sex. Improvements in the quality of competition, and of other athletic benefits, provided to women athletes, while not considered under the three-part test, can be considered by OCR in making an overall determination of compliance with the athletics provision of Title IX.

However, under this part of the test an institution is not required, as it is under part three, to accommodate all interests and abilities of the underrepresented sex. Moreover, under part two an institution has flexibility in choosing which teams it adds for the underrepresented sex, as long as it can show overall a history and continuing practice of program expansion for members of that sex.

However , OCR does examine an institution's recruitment practices under another part of the Policy Interpretation. See 44 *Fed. Reg.* 71417. Accordingly, where an institution recruits potential student athletes for its men's teams, it must ensure that women's teams are provided with substantially equal opportunities to recruit potential student athletes. While these indications of interest may be helpful to OCR in ascertaining likely interest on campus, particularly in the absence of more direct indicia, an institution is expected to meet the actual interests and abilities of its students and admitted students.

APPENDIX D

1998 Clarification Letter (Guidance on Financial Aid)

Note: *On July 23, 1998, the Office for Civil Rights issued a "guidance" concerning the granting of financial aid in athletics. The guidance took the form of a letter to Bowling Green State University, which had previously inquired about the matter. What follows is an abridgment of the guidance with emphasis on the salient points relating to financial aid in athletics.*

This is in response to your letter requesting guidance in meeting the requirements of Title IX specifically as it relates to the equitable apportionment of athletic financial aid. . . . You have asked us to provide clarification regarding how educational institutions can provide intercollegiate athletes with nondiscriminatory opportunities to receive athletic financial aid. Under the Policy Interpretation, the equitable apportioning of a college's intercollegiate athletics scholarship fund for the separate budgets of its men's and women's programs—which Title IX permits to be segregated—requires that the total amounts of scholarship aid made available to the two budgets are "substantially proportionate" to the participation rates of male and female athletes. 44 *Fed. Reg.* 71413, 71415 (1979).

. . .

Athletics: Scholarship Requirements

With regard to athletic financial assistance, the regulations promulgated under Title IX provide that, when a college or university awards athletic scholarships, these scholarship awards must be granted to "members of each sex in proportion to the number of students of each sex participating in . . . intercollegiate athletics," 34 C.F.R. 106.37(c). Since 1979, OCR has interpreted this regulation in conformity with its published "Policy Interpretation: Title IX and Intercollegiate Athletics," 44 *Fed. Reg.* 71413 (December 11, 1979). The Policy Interpretation does not require colleges to grant the same number of scholarships to men and women, nor does it require that individual scholarships be of equal value. What it does require is that, at a particular college or university, "the total amount of scholarship aid made available to men and women must be substantially proportionate to their [overall] participation rates" at that institution. Id. at 71415. It is important to note that the Policy Interpretation only applies to teams that regularly compete in varsity competition. Id. at 71413 and n. 1.

Under the Policy Interpretation, OCR conducts a "financial comparison to determine whether proportionately equal amounts of financial assistance (scholarship aid) are available to men's and women's athletic programs," Id. The Policy Interpretation goes on to state that "[i]nstitutions may be found in compliance if this comparison results in substantially equal amounts or if a disparity can be explained by adjustments to take into account legitimate nondiscriminatory factors." Id.

A "disparity" in awarding athletic, financial assistance refers to the difference between the aggregate amount of money athletes of one sex received in one year, and the amount they would have received if their share of the entire annual budget for athletic scholarships had been awarded in proportion to their participation rates. Thus, for example, if men account for 60% of a school's intercollegiate athletes, the Policy Interpretation presumes that—absent legitimate nondiscriminatory factors that may cause a disparity—the men's athletic program will receive approximately 60% of the entire annual scholarship budget and the women's athletic program will receive approximately 40% of those funds. This presumption reflects the fact that colleges typically allocate scholarship funds among their athletic teams, and that such teams are expressly segregated by sex. Colleges' allocation of the scholarship budget among teams, therefore, is invariably sex-based, in the sense that an allocation to a particular team necessarily benefits one sex to the exclusion of the other. See Brown, 101 F. 3d at 177. Where, as here, disparate treatment is inevitable and a college's allocation of scholarship funds is "at the discretion of the institution," Brown 101 F. 3d at 177, the statute nondiscrimination requirements obliges colleges to ensure that men's and women's separate activities receive equitable treatment. Cf. United States v.Virginia, 518 U.S. 515, 554 (1996).

Nevertheless, in keeping with the Policy Interpretation allowance for disparities from "substantially proportionate" awards to the men's and women's programs based on legitimate nondiscriminatory factors, OCR judges each matter on a case-by-case basis with due regard for the unique factual situation presented by each case. For example, OCR recognizes that disparities may be explained by actions taken to promote athletic program development, and by differences between in-state and out-of-state tuition at public colleges, 44 *Fed. Reg.* at 71415. Disparities might also be explained, for example by legitimate efforts undertaken to comply with Title IX requirements, such as participation requirements. See e.g. Gonyo v. Drake Univ. 879 F. Supp. 1000, 1005-06 (S.D. Iowa 1995). Similarly, disparities may be explained by unexpected fluctuations in the participation rates of males and females. For example, a disparity may be explained if an athlete who had accepted an athletic scholarship decided at the last minute to enroll at another school. It is important to note it is not enough for a college or university merely to assert a nondiscriminatory justification. Instead, it will be required to demonstrate that its asserted rationale is in fact reasonable and does not reflect underlying discrimination. For instance, if a college, consistently awards a greater number of out-of-state scholarships to men, it may be required to demonstrate that this does not reflect discriminatory recruitment practices. Similarly, if a university asserts the phase-in of scholarships for a new team as a justification for a disparity, the university may be required to demonstrate that the time frame for phasing-in of scholarships is reasonable in light of college sports practices to aggressively recruit athletes to build start-up teams quickly.

In order to ensure equity for athletes of both sexes, the test for determining whether the two scholarship budgets are "substantially proportionate" to the respective participation rates of athletes of each sex necessarily has a high threshold. The Policy Interpretation does not, however, require colleges to achieve exact proportionality down to the last dollar. The "substantially proportionate" test permits a small variance from exact proportionality. OCR recognizes that, in practice, some leeway is necessary to avoid requiring colleges to unreasonably fine-tune their scholarship budgets.

When evaluating each scholarship program an a case-by-case basis, OCR's first step will be to adjust any disparity to take into account all the legitimate nondiscriminatory reasons provided by the college, such as the extra costs for out-of-state tuition discussed earlier. If any unexplained disparity in the scholarship budget for athletes of either gender is 1% or less for the entire budget for athletic scholarships, there will be a strong presumption that such a disparity is reasonable and based on legitimate and nondiscriminatory factors. Conversely, there will be a strong presumption that an unexplained disparity of more than 1% is in violation of the "substantially proportionate" requirements.

Thus, for example, if men are 60% of the athletes, OCR would expect that the men's athletic scholarship budget would be within 59%-61% of the total budget for athletic scholarships for all athletes, after accounting for legitimate nondiscriminatory reasons for any larger disparity. Of course, OCR will continue to judge each case in terms of its particular facts. For example, at those colleges where 1% of the entire athletic scholarship budget is less than the value of one full scholarship, OCR will presume that a disparity of up to the value of one full scholarship is equitable and nondiscriminatory. On the other hand, even if an institution consistently has less than a 1% disparity, the presumption of compliance with Title IX might still be rebutted if, for example, there is direct evidence of discriminatory intent. OCR recognizes that there has been some confusion in the past with respect to the Title IX compliance standards for scholarships. OCR's 1990 Title IX Investigator's Manual correctly stated that one would expect proportionality in the awarding of scholarships, absent a legitimate, nondiscriminatory justification. But that Manual also indicated that compliance with the "substantially proportionate"' test could depend, in part, upon certain statistical tests. In some cases, application of such a statistical test would result in a determination of compliance despite the existence of a disparity as large as 3-5%.

We would like to clarify that use of such statistical tests is not appropriate in these circumstances. Those tests, which are used in some other discrimination contexts to determine whether the disparities in the allocation of benefits to different groups are the result of chance, are inappropriate in the athletic scholarship context because a college has direct control over its allocation of financial aid to men's and women's teams, and because such decisions necessarily are sex-based in the sense that an allocation to a particular team will affect only one sex. See Brown 101 F. 3d at 176-78 (explaining why college athletics "presents a distinctly different situation from admissions and employment," and why athletics requires a different analysis than that used "in such other contexts "in order to determine the existence of nondiscrimination"). In the typical case where aid is expressly allocated among sex-segregated teams, chance simply is not a possible explanation for disproportionate aid to one sex. Where a college does not make a substantially proportionate allocation to sex-segregated teams, the burden should be on the college to provide legitimate, nondiscriminatory reasons for the disproportionate allocation. Therefore, the use of statistical tests will not be helpful in determining whether a disparity in the allocations for the two separate athletic scholarship budgets is nondiscriminatory.

While a statistical test is not relevant in determining discrimination, the confusion caused by the manual's inclusion of a statistical test resulted in misunderstandings. Therefore, OCR is providing this clarification regarding the substantial proportionality provision found in the 1979 Policy Interpretation to confirm the substance of a longstanding standard. In order to ensure full understanding, OCR will apply the presumptions and case-by-case analysis described in this letter for the

1998-99 academic year. OCR strongly encourages recipients to award athletic financial assistance to women athletes in the 1997-98 academic year consistent with this policy clarification, both as a matter of fairness and in order to ensure that they are moving towards the policy clarification stated in this letter.

Further Clarification Letter of 2003
[Reaffirmation of Title IX's Requirements in General and Proportionality in Particular]

July 11, 2003

Dear Colleague:

It is my pleasure to provide you with this Further Clarification of Intercollegiate Athletics Policy Guidance Regarding Title IX Compliance.

Since its enactment in 1972, Title IX has produced significant advancement in athletic opportunities for women and girls across the nation. Recognizing that more remains to be done, the Bush Administration is firmly committed to building on this legacy and continuing the progress that Title IX has brought toward true equality of opportunity for male and female student-athletes in America.

In response to numerous requests for additional guidance on the Department of Education's (Department) enforcement standards since its last written guidance on Title IX in 1996, the Department's Office for Civil Rights (OCR) began looking into whether additional guidance on Title IX requirements regarding intercollegiate athletics was needed. On June 27, 2002, Secretary of Education Rod Paige created the Secretary's Commission on Opportunities in Athletics to investigate this matter further, and to report back with recommendations on how to improve the application of the current standards for measuring equal opportunity to participate in athletics under Title IX. On February 26, 2003, the Commission presented Secretary Paige with its final report, "Open to All: Title IX at Thirty," and in addition, individual members expressed their views.

After eight months of discussion and an extensive and inclusive fact-finding process, the Commission found very broad support throughout the country for the goals and spirit of Title IX. With that in mind, OCR today issues this Further Clarification in order to strengthen Title IX's promise of non-discrimination in the athletic programs of our nation's schools. Title IX establishes that: "No person in the United States shall, on the basis of sex, be excluded from participation in, be denied the benefits of, or be subjected to discrimination under any education program or activity receiving Federal financial assistance."

In its 1979 Policy Interpretation, the Department established a three-prong test for compliance with Title IX, which it later amplified and clarified in its 1996 Clarification. The test provides that an institution is in compliance if 1) the intercollegiate-level participation opportunities for male and female students at the institution are "substantially proportionate" to their respective full-time undergraduate enrollments, 2) the institution has a "history and continuing practice of program expansion" for the underrepresented sex, or 3) the institution is "fully and effectively" accommodating the interests and abilities of the underrepresented sex.

First, with respect to the three-prong test, which has worked well, OCR encourages schools to take advantage of its flexibility, and to consider which of the three prongs best suits their individual situations. All three prongs have been used successfully by schools to comply with Title IX, and the test offers three separate ways of assessing whether schools are providing equal opportunities to their male and female students to participate in athletics. If a school does not satisfy the "substantial proportionality" prong, it would still satisfy the three-prong test if it maintains a history and continuing practice of program expansion for the underrepresented sex, or if "the interests and abilities of the members of [the underrepresented] sex have been fully and effectively accommodated by the present program." Each of the three prongs is thus a valid, alternative way for schools to comply with Title IX.

The transmittal letter accompanying the 1996 Clarification issued by the Department described only one of these three separate prongs—substantial proportionality—as a "safe harbor" for Title IX compliance. This led many schools to believe, erroneously, that they must take measures to ensure strict proportionality between the sexes. In fact, each of the three prongs of the test is an equally sufficient means of complying with Title IX, and no one prong is favored. The Department will continue to make clear, as it did in its 1996 Clarification, that "[i]nstitutions have flexibility in providing nondiscriminatory participation opportunities to their students, and OCR does not require quotas."

In order to ensure that schools have a clear understanding of their options for compliance with Title IX, OCR will undertake an education campaign to help educational institutions appreciate the flexibility of the law, to explain that each prong of the test is a viable and separate means of compliance, to give practical examples of the ways in which schools can comply, and to provide schools with technical assistance as they try to comply with Title IX.

In the 1996 Clarification, the Department provided schools with a broad range of specific factors, as well as illustrative examples, to help schools understand the flexibility of the three-prong test. OCR reincorporates those factors, as well as those illustrative examples, into this Further Clarification, and OCR will continue to assist schools on a case-by-case basis and address any questions they have about Title IX compliance. Indeed, OCR encourages schools to request individualized assistance from OCR as they consider ways to meet the requirements of Title IX. As OCR works with schools on Title IX compliance, OCR will share information, on successful approaches with the broader scholastic community.

Second, OCR hereby clarifies that nothing in Title IX requires the cutting or reduction of teams in order to demonstrate compliance with Title IX, and that the elimination of teams is a disfavored practice. Because the elimination of teams diminishes opportunities for students who are interested in participating in athletics instead of enhancing opportunities for students who have suffered from discrimination, it is contrary to the spirit of Title IX for the government to require or encourage an institution to eliminate athletic teams.

Therefore, in negotiating compliance agreements, OCR's policy will be to seek remedies that do not involve the elimination of teams.

Third, OCR hereby advises schools that it will aggressively enforce Title IX standards, including implementing sanctions for institutions that do not comply. At the same time, OCR will also work with schools to assist them in avoiding such sanctions by achieving Title IX compliance.

Fourth, private sponsorship of athletic teams will continue to be allowed. Of course, private sponsorship does not in any way change or diminish a school's obligations under Title IX. Finally, OCR recognizes that schools will benefit from clear and consistent implementation of Title IX. Accordingly, OCR will ensure that its enforcement practices do not vary from region to region.

OCR recognizes that the question of how to comply with Title IX and to provide equal athletic opportunities for all students is a challenge for many academic institutions. But OCR believes that the three-prong test has provided, and will continue to provide, schools with the flexibility to provide greater athletic opportunities for students of both sexes.

OCR is strongly reaffirming today its commitment to equal opportunity for girls and boys, women and men. To that end, OCR is committed to continuing to work in partnership with educational institutions to ensure that the promise of Title IX becomes a reality for all students. Thank you for your continuing interest in this subject.

Sincerely,
Gerald Reynolds
Assistant Secretary for Civil Rights

APPENDIX F

Tools for Finding Help and Perspective

Title IX is as static as the words on the pages of its regulations. Title IX is as dynamic as the interpretation of those words in the offices of OCR, the hallways of Congress, the courtrooms of the nation, and the minds of athletics directors, coaches, athletes, and parents. The stakeholders of Title IX are diverse. They are diverse in the degree of their knowledge of the static portion of Title IX and perhaps more diverse in their points of view concerning the dynamic nature and influence of Title IX in its fourth decade. It will ever be thus.

Consider this appendix as a reading list for a continuing education on Title IX. The body of literature grows with each new court decision, each new OCR investigation, and each new discussion in the press and in the locker room. The references, some annotated, to resources noted herein provide in-depth readings of case decisions, a broad variety of media points of view, academic discourses on the relation of Title IX to the broader world, association-based recommendations for compliance mechanisms, databases on the changing face of athletics, and a few other goodies that you, the kind and gentle reader, might find either of use or of interest. Have fun.

PLANNING FOR COMPLIANCE

Minnesota High Schools

Minnesota reviewed its high schools for compliance with Title IX. Their materials and report provide a good blueprint for the process applicable to other states. The report "Gender Equity in Athletics Manual: Minnesota State High School League" is available from

MSHSL
2100 Freeway Blvd.
Brooklyn Center, MN 55430
612-560-2260

Washington State Public Schools

Washington State's superintendent of public instruction has prepared a Web site that includes extremely useful information about Title IX as it applies to middle and senior high schools. Included in the information is an approach to evaluating equity that would serve other states well as a starting place for designing compliance surveys, as well as material useful in educating the school population about the rights and responsibilities of Title IX. The main Web address for the office is

www.k12.wa.us

The Web address for direct access to the list of Title IX materials is

www.k12.wa.us/search.aspx?SearchTermsheader=title%20ix

NCAA

The NCAA's Web site includes access to compliance plans generated at many colleges and universities. The plans may provide ideas for the development of one at your school. Check the NCAA Web site at

www.ncaa.org

NWLC

The National Women's Law Center has developed a useful checklist for evaluating compliance called Check It Out, which is downloadable at no cost at

nwlc.org/index.cfm
Click on Athletics.
Scroll down to "Is Your School Complying with Title IX?"
Click on "Check It Out."

ASSOCIATION-BASED MATERIAL

NAGWS

The National Association for Girls and Women in Sport provides a variety of Title IX information including several publications such as workshop kits for increasing knowledge of Title IX for parents and teachers. In addition, the association's Web site carries links to a helpful array of materials on Title IX and data on the status of women in sport. Their general, searchable Web site address is

www.nagws.org

The NAGWS Web site that takes you most directly to Title IX link, is

www.aahperd.org/nagws/template.cfm?template=title9/
bush.html

NCWGE

The National Coalition for Women and Girls in Education is made up of a group of organizations, many of which focus on sports and athletics opportunities for girls and women. Besides providing access to their Title IX materials, the site carries links to several other associational sites with useful Title IX information. Their main site address is

www.ncwge.org

NCAA

The National Collegiate Athletics Association (NCAA) has extensive links to materials available online relating to Title IX. The main NCAA Web site is

www.ncaa.org

The list of materials, available from the 2003 NCAA Title IX Seminar is found at

www1.ncaa.org/membership/ed_outreach/gender_equity/
resource_materials/Resources.html

NWLC

The National Women's Law Center provides legal information concerning Title IX including the organization's new Check It Out manual for evaluating Title IX compliance in a downloadable form. The organization's main Web site is

www.nwlc.org

The Check It Out manual, as well as other materials, is downloadable at

nwlc.org/index.cfm
Click on Athletics.
Scroll down to "Is Your School Complying with Title IX?"
Click on "Check It Out."

NACWAA

The National Association of Collegiate Women Athletic Administrators provides programs, forums, and executive training sessions for coaches and athletic administrators. The association also provides great leadership in the area of intercollegiate athletics administration. The main Web site for the association is

www.nacwaa.org

The association also provides useful links to other organizations at

http://nacwaa.org/rc/rc_titleix_main.php

NWCA

The National Wrestling Coaches Association, the lead plaintiff in the 2002-2003 "wrestlers" lawsuit that unsuccessfully sought to throw out the proportionality prong along with other aspects of Title IX, includes in its Web site articles and information concerning its point of view on Title IX including a school-by-school listing of discontinued teams. The main site address for the association is

www.nwcaonline.com/

Title IX information is at http://www.nwcaonline.com/titleix.cfm

NOW

The National Organization for Women provides access to its press releases and position statements regarding Title IX as well as links to a variety of other governmental and associational sites. The main site address for NOW's Title IX material is

http://now.org/search/search.cgi?query=title+ix&metaname=swishdefault&si=0

WEEA

The Women's Education Equity Act Equity Resource Center provides links to other associations' material on Title IX as well as providing its own. The main Web address for the association is

www.edc.org/WomensEquity

Specific materials and links relating to Title IX are found at

www.edc.org/WomensEquity/resource/title9/index.htm

You'll find state folks to contact to assist with equity questions on a more local basis at

www.edc.org/WomensEquity/resource/title9/state.htm

Save Title IX

Save Title IX is an organization focused on, as its name implies, maintaining the vitality and current formulation of Title IX. The organization developed an active Web site particularly at the time of the commission. The Web site provides useful links as well as brief position statements on a variety of Title IX issues and links to the minority report on the commission at

www.savetitleix.org

WSF

The Women's Sports Foundation includes in its materials short, single-topic issue papers as well as links to other associations where you'll find even more information and a variety of the association's own useful information and reports. The main site for the Women's Sports Foundation is

www.womenssportsfoundation.org

The list of Title IX–related reports and links is found at

www.womenssportsfoundation.org/cgi-bin/iowa/search/index.html

GOVERNMENTAL

Department of Education

The Department of Education provides online access to all of the 2003 commission hearings, final report, and related information in downloadable form. The final report and transcripts are also available on many other sites, particularly organizational sites with a focus on Title IX. The Department of Education site that takes you directly to a main search list is

http://ed.gov/index.jhtml

From this site, search for "Commission on Athletics Opportunities."

GAO

The Government Accounting Office has created several documents that bring together data on various aspects of gender equity in athletics. The main Web site for the GAO is

www.gao.gov

Several of the more interesting documents are:

Intercollegiate Athletics Four-Year Colleges' Experiences Adding and Discontinuing Teams, March 2001

(Search at main Web site for "Experiences Adding and Discontinuing Teams")

Status of Efforts to Promote Gender Equity in Intercollegiate Athletics, October 1996

(Search at main Web site for "Promote Gender")

Comparison of Selected Characteristics for Men's and Women's Intercollegiate Athletics, June 18, 1999

(Search at main Web site by entire title)

OCR

The U.S. Department of Education's Office for Civil Rights (the administrative agency charged with enforcing Title IX) has useful Title IX information available on its main site at

www.ed.gov/about/offices/list/ocr/index.html

Materials relating to the commission's activities as well as copies of the regulations and policy interpretations are downloadable from OCR. Specifically the full regulations can be found at:

www.ed.gov/policy/rights/reg/ocr/edlite-34cfr106.html

Specifically, the full policy interpretations are downloadable at

www.ed.gov/about/offices/list/ocr/docs/t9interp.html

Specifically, the full 2003 further clarification letter is downloadable at

www.ed.gov/about/offices/list/ocr/title9guidanceFinal.html

Online complaint forms are available at

www.ed.gov/about/offices/list/ocr/complaintintro.html

http://wdcrobcolp01.ed.gov/CFAPPS/OCR/complaintform.cfm

Department of Justice

The United States Department of Justice Web site carries substantial Title IX enforcement information. Its main site for such material is

www.usdoj.gov/crt/cor/coord/titleix.htm

Clear guidance about the duties of the campus "designated Title IX employee," who has the responsibility for educating the campus community about the rights and responsibilities of Title IX as well the responsibility for handling in-house complaints and developing complaint procedures, is found at

www.usdoj.gov/crt/cor/coord/TitleIXQandA.htm

One of the emerging areas of discussion about Title IX jurisdiction noted in chapter 3 is the definition of federal financial assistance. The Department of Justice site includes useful information on the topic as well as links to more information elsewhere at

www.usdoj.gov/crt/cor/federalfundingsources.htm

LAW AND CASE RELATED

Some of the cases below are landmarks; others such as *Grove City* are landmarks that, in part, no longer apply. Reading the cases can help you understand the legal logic used, and many of the cases include thorough reviews of the legislative and judicial history of Title IX.

If your institution permits access to Lexis-Nexis or Westlaw online, finding court opinions is easy. If not, here are a few open-to-anyone sites and the cases that you'll find at each.

Supreme Court

Supreme Court opinions handed down since 1999 are readily available at the following Web site:

www.supremecourtus.gov/

For earlier cases, you might find access easier through the findlaw.com Web site, which allows a broad search of many opinions. Here are a few samples and the sites that take you immediately to a downloadable copy of the decision.

Franklin v Gwinnett
http://caselaw.lp.findlaw.com/scripts/getcase.pl?court=us&vol=503&invol=60

Grove City College v Bell
http://caselaw.lp.findlaw.com/scripts/getcase.pl?court=us&vol=465&invol=555

Cannon v University of Chicago
http://caselaw.lp.findlaw.com/scripts/getcase.pl?court=us&vol=441&invol=677

North Haven Board of Education v Bell
http://caselaw.lp.findlaw.com/scripts/getcase.pl?court=us&vol=456&invol=512

Oncale v Sundowner
http://caselaw.lp.findlaw.com/scripts/getcase.pl?court=us&vol=000&invol=96-568

Gebser v Lago Vista Independent School District
http://caselaw.lp.findlaw.com/scripts/getcase.pl?court=us&vol=000&invol=96-1866

Davis v Monroe County Board of Education
http://caselaw.lp.findlaw.com/scripts/getcase.pl?court=us&vol=000&invol=97-843

Faragher v City of Boca Raton
http://caselaw.lp.findlaw.com/scripts/getcase.pl?court=us&vol=000&invol=97-282

Courts of Appeal

Court of appeal cases are usually searched for within the specific district in which they reside. For court of appeal cases see

www.findlaw.com/casecode/index.html#federal

OCR Complaints, High School Cases, Miscellaneous

The University of Iowa hosts a comprehensive Web site that contains a variety of links to other useful Title IX sites. The site also includes extensive information about OCR complaints on both the high school and the college level. The main address for the site is

http://bailiwick.lib.uiowa.edu/ge

PARTICIPATION DATA

Acosta and Carpenter

Acosta and Carpenter's *Women in Intercollegiate Sport—A Longitudinal, National Study—Twenty Seven Year Update: 1977-2004* tracks participation as well as coaching and administrative data from one year before Title IX compliance (1978) to 2004. Copies of the 27-page summary are available for downloading at

webpages.charter.net/womeninsport/

NCAA Gender Equity Study

The NCAA issued its first *Gender Equity Study* in 1992. Besides the *Gender Equity Report,* you'll find other related studies available for downloading. The 1999-2000 report is available online at

www.ncaa.org

NFSHSA

The National Federation of State High School Associations has kept data on the participation of boys and girls in athletic programs across the nation. The main site is

www.nfhs.org

The most recent reports are available at

www.nfhs.org/scriptcontent/Va_custom/va_cm/contentpage
display.cfm?content_ID=133

U.S. Commission on Civil Rights

The United States Commission on Civil Rights collected reports and data on the participation of boys and girls, and men and women in athletics and intramural programs in the early days of Title IX. The data included in the report do not extend past 1980, but the early data are well worth the look. The commission's main Web site address is

www.usccr.gov/

The commission's Web site for their publications is

www.usccr.gov/pubs/catalog/clear.htm

More Hurdles to Clear: Women and Girls in Competitive Athletics
This 1980 document reviews the history and assesses the status of females in intercollegiate and interscholastic athletics. It summarizes HEW's enforcement of Title IX of the Education Amendments of 1972 that prohibit discrimination based on sex in education and athletic programs receiving federal financial assistance. CHP 63. 87 pp. No. 005-902-00016-9.

BOOKS

Books regarding gender equity or gender equity in sport could generate a long list, but two give valuable perspective to (1) those who want to examine the changing milieu in which sports for women have existed for decades both before and after Title IX and (2) those who want to gain empathy for the effect that exercising Title IX rights has on the complainant or plaintiff.

Greta Cohen, editor, *Women in Sport—Issues and Controversies, 2d Edition*, National Association for Girls and Women in Sport, 2001.

Cynthia Pemberton, *More Than a Game: One Woman's Fight for Gender Equity in Sport*, Northeastern University Press, 2002.

LAW REVIEWS

If your institution's library has Lexis-Nexis or Westlaw, finding the law review articles will be easy. Many law reviews deal with Title IX, but the following short starter list includes two that give a cogent history and an easily understood perspective:

Diane Heckman, "The Glass Sneaker: Thirty Years of Victories and Defeats Involving Title IX and Sex Discrimination in Athletics," 13 *Fordham Intellectual Property, Media & Entertainment Law Journal*, 551, winter 2003.

Deborah Brake, "The Struggle for Sex Equality in Sport and the Theory Behind Title IX," 34 *University of Michigan Journal of Law Reform*, 13, fall 2000/winter 2001.

OCR OFFICE LOCATIONS

The Office for Civil Rights has 10 regional offices. A listing of those offices may be found on the Web at

http://wdcrobcolp01.ed.gov/CFAPPS/OCR/contactus.cfm

or may be obtained by calling the national office in Washington, D.C., at 800-421-3481.

BIBLIOGRAPHY

AAHPER Update, May 1973, 11.

AAHPER Update, February 1975, 1, 3.

AAUW. *Title IX at Thirty—Report Card on Gender Equity.* Washington, D.C., 2002.

Aaron, D.J., S.R. Dearwater, S.R. Anderson, et al. "Physical Activity and the Initiation of High-Risk Health Behaviors in Adolescents." *Medicine and Science in Sports and Exercise* 27 (1996): 1639-1645.

A License for Bias. American Association of University Women, Legal Advocacy Fund, Washington, D.C., 2000.

Acosta, R.V., and L. Carpenter. *Women in Intercollegiate Sport—A Twenty Seven Year Update.* Unpublished manuscript, available at webpages.charter.net/ womeninsport.

Alexander v Sandoval, 121 S. Ct. 1511 (2001).

"Amateur Hockey Association of Illinois Is Not Subject to Title IX Because It Doesn't Receive Federal Funding." *Entertainment Law Reporter* 23, no. 5 (October 2001).

Association for Intercollegiate Athletics for Women v NCAA 735 F. 2d 577 (1984)

Auer v Robbins, 519 U.S. 452 (1997).

Bennett v West Texas State University, 799 F. 2d 155 (5th Cir. 1986).

Blair v Washington State University, 740 P. 2d 1379 (1987).

Board of Trustees of the University of Alabama v Patricia Garrett, 531 U.S. 356, 121 S. Ct. 955 (2001).

Bock, Hal. "Title IX-Equalizer or Quota Enforcer?" *Valley News* (West Lebanon, NH), June 23, 2002, D5.

Boucher v Syracuse University, 164 F. 3e 113 (1999).

Bougher v University of Pittsburgh, 882 F. 2d 74 (3d Cir. 1989)

Boulahanis v Board of Regents, 198 F. 3d 633 (7th Cir.) (1999), 530 U.S. 1284 (2000) cert. denied.

Brake, Deborah. "The Struggle for Sex Equity in Sport and the Theory Behind Title IX." *34 University of Michigan Law Journal of Law Reform, 13,* fall 2000/winter 2001.

Brentwood Academy v Tennessee Secondary School Athletic Association, 121 S. Ct. 924 (2001).

Brown v Board of Education, 347 U.S. 483 (1956)

Bryant v Colgate, New York District Court, no. 93-CV-1029, 1997.

Burnett v Gratan, 486 U.S. 42 (1984)

California NOW v Board of Trustees of California State Universities, case no. 949297 (Cal. Super. Ct. San Francisco County, October 20, 1993).

Cannon v University of Chicago, 441 U.S. 677 (1979).

Carpenter, L. "Letters Home: My Life With Title IX." In *Women in Sport: Issues and Controversies,* 2d edition, edited by Greta Cohen. National Association for Girls and Women in Sport, Reston, VA, 2001.

Chalenor et al. v University of North Dakota, 291 F. 3d 1042 (8th Cir. 2002).

Chevron USA v Natural Resources Defense Council, Inc., 467 U.S. 837 (1984)

Chronicle of Higher Education, "Federal Panelists' Ideas for Changing Title IX," Washington, D.C., January 3, 2003.

Chronicle of Higher Education, "Title IX at Thirty" (comments of Sen. Birch Bayh), Washington, D.C., June 21, 2002.

Civil Rights Restoration Act of 1987, 20 U.S.C. section 1687 (1988).

Clark v Arizona Interscholastic Association, 695 F. 2d 1126 (1982), cert. denied at 46 U.S. 818 (1983).

Cohen v Brown University, 991 F. 2d 888 (1st Cir. 1993); 101 F. 3d 155 (1st Cir. 1996), cert. denied 520 U.S. 1186 (1997).

Colton, M.E., and S. Gore. *Risk, Resiliency, and Resistance: Current Research on Adolescent Girls.* Ms. Foundation, New York, 1991.

Cook v Colgate University, 802 F. Supp. 737 (N.D.N.Y., 1992) vacated as moot, 992 F. 2d 17 (2d Cir. 1993).

Cordoba, Rocio De Lourdes. "In Search of a Level Playing Field: *Baca v City of Los Angeles* as a Step Toward Gender Equity in Girls' Sports Beyond Title IX,"*Harvard Women's Law Journal* 24 (spring 2001): 139.

Davis v Monroe County Board of Education, 526 U.S. 629 (1999).

Dobie, Michael, "Title IX Hearings Not Encouraging," *Newsday,* New York, February 3, 2003.

Equity in the Gymnasium: Coed Physical Education: Finding Solutions and Meeting the Challenges. National Association for Girls and Women in Sport, Reston, VA, 2000.

Faragher v City of Boca Raton, 524 U.S. 775 (1998).

Favia v Indiana University of Pennsylvania, 812 F. Supp. 578 (W.D. Pa) (1992), motion to modify [substitute one team for another] order denied, 7 F. 3d 332 (3d Cir. 1993).

Figler, Stephen. *Sport and Play in American Life.* Saunders, New York, 1981.

Flores, Christopher. "Wrestling Coaches Sue Education Department Over Title IX Enforcement," *Chronicle of Higher Education,* Washington, D.C., February 1, 2002.

Franklin v Gwinnett County Public Schools, 112 S. Ct. 1028 (1992).

Gaines, Patrice. "Title IX at 30—Making the Grade?" *AAUW Outlook,* spring-summer 2002.

Gebser v Lago Vista Independent School District, 96-1866, U.S. Supreme Court, 524 U.S. 274 (1998).

Glover v Standard Fed. Bank, 283 F. 3d 953 (8th Cir. 2002).

Gonyo v Drake University, Civ. No. 4-93-70470, 1993 U.S. Dist. LEXIS 16537 (S.D. Iowa Oct. 7, 1993).

Grove City College v Bell, 465 U.S. 555 (1984).

Guardians Association v Civil Service Commission of the City of New York, 463 U.S. 582 (1983).

"Guidelines on Title IX Requirements," *Federal Register* vol. 67, no. 89 (May 8, 2002): 31102-31103.

Haffer v Temple University, 678 F. Supp. 517 (E.D. Pa. 1987) and C.A. No. 80-1362 (E.D. Pa. September 6, 1988) (entry of consent order).

Halpin, Ty. "Wrestling With Reality: Women Wrestlers Try to Pioneer Their Way to a Sanctioned Sport," *NCAA News*, Indianapolis, November 22, 1999.

Hanson, S.L., and R.S. Kraus. "Women, Sports, and Science: Do Female Athletes Have an Advantage?," *Sociology of Education* 71 (1988): 93-110.

Haworth, Karla. "Statement on Sports Scholarships Frustrates and Confuses Colleges," *Chronicle of Higher Education*, Sept. 4, 1998.

Heckman, Diane, "The Glass Sneaker: Thirty Years of Victories and Defeats Involving Title IX and Sex Discrimination in Athletics," *13 Fordham Intellectual Property, Media & Entertainment Law Journal*, 551, winter 2003.

Helwig, Carol, "Bias Ruling Applauded by Officials, *USA Today*, February 27, 1992.

Helwig, Carol, "Decision Sends Clear Message to Violators: Money Increases Incentive," *USA Today*, February 27, 1992.

Helwig, Carol. "Study Results Echo Inequity Women Know All Too Well," *USA Today*, March 12, 1992.

Hu, Frank, et al., "Physical Activity and Risk of Stroke in Women," *Journal of the American Medical Assn.*, 283: 2961-2967, June 2000.

Journal of Sport and Exercise Psychology, "Parents Play=Daughters Play" December 1997, Vol. 19, No. 4, pp. 435-36.

Justus, J., et al. "Sports Reform: College Athletics in Flux." *Journal of College and University Law* 22 (1995): 48-62.

Kelley v Board of Trustees of University of Illinois, 35 F. 3d 265 (7th Cir. 1994), 531 U.S. 1128 (1995) cert. denied.

Kiechel v Auburn University, C.A. File No. 93-V-474-F (M.D. Ala. July 19, 1993).

King, Billie Jean. "For All the Good Things It Has Done, Title IX Is Still Plagued by Myths." *New York Times*, Sunday, June 23, 2002, 7.

Kleczek v Rhode Island Interscholastic League, Inc., 768 F. Supp. 951 (D.R.I. 1991).

Labinger, Lynette, quoted in opinion article, *NCAA News*, Indianapolis, November 9, 1998.

Lakoski v James, 66 F. 3d 751 (5th Cir. 1995), cert. denied, 117 S. Ct. 357 (1996).

Louisiana High School Athletic Association v St. Augustine High School, 396 F. 2d 224 (1968).

Lowrey v Texas A&M University, 96-20157 (5th Cir. 1997).

Lujan v Defenders of Wildlife, 504 U.S. 555 (1992).

Martin v Occupational Safety and Health Commission, 499 U.S. 133 (1991).

Mauro, Tony. "Sex Bias Law Applied to Schools," *USA Today*, February 27, 1992.

Mercer v Duke University, no. 01-1512, U.S. Court of Appeals for the Fourth Circuit, unpublished, decided November 15, 2002.

Miami Univ. Wrestling Club v Miami University, 302 F. 3d at 609-10.

Minor v Northville Pub. Sch., 605 F. Supp. 1185 (E.D. Mich. 1985).

National Collegiate Athletic Association v Tarkanian, 488 U.S. 179 (1988).

National Federation of State High School Associations, 2003 Participation Survey.

National Women's Law Center, press release, Washington, D.C., June 18, 2002.

National Wrestling Coaches Association et al. v United States Department of Education, 263 F. Supp. 2d 882 (D.C. Cir. 2003).

NACAA, Equity definition, Summer 1993.

NCAA, *NCAA News*, comment by Dale Anderson, February 1, 1999.

NCAA. *Division I NCAA Study on Graduation Rates*, Indianapolis, 2000.

NCAA. *Gender Equity Study*, Indianapolis, 2002.

Neal v Board of Trustees of California State Universities, 198 F. 3d 763 (9th Cir. 1999).

Nevada Department of Human Resources v Hibbs, 123 S. Ct. 1972 (2003).

NFSHSA. *Study on Participation*, Indianapolis, 2003.

Nike television ad, aired 1995.

"Nondiscrimination on the Basis of Sex in Education Programs or Activities Receiving Federal Assistance; Proposed Rule," *Federal Register vol. 67*, no. 89 (May 8, 2002): 31098-31099.

North Haven Board of Education v Bell, 456 U.S. 512 (1982).

Oncale v Sundowner Offshore Services, Inc., 523 U.S. 75 (1998).

Pederson v Louisiana State University, 213 F. 3d 858 (5th Cir. 2000).

Pemberton, Cynthia. *More Than a Game: One Woman's Fight for Gender Equity in Sport*, Northeastern University Press, 2002.

P.H. v School District of Kansas City, 265 F. 3d 653 (8th Cir. 2001).

President's Council on Physical Fitness and Sport. *Physical Activity & Sport in the Lives of Girls*. Washington, D.C., 1997.

R.M. Smith v National Collegiate Athletic Association, 525 U.S. 459 (1999).

Roberts v Colorado State University, 814 F. Supp. 1507 (D. Colo) (Roberts I), aff'd in part, 998 F. 2d 824 (10th Cir. 1993) (Robert II), cert. denied, 114 S. Ct. 580 (1993).

Sanders v Texas A&M University, No A-92-CA-405 (W.D. Texas), July 1, 1992.

Sangree, Suzanne. "Title IX and the Contact Sports Exemption: Gender Stereotypes in a Civil Rights Statute," *Connecticut Law Review* 32 (winter 2000): 381.

Seminole Tribe of Florida v Florida, 517 U.S. 44, 116 S. Ct. 1114 (1996).

Sex Discrimination Regulations, Hearings Before the House Subcommittee on Post Secondary Education of the Committee on Education and Labor, 94th Congress, 1st Session (1975).

"Sixth Circuit Dropped the Ball: An Analysis of *Brentwood Academy v Tennessee Secondary School Athletic Ass'n* in Light of the Supreme Court's Recent Trends in State Action Jurisprudence." *2001 Brigham Young University Law Review* 1313 (2001).

Silva, Elaine, "Women at Work—Changes and Challenges," *AAUW Outlook*, Spring/Summer, Washington, D.C., 2003

Staurowsky, Ellen. "The Title IX Commission's Flawed Lineup." *Chronicle of Higher Education,* February 14, 2003.

Steel Co. v Citizens for a Better Environment, 523 U.S. 83 (1998).

Suggs, Welch. "Cheers and Condemnation Greet Report on Gender Equity," *Chronicle of Higher Education,* March 7, 2003.

Suggs, Welch. "Men's Sports Coaches Announce New Challenge to Title IX Guidelines," *Chronicle of Higher Education,* August 18, 2003.

Sweet, Judith (former NCAA president), *NCAA News,* Indianapolis, January 27, 1993.

"Tax Expenditures, Social Justice, and Civil Rights: Expanding the Scope of Civil Rights Laws to Apply to Tax-Exempt Charities." *2001 Brigham Young University Law Review* 167 (2001).

Teegarden, D., and W. Proulx, et al. 1996, *Medicine and Science in Sports and Exercise* 28: 105.

Thomas Jefferson University v Shalala, 512 U.S. 504 (1994).

Warren v Reading School District, 278 F. 3d 163 (2002).

White, Ernest A., and Connie Sheets, "If You Let Them Play They Will." *JOPERD* 72, no. 4 (2001): 27.

White, Kerry, A. "States Step Up to Push for Equity in Absence of Federal Enforcement," *Education Week,* June 18, 1997.

Williams v School Dist. of Bethlehem, 998 F. 2d 168 (3d Cir. 1993).

Women's Sports Foundation. *Miller Lite Report.* 1985.

Women's Sports Foundation. *Minorities in Sports.* 1989.

Women's Sports Foundation. *Gender Equity Report Card: A Survey of Athletic Opportunity in American Higher Education—Then and Now,* East Meadow, NY, 1997.

Women's Sports Foundation. *Sport and Teen Pregnancy.* 1998.

Women's Sports Foundation. *Health Risks and the Teen Athlete.* 2000.

Women's Sports Foundation, Internet Resource Center, March 8, 2000.

Women's Sport Foundation, *Title IX and Race in Intercollegiate Sport,* 2003.

Women's Sports Foundation, Media Relations, December 15, 2003, womensports foundation.org

Wyshak, G., and R.E. Frisch, "Breast Cancer Among Former College Athletes Compared to Non-Athletes; a 15-Year Follow Up," *British Journal of Cancer* 82, no. 3 (2000): 725-730.

Yellow Springs Exempted Village Sch. Dist. Bd. of Ed. v Ohio High School Athletic Association, 647 F. 2d 651, 658 (6th Cir. 1981).

INDEX

Note: The italicized *f* and *t* following page numbers refer to figures and tables, respectively.

ABOUT THE AUTHORS

Linda Jean Carpenter, PhD, JD, (right) has been involved in Title IX and gender equity issues in sport for over three decades. Studies on various topics related to women in sport have characterized her research efforts with coauthor Dr. Acosta. In addition to writing extensively on the subject of equity, she is a sought-after speaker at national, regional, and local conferences.

Dr. Carpenter is professor emerita at the City University of New York's Brooklyn College. She has received numerous national awards, including the 2004 Sport and Recreation Law Association Leadership Award, the 2003 American Bar Association Outstanding Nonprofit Lawyers Award (Outstanding Academic), and the 1998 Honor Award from the National Association for Girls and Women in Sport. She is also a charter member of the North American Society for Health, Physical Education, Recreation, Sport, and Dance.

Dr. Carpenter, a member of the New York State and United States Supreme Court bars, earned her JD from Fordham University School of Law in 1981 and her PhD in sport administration in 1974 from the University of Southern California.

R. Vivian Acosta, PhD, (left) has also been involved in Title IX and gender equity issues in sport for more than 30 years. A professor emerita at the City University of New York's Brooklyn College, she has written extensively on the subject and served as a presenter at national, regional, and local conferences. Dr. Acosta's well-known 27-year longitudinal national study on the status of women in intercollegiate sport, conducted with coauthor Dr. Carpenter, has been frequently cited in the media, Congress, and gender equity lawsuits.

A former president of the National Association for Girls and Women in Sport, Dr. Acosta served on the Board of Governors for the American Alliance for Health, Physical Education, Recreation, and Dance. She received the National Association of Collegiate Women Athletic Administrators' Lifetime Achievement Award in 2001, and in 2003 she received the Rachel Bryant Award from the National Association for Girls and Women in Sport.

Experienced as an athletic director and coach of many sports, including men's teams, Dr. Acosta earned her PhD in sport administration in 1974 from the University of Southern California.